Tortured into
Fake Confession

Tortured into Fake Confession

The Dishonoring of Korean War Prisoner Col. Frank H. Schwable, USMC

RAYMOND B. LECH

McFarland & Company, Inc., Publishers
Jefferson, North Carolina, and London

Frontispiece: Colonel Frank H. Schwable, 1949 (official U.S. Marine Corps photograph). While a prisoner of the Chinese during the Korean War, Colonel Schwable composed and signed a confession stating that he planned a germ warfare campaign over North Korea and parts of China in conjunction with the Joint Chiefs of Staff and senior subordinate commands.

LIBRARY OF CONGRESS CATALOGUING-IN-PUBLICATION DATA

Lech, Raymond B., 1940–
    Tortured into fake confession : the dishonoring of Korean War prisoner Col. Frank H. Schwable, USMC / Raymond B. Lech.
        p.   cm.
    Includes bibliographical references and index.

    ISBN 978-0-7864-6548-4
    softcover : 50# alkaline paper ∞

    1. Schwable, Frank H.— Trials, litigation, etc. 2. Courts-martial and courts of inquiry — United States. 3. Korean War, 1950–1953 — Prisoners and prisons. I. Title.
KF7654.5.S3L43   2011
343.73'0143 — dc23   2011028711

BRITISH LIBRARY CATALOGUING DATA ARE AVAILABLE

© 2011 Raymond B. Lech. All rights reserved

No part of this book may be reproduced or transmitted in any form or by any means, electronic or mechanical, including photocopying or recording, or by any information storage and retrieval system, without permission in writing from the publisher.

Front cover: Colonel Frank H. Schwable, 1949 (official U.S. Marine Corps photograph). Cover design by David K. Landis (Shake It Loose Graphics)

Manufactured in the United States of America

McFarland & Company, Inc., Publishers
  Box 611, Jefferson, North Carolina 28640
    www.mcfarlandpub.com

To Yolanda Michele Saldana-Lech
and Michael Christopher Daly

And to always remember Mademoiselle Sadie

Contents

Acknowledgments ix
Preface 1

1 — The Inquiry 5
2 — The Wing 24
3 — The Preparation 39
4 — The Capture 49
5 — The Camp 59
6 — The Menticide (Part I) 76
7 — The Menticide (Part II) 96
8 — The Transfer 109
9 — The Ship 132
10 — The Arrival 150

Epilogue 164
Appendix: Deposition by the Captured United States Colonel Frank H. Schwable 171
Notes 181
Bibliography 187
Index 191

Acknowledgments

Over 10 years ago, when I was writing *Broken Soldiers*, in the process of gathering documents I received the entire transcript of Col. Frank H. Schwable's court of inquiry together with various supplements, which I barely used. After letting it gather dust for many years, I decided to dig into the transcript for this book. As a whole, the U.S. Navy and U.S. Marine Corps have been extremely helpful to me in the gathering of these primary sources and my sincere appreciation goes out to them.

In today's electronic age, with Facebook, Twitter, and a host of other electronic means of communication, almost everyone has "friends," and tons of them. I have five, and two of them are to whom the book is fondly dedicated. The other three I hardly ever see but we communicate on a regular basis.

I met Lt. Col. William Latham, USA, at West Point many years ago when he was an assistant professor of English. After retiring in 2006, Bill accepted a position as an assistant professor at the U.S. Army Command and General Staff College. Bill is an author in his own right. While I was writing my book, he and I became close and he was always there when I needed guidance and advice. Friends must be there when one needs them and the colonel was always there for me.

Dr. Carol Johnson is an associate professor in the Department of Humanities at the New Jersey Institute of Technology. Carol wrote *The Language of Work* and is presently putting together another manuscript. It has been said that "the fall will never kill you, it's the sudden stop," and whenever I was sure I was hitting bottom, my friend Carol was always there. In particular, she was a lifesaver when it came to photos. Without her outstanding assistance, I would have been totally lost. Thanks, Carol.

And then there's Sheila. Dr. Sheila Miyoshi Jager is an associate professor and the director of East Asian studies at Oberlin College, Oberlin, Ohio. She also is an author. Like Carol, Sheila never hesitated to help me when I needed it. Most importantly is that she introduced me to her husband, Colonel Jiyul Kim, USA (Ret.).

Jiyul was director of Asian studies at the Army War College in Carlisle, Pennsylvania. When I needed any guidance as to where to go to find something, Colonel Kim was right on top of it. I have pages of emails from him suggesting sources to me. In fact, the colonel, together with his wife, Sheila, and Colonel Latham, were instrumental in placing my 60,000 pages of primary source documents about POWs in Korea with the U.S. Army Heritage and Education Center in Carlisle for safekeeping. My gratitude to Sheila and the colonel.

A daunting task is to gather photographs for a book — and this is only gathering and does not include permissions and captioning. Gunnery Sergeant Matthew Butler of the marine's public affairs office in New York City got me started on the right foot by introducing me to Gunnery Sergeant Chanin Nuntavong who was the media chief of the Division of Public Affairs at Headquarters, Marine Corps. The gunny was a good interrogator and I had to fill out various forms, submit a resume, a book proposal form, and even a copy of my publishing contract. Once he approved me, however, I was assigned First Lieutenant Joshua Diddams, Headquarters, Marine Corps at the Pentagon. In a sense, the lieutenant was now working with me.

Lieutenant Diddams knew what buttons to press, and if he didn't have what I wanted, he didn't send me somewhere else but went there himself. I had a tough time getting a photo of General Bare, for example, and in a short time, an email came in and attached was his picture. Thank you, Lieutenant.

I need to show my appreciation to Rebecca Eisenman and Polly Gilgenbach at the Mayo Clinic for the photograph of Dr. Mayo. It wasn't as easy as I thought it would be; the Mayo family is big and Charles Mayo is the grandson of the founder. The ladies did not stop until we got the right Dr. Mayo.

Digging into the *New York Times* for something over a half century old makes one lose patience. I approached an old pal, Anne Marie Tognella, who's with the Sachem (NY) Public Library, to assist in getting for me one particular article from 1954. She went to her co-worker Lauren Gilbert, who in turn went into her historical database. A few days later I had what I wanted. My appreciation goes to Anne Marie and Lauren.

Rachel Johnstone, Combat Camera Archives, Marine Corps Base, Camp Lejeune, worked hard in attempting to get me a photo of General Linscott. She finally found a formal portrait of him in *The Globe*, the weekly newspaper at Lejeune. I couldn't use it because it was too blurry, but at least I knew the photo existed — somewhere. Thanks, Rachel.

A super find was Andre B. Sobocinski, Office of Medical History, and archivist, Benjamin Rush Education and Conference Center, Navy Medicine

Institute for the Medical Humanities. Andre is a really nice man and knows his stuff. I asked for a picture of Admiral Cooper and in a few days I had it. Using a "While I have your ear," ploy, I asked Andre if he knew anyone in the marines who could get me a picture of General Linscott. I had spent weeks trying to find him but with no luck. He referred me and said, "Just make sure you mention my name." I won't forget your name, Andre.

I called Dr. Annette Amerman at the Marine Corps Historical Center and asked her if she could direct me to where I can get General Linscott's photograph. I mentioned Andre's name. She asked if I could hold on a minute and I said I'd hold for an hour if she can assist. Within two minutes she got back and said, "I've got it." Within another ten minutes, I had it on my desk. I sincerely appreciate the help of Dr. Amerman.

Without the father-and-son team of Fred and Matthew Gelfand, I would be totally stuck. The Gelfands own a nice regional real estate company and they gave me a great desk, an up-to-date computer system, a huge copy machine, fax, and anything else I needed to do a book. All they asked in return is that I answer the phones once in a while. Not a bad trade. Fred and Matthew are good and very generous people. Thanks, guys.

Preface

> *We cannot urge too strongly that all the facts be published far and wide, in the press, on our movie screens, on television, and through every media of information which may be at our disposal. Spread the word of truth. Against that kind of light, even our enemies would not dare to appear so ridiculous as to attempt to repeat this sort of thing.*
> — Col. Paul Sherman, USMC, Court of Inquiry, Vol. 3, 1153

Col. Frank Hawse Schwable was a U.S. Marine who served his country faithfully and loyally. During his term of service, the colonel was awarded numerous decorations, including the Legion of Merit with a combat "V" and two gold stars, the Distinguished Flying Cross with three gold stars, and the Air Medal with two silver stars in lieu of 10 awards. Colonel Schwable put his life on the line many times while in air combat against the Japanese during World War II.[1]

The colonel's father, Col. Frank J. Schwable, was a 30-year marine and a veteran of both the Boxer Rebellion and the Philippine Insurrection. His wife, Beverly, was the daughter of Capt. John B. Pollard (M.D.), USN. Frank and Beverly Schwable had two children together, David and Susan. Simply because of his lineage, it therefore wasn't unusual for the colonel to go to the finer prep schools in the Washington, D.C., area and then receive his appointment to the U.S. Naval Academy; he graduated in 1929, one month short of his 21st birthday, as a second lieutenant of marines. Two years later he was a marine aviator.[2]

One day during the summer of 1952 (the Korean War was two years old), Colonel Schwable was shot down and captured while flying over the front lines. He was imprisoned and mentally and physically tortured by the Chinese until eventually, after months of agony, the colonel signed a germ warfare confession. He didn't confess that he flew the actual missions because everyone knew he was too old for that; furthermore, his position as chief of staff of the First Marine Aircraft Wing (and previously assigned to very sensitive work at the Pentagon), didn't permit him to fly anywhere near the battle area. His confession, however, stated that he planned the campaign. And not by himself either; he designed it together with the Joint Chiefs of Staff and senior subordinate staffs below that level. In the confession, Colonel Schwable furnished to the enemy the names of generals and other colonels who were also involved and making them, in addition to himself, instrumental in the conspiracy of implementing the strategy and tactics involved in a germ warfare campaign by the United States against North Korea and parts of China. In 1953 and 1954, Col. Frank Schwable, second-highest-ranking officer held as a POW during the Korean War (after Maj. Gen. William Dean) was a very famous man. It wasn't unusual to see his name on the front page of newspapers worldwide.

After his release from captivity, there was a major investigation into his activities as a POW. To many, Colonel Schwable was a disgrace to his corps and his country. He was a fallen marine.[3]

* * * *

There are four particulars that constantly appear within this book that should be addressed now:

Name, Rank, and Serial Number

This is incorrect. Technically it's *name, grade, and service number.* Rifles have serial numbers, not people. A rank is within a grade. An example of this is when Paul Liles and Harry Fleming were captured and brought to the same collection point. They were the two senior officers present, but who was in charge? They compared dates of promotion and discovered that Liles had been advanced to lieutenant colonel two years prior to Fleming. Liles was in charge; he outranked Fleming within the grade of lieutenant colonel by two years.

But who in the world ever heard of—or, more importantly, says—"name, grade, and service number?" Certainly none of the officers (including generals) in this book ever did. Common usage dictates that one stay with what one knows and not get too technical or fancy when common jargon will suffice.

Time

Mind is conditioned by time; practically everything a person does is related to time. For the most part, time controls our lives. Time is a unit of measurement; it measures things. Most important, however, is that it's used to measure distance. Included in this is the space (time) between one event and another. A Korean War POW did not have this privilege; he had no unit of measurement; he had no time.

Lt. Col. William Thrash, USMC, was in solitary confinement for several months and he said, "I had lost track of time to some degree." He's putting it mildly. Days meant nothing, hours were meaningless and one did not have to be in solitary to realize this; just be a regular POW. Two men would be in the same room at the same time with the same interrogator asking the same question to both and one would say the event took place in January 1952 and the other January 1953. When you lose time, you're absent a sense of self because you don't know where you are at any given time. No one knew what time it was and therefore, in many instances in this book, if we come within a week or so of something happening, consider it a bull's-eye.[4]

Surrender/Capture

Many former POWs strenuously object to the word "surrender" and categorically state, "Oh, no, we didn't surrender; we were captured." The difference, however, is that one is a cause and the other an effect. During the Persian Gulf War, some Iraqi troops actually surrendered to helicopters but weren't captured until later, sometimes days. It seems that if a soldier is wounded, or out of ammo, or has no weapon at all, he's captured. On the other hand, if he has a fully loaded working rifle, drops it and raises his hands, he surrendered. The GIs in Korea, for the most part, surrendered; a little over 7,000 of them.

But it's necessary to ease up on this somewhat because surrender is not generally an individual act. Units surrender as a group (large or small) and that group has a commander who makes the decision for them. The average soldier, upon surrendering, does not do so of his own free will but is obeying orders from his commander.

Eloquence

This is a book whose characters are very intelligent men. All had, at the minimum, their undergraduate diploma and the majority held advanced degrees. When they speak, they do so with a sense of power, rhythm, harmony, and quite often beauty. Furthermore, the eloquence is extemporaneous; whoever speaks does not have the advantage of editing the written word. It has been said of Colonel Schwable, for example, that "his words are eloquence itself; conceived in an agony of spirit; nurtured through months of restraint and given to you in an honest spirit of truth which no man can belie."[5]

It's extremely difficult, however, to tie together this oftentimes romantic articulation with their profession. These men are trained killers; they're trained to kill people and the majority of men introduced in this work have killed at least one man in their life, especially among the more senior officers.

* * * *

The fame (or infamy, depending on which side one was on) of Frank Schwable reached the very highest levels of the United Nations. The Soviet Union was on the attack and the United States on the defensive, trying in every which way it could to refute the germ warfare confession of Colonel Schwable.

Six weeks after the colonel's release from captivity (in September 1953), Dr. Charles Mayo, on behalf of the United States, presented before the 648th meeting of the political committee of the United Nations General Assembly a long statement denying any U.S. involvement in germ warfare. He began by saying:

> It is not a pretty story that confronts us. It is a story of terrible physical and moral degradation. It concerns men shaken loose from their foundation of moral value — men beaten down by the conditioning which the science of Pavlov reserves for dogs and rats — all in a vicious attempt to make them accomplices to a frightful lie.[6]

The confession the colonel signed would have long-lasting personal and national effects not only during his imprisonment but long after his release. Four months after the colonel gained his freedom, the commandant of the Marine Corps convened a court of inquiry to investigate what actually happened in the mountains of North Korea that forced him to do what he did. The four members of the court, all flag officers, finally determined that Colonel Schwable underwent such drastic torture of the mind that his only choices were to sign, go insane, or die.

In the end, the panel recommended to the commandant that no court-martial and subsequent punishment be instituted but that Colonel Schwable, during his final years in the marines before retirement, never again be permitted to command troops. He was transferred to Norfolk, Virginia, where he spent his last years as an aviation safety officer. He investigated accidents.

1

The Inquiry

This court is not dealing with any person of marginal reputation. They are dealing with a person of demonstrated courage and outstanding efficiency.
—John H. Pratt, Esq., Court of Inquiry, Vol. 3, 1123

The image of the U.S. Marine Corps had been tarnished, stained as never before in its entire history. One of the corps' best, a future general, "An excellent officer, very attentive to his duties," chief of staff of the First Marine Aircraft Wing in Korea, had done the unthinkable. Col. Frank H. Schwable had signed a germ warfare confession while a prisoner of the Chinese during the Korean War. Some marines in very high places, including headquarters, thought he should have died or, if it came down to it, killed himself.[1]

Lemuel C. Shepherd, Jr., general, U.S. Marine Corps and its 20th commandant, had some serious damage control to perform because his corps was listing. The general basically had only two options: first was don't do anything and hope that the entire affair would go away, and the second was to court-martial his colonel. He didn't like either one and so he chose a third option, which was to convene a court of inquiry to thoroughly investigate why one of his senior officers, whom he knew personally, would do what he did. There had to be more than met the eye.

The order to inquire into the behavior of Colonel Schwable while a POW was personally signed by General Shepherd on Thursday, January 21, 1954. He received "outspoken criticism from many quarters" concerning this decision because a court-martial carries a penalty if wrongdoing is confirmed while an inquiry carries nothing; it has absolutely no authority to punish. The court did have a function, though, and a very serious and publicized one:

1. Find out what the *FACTS* were. What caused Colonel Schwable to utterly collapse? What were the circumstances?

2. Express *OPINIONS* on these facts.
3. Make *RECOMMENDATIONS* (in this case, including disciplinary action) back to the convening authority, which was the commandant, who could accept or reject any or all of the above.²

This was not a typical convening order, however, because more was asked of this about-to-be-formed board. The board was also told to look into "any other action on the part of Colonel Schwable ... which would tend to bring discredit upon the Armed Forces of the United States." Notice that the order does not say discredit upon the marines. There was a lot more at stake here than the marines; the U.S. government (including President Eisenhower), the United Nations, and people everywhere didn't know why a well-trained and disciplined senior U.S. Marine would admit to participating in the hideous act of indiscriminately killing civilians by dropping germs on them. Could it be true? Much of the world in 1952, 1953, and 1954 believed, or tended to believe, that the United States dropped germ-laden bombs on North Korea and parts of China.³

An inquiry, vis-à-vis a court-martial, was a great choice. The commandant was "determined that the right way, the fair way, the American way of settling an issue which had aroused an intense and vociferous public concern was to order a hearing before a legally constituted judicial tribunal, wherein all the facts could be brought into their true light and proper perspective." Furthermore, in an unusual move for an inquiry, the public and press were invited. Except for

General Lemuel C. Shepherd, Jr., 20th Commandant of the Marine Corps. As the convening authority for the Court of Inquiry, the general instructed that the four members investigate any "action on the part of Colonel Schwable ... which would tend to bring discredit upon the Armed Forces of the United States" (official U.S. Marine Corps photograph).

secret portions, it was an open-door policy. Some thought this inappropriate, but General Shepherd retorted, "This was a national and international problem and for that reason we should have a public hearing."[4]

Comparing a court of inquiry to a court-martial is like comparing apples to oranges. Most people who read court-martial transcripts find them boring. Both a defense attorney or counsel for the court would object to a question (or answer) and off they would go with pages of quoting, analyzing, and arguing law. After becoming familiar with them, one would know when to stop reading and start turning bland pages. Not so with an inquiry; for the most part there are no objections. Opinions are solicited, and before a witness leaves the stand, he's indeed asked if he wants to say anything else. There's not even a manual for the conduct of this type of proceeding. The Manual for Courts-Martial is used as a procedural guide. It's quite common at an inquiry for a talkative witness to go on for three or four pages of testimony without another question being asked or any other interruption.[5]

"My duty is to protect Colonel Schwable. I have another duty to protect our country. I am anxious that this court get every piece of information about this important subject that can be brought in, no matter how it is brought in, and we certainly will wave [sic] any objection." This was the mind-set of Colonel Schwable's military attorney and of all others taking part in the investigation. Counsel ended by noting, "This body can do more than a court-martial [in] doing justice and acting in the best interests of our national welfare."[6]

But there was one last thing on the commandant's mind and it was more important than whether to have an open or closed-door policy. The question before the court, and this is extremely important to remember, was not *if* Frank Schwable signed a germ warfare confession — that was a given before the doors opened as he had signed one. It was *why*? In his gut, the commandant felt that it had to be a torture of some kind. But the colonel publicly admitted to the press as soon as he was repatriated that he wasn't tortured — at least not physically. What other kind of torture was there? Could it have been the mind?

General Shepherd just instinctively knew from statements written by Colonel Schwable after his release that the Chinese held tremendous power over him while he was their prisoner, enough power to have the colonel relinquish his free will and do anything they wanted him to do, including defame his country. But power, as such, is not isolated. It stems from an energy source, and energy requires force. General Shepherd mandated that the inquiry discover that force:

> The court, after giving due consideration to all factors affecting Colonel Schwable's mental and psychological condition during the period of his captivity, shall state, whether in its opinion, any of the alleged acts ... performed by Colonel Schwable

during the period in question, occurred as the result of duress, or physical or mental torture of such severity, or threats of death of such compelling nature as, in either case, would constitute reasonable justification for entering into any such acts or of thereafter continuing such acts.[7]

* * * *

At 10:00 A.M. on a cold Tuesday, February 16, 1954, four distinguished, scholarly, powerful men walked into the courtroom and took their assigned places. Three of them wore the marine officer's winter uniform with green blouse and decorations and the fourth the blue uniform of an officer in the U.S. Navy.[8]

> *Linscott, Henry D., Major General, USMC:* General Linscott was president of the court. The president is also the judge, as it will, since an inquiry does not have a law officer (as a court-martial would) who acts as the civilian equivalent of a judge. Kansas born, the general graduated from Kansas State Agricultural College, saw action in the South Pacific during World War II and, at the time of this inquiry, was commanding general of the sprawling marine base at Camp Lejeune.[9]
>
> *Schilt, Christian F., Major General, USMC:* Former commanding general of the First Marine Aircraft Wing, he was relieved by Brig. Gen. Clayton "Jerry" Jerome on April 12, 1952. Colonel Schwable relieved Schilt's chief of staff a few weeks later. The general is the holder of the Medal of Honor, for heroism in Nicaragua in 1928.[10]
>
> *Bare, Robert E., Major General, USMC:* A veteran of the Normandy and Okinawa invasions, he attended the same prep school in the Washington area as Colonel Schwable (Severn School in Boone, Maryland) and graduated from the naval academy in 1920. Promoted to major general just a few weeks before the inquiry, he was director of the Marine Corps Development Center at Quantico.[11]
>
> *Cooper, Thomas F., Rear Admiral (M.D.), USN:* The admiral received his B.A. degree from the University of Missouri and his doctor of medicine degree from Jefferson Medical College in Philadelphia. At the time of the inquiry, Dr. Cooper was assistant chief at the Bureau of Medicine and Surgery for Planning and Logistics, United States Navy.[12]

These men were the members of the court and chosen to find the force that made Colonel Schwable sign the confession. There wasn't anyone present in the courtroom to convince them of anything; there was no prosecutor and no defense attorney, for this was not a trial. But there were other players there, not to convince but to inform. The court, per se, was represented by an attorney (and his assistant), and Colonel Schwable, not a defendant but a "party to the inquiry," was also represented.

Left: Major General Christian F. Schilt, Member of the Court of Inquiry. Former commanding general, First Marine Aircraft Wing, and recipient of the Medal of Honor (official U.S. Marine Corps photograph). *Right:* Major General Robert E. Bare, Member of the Court of Inquiry. The general was director of the Marine Corps Development Center at Quantico, Virginia (official U.S. Marine Corps photograph).

Murphy, Kenneth E., Lieutenant Colonel, USMCR: Colonel Murphy was "counsel to the court": and when he spoke, the court spoke. There's not much information about the colonel's background from the marines because they had nothing. It's a good guess that he was a civilian, brought onto active duty specifically for the proceeding (he was stationed at headquarters) and subsequently released back to reserve status after the investigation. Whatever it was, he was good. No rambling, no speeches and, most importantly, support for and general agreement with Colonel Schwable's counsel, and vice versa. This inquiry was to find facts, not fault.

Bennett, Nalton M., Captain, USMC: The captain was "assistant counsel to the court" and Colonel Murphy's assistant. He had to be in his mid to late 20s because just weeks before the inquiry, he was a first lieutenant. It can be safely assumed that he received this promotion because you just did not have a lieutenant questioning colonels and generals. Captain Bennett posed about half of all the questions asked on behalf of the court during the proceeding. He was very good, and what was impressive was that he wasn't impressed. He didn't care whether you were a colonel or a corporal, he asked questions of both in the same manner: directly but with extreme courtesy.

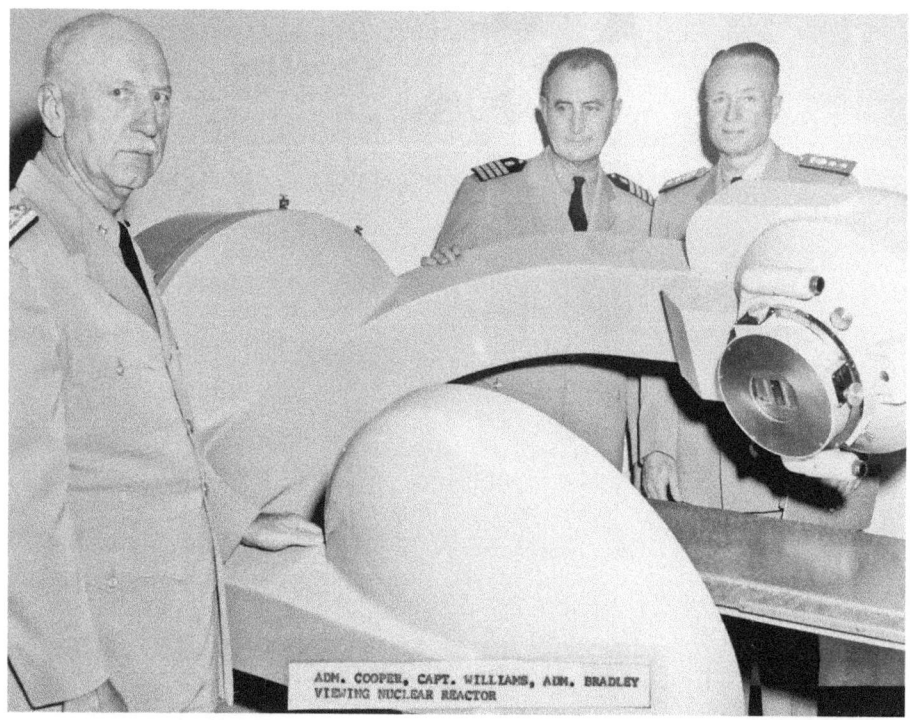

Rear Admiral Thomas F. Cooper, M.D., Member of the Court of Inquiry (left) with Captain Williams (middle) and Rear Admiral Bradley (right) viewing a hospital's nuclear reactor. Admiral Cooper was assistant chief, Bureau of Medicine and Surgery for Planning and Logistics (official U.S. Navy photograph, Bureau of Medicine and Surgery Library and Archives).

During their careers, all four members of the court had, at one time, experienced intense combat in the service of their country. This includes Admiral Cooper, who was senior medical officer aboard the cruiser USS *Atlanta* when the Japanese sank her off Guadalcanal on November 13, 1942. Colonel Murphy may have seen combat during World War II and/or Korea and Captain Bennett probably didn't see any. It's a different story when it comes to the parties (and their lawyers) to the inquiry.[13]

Sherman, Paul D., Colonel, USMC: Colonel Sherman had just turned 57 years old. He held a B.A. from Boston University and a law degree from George Washington University. Originally an aviator, he quit flying in 1932 and became a ground officer. He fought on Guadalcanal during World War II and after the war became commanding officer, Twenty-First Marine Regiment, Second Marine Division.[14]

Colonel Sherman's brother, who died two and a half years before the inquiry, was Admiral Forrest P. Sherman, the 12th chief of naval operations. Colonel Schwable knew Paul Sherman because they attended Marine Corps Basic School together in 1929. When he learned of the pending investigation into his conduct while a POW, Schwable approached Colonel Sherman and asked if he would represent him during the proceedings. Sherman's reply was that he'd be delighted to do it.[15]

Possibly with the exception of authorities at higher levels, the majority of the military and civilian populations of North Korea and China believed that germ warfare was being conducted by the United States. Not so Colonel Sherman. One Saturday evening during a normal weekend break, the colonel was at his dining room table preparing for Tuesday's hearing. His family was present and general conversation was taking place when his 11-year-old daughter asked, "Daddy, what is germ warfare?"

"Nothing, Barbie, it is just a fairy story."

"Oh," she questioned, "You mean like Hans Christian Andersen?"

"Yes."[16]

Pratt, John H., Esq., Morris, Pearce, Gardner and Pratt, Washington, D.C.: Colonel Schwable rightly felt that there was more required in counsel than a very good military lawyer — someone was needed who understood the mind and could concentrate on it, someone who knew what questions to ask of the psychologists and psychiatrists who would appear as witnesses. One day he personally went to visit retired admiral Ozzie Colclough, then president of George Washington University and former judge advocate general of the navy (JAG). Admiral Colclough advised Schwable to ask an attorney he knew, John Pratt, if he would assist. After he contacted Mr. Pratt, the lawyer immediately accepted.[17]

On the surface, this was a very bad move by Colonel Schwable; a civilian attorney representing a member of the armed forces in a military courtroom is generally a disaster. Military law is somewhat different than civilian law, and civilian lawyers don't know it as well as military attorneys. They don't know procedure (which is very different), they don't know protocol (or tradition), and most important, they can lack respect (when a general speaks, you listen). In a word, they're an annoyance, at times coupled with arrogance.

The exception (and there are rare exceptions), was Pratt. He was 43 years old and had received his law degree from Harvard University. A member of the Washington, D.C., bar, he was also a former marine and therefore one of them. His two brothers were Capt. William V. Pratt, USN, and Rear Admiral Richard R. Pratt. John Pratt was proud of his

Bronze Star for bravery and his Purple Heart—he had lost part of an arm while fighting as a marine in the Philippines.[18]

Sherman and Pratt worked very well together. Colonel Sherman was in charge, but he handled, for the most part, the military side of the issues while Pratt studied and was responsible for the psychological side. Colonel Schwable was pleased with the two men: "Both were very helpful to me—very cooperative."*[19]

Bley, Roy H., Major, USMC: There were only two marines who signed germ warfare confessions during the Korean War and Major Bley was the other. He was Colonel Schwable's co-pilot. On the third day of the inquiry, Thursday, February 18, 1954, the major was called to the stand. While describing his experiences, he mentioned that the Chinese kept telling him that he had a problem which must be cleared. (To the Chinese, all POWs had a problem.) "What did they mean by problem?" asked Sherman. Bley replied, "The problem to them was germ warfare." At that moment, the colonel brought everything to a halt. "Major, you are suspected of committing an offense in violation of the Uniform Code of Military Justice, of having had dealings with the enemy in general terms. You don't have to make any statement and any statement you make can be used against you in a court-martial." Obviously, this was all rehearsed between Sherman and Bley prior to him taking the stand because Bley's reply was, "Well, sir, I request to become an interested party." He asked that Sherman become his counsel, to which the colonel agreed. He was now representing the pilot and co-pilot while Pratt represented only Colonel Schwable.[20]

What's an "interested party?" There's nothing in any manual about this; it was unprecedented. But it made sense. Major Bley was shot down with his colonel, captured at the same time, and essentially went through the same tortures as Colonel Schwable. To have a separate court of inquiry for the major would obviously have been a waste of time and money, so he was simply incorporated into the present inquiry. The recommendations of the court to the commandant were going to have the same effect on the major as on Colonel Schwable. In a way, Bley's future was in the colonel's hands. Although he sat at the table for the parties to the inquiry, except for his time on the stand, his name was hardly ever mentioned during the term of the investigation.

General Linscott, as president, did not have the authority to allow this and therefore, on the same day, he wrote a memo to the commandant warning him that there was nothing in any manual on this "interested party" concept,

---

*The marines paid Colonel Sherman, but John Pratt received his compensation from Colonel Schwable personally.

but to convene a separate inquiry would entail "a large number of additional witnesses, delay while counsel assembles his evidence relating to Major Bley and a protracted adjournment for the purposes." General Shepherd, therefore, gave the okay for Major Bley to be an interested party with further instructions that General Linscott should "confine the scope of the inquiry and its findings to the case of Colonel Schwable." This was also an excellent move because it accorded to Roy Bley "those rights which would not be available to him were he not made a party."[21]

* * * *

"For a month a tense military drama has been unfolding in the grave quiet of a barrack courtroom at Marine Corps Headquarters in Arlington, Va." reported the *New York Times*. Four days later, on March 18, 1954, their renowned military correspondent, Hanson W. Baldwin, editorialized by saying that "The court of inquiry, composed of distinguished officers, has been an example to other investigators. It has been judicious, thorough, fair, and it has demonstrated by its questioning that it knows the quality of mercy is not strained."[22]

The inquiry took place in Building Four, Henderson Hall, Arlington, Virginia. When a marine thinks of Henderson Hall, he thinks of Headquarters, U.S. Marine Corps, which encompasses over 22 acres. It also supplies barracks and support to marines stationed at or temporarily assigned to headquarters. Henderson Hall sits on the southern border of Arlington National Cemetery and is just west of the Pentagon. Its next-door neighbor is Fort Myer. Within the building is the courtroom, which once was a barrack. Heavy wooden beams braced its high ceiling.[23]

Although this was not a trial, Colonel Schwable was a suspect. He was suspected of some very serious things including (a) aiding or attempting to aid the enemy, (b) failure to obey a lawful regulation of the navy department; i.e., furnishing the enemy more than name, rank, and serial number, and (c) conduct tending to bring discredit upon the naval service.[24]

Colonel Schwable was the first marine in the illustrious heritage of the corps to have his conduct as a POW investigated. No other inquiry in American military history received as much publicity, press coverage, and wide distribution as this one except, possibly, the inquiry that investigated the Japanese attack on Pearl Harbor. This was news. During the first few days, the courtroom was described as having "had much of the tension that has made a success of 'The Caine Mutiny Court-Martial.'" It was very, very quiet.[25]

Beverly and Frank Schwable had a loving marriage and while a prisoner, he constantly thought of her and their two children. Colonel Schwable was a devoted father and loving husband. Beverly attended court every day and, being a military wife from a military family, she had probably learned to take things in stride. On Tuesday morning, the first day, she sat among the spectators, "working on embroidery as the proceedings opened."[26]

General Linscott, who was "round faced" with a "little mustache," was no-nonsense. He conducted his court in a "rigidly formal" manner, and one can just imagine the general "peering solemnly at the witnesses over his spectacles."[27]

The general had a mandate from his commandant to keep the doors open, and he did his best to obey this order. However, he informed the packed room at inception, "in those cases where it becomes necessary to take classified testimony or introduce classified documents involving national security, it will be necessary to ask you ladies and gentlemen to leave the court." This was logical because all the equipment was in the courtroom; either move the equipment or move the people. There was one other thing that the general closed the doors for — closed them, that is, to ladies — and that was cursing. If he felt a witness would use foul language (or was warned so by one of the attorneys), the general cleared the room of women. But he was once caught off guard.[28]

Major General Henry Linscott, President of the Court of Inquiry. General Linscott was commanding general, Camp Lejeune, North Carolina (official U.S. Marine Corps photograph).

There was an enlisted man on the stand testifying to certain things he overheard in a conversation between Colonel Schwable and a Chinese interrogator. When he was asked what the colonel's answer was to a specific question, the witness replied, "Fuck you." "And with that," Colonel Schwable recalled, "Gen. Linscott rose up and he put his two hands on his desk and he stood up like this, face flushed and red, and he said, 'If any one of you reporters report this, I will throw you out of the court,' and he sat down and fell over backwards in his chair. And the next thing we saw of him, he had his two hands on the desk, and up comes this red face like that."

People wanted to just crack up but the commanding presence of the general kept the whole place as quiet as a church.²⁹

Then in walked Maj. Gen. William Dean, USA. At this point, in the courtroom were the highest and second-highest-ranking officers of the armed forces of the United States (and the United Nations Command) captured during the Korean War in the same space for the first time.

* * * *

The former commanding general of the 24th Infantry Division carried a presence for his 55 years. Easily recognized with his gray crew cut, the general was captured at the end of August 1950 and was a prisoner of war for three years.* When he was captured, he weighed about 100 pounds. He had been on the lam for 36 days, constantly attempting to avoid the North Korean army after being separated from his division. He walked 15 to 20 miles every night over Korean mountains, many times going nowhere but in circles. Sometimes a kind Korean would give him a bowl of rice (once, two eggs) but he wasn't really eating, "so the weight poured off me. And during 32 [of the 36] days, I didn't have one bowel movement. So I was not a well man. As soon as I was captured, then the next day the dysentery started."³⁰

He was taken care of, and two days after his capture he was given a shave, shower, and haircut. Before and after pictures were snapped of him and, looking at the finished product, the photographer remarked, "You will be amazed at the

Major General William F. Dean, Commanding General, 24th Infantry Division. Within the United Nations command in Korea, the general was the highest-ranking officer captured during the war. For three years, he was a prisoner of the North Koreans (official U.S. Army photograph).

*Except for the inquiry transcripts, no other sources for General Dean have been used in this work. Every statement is extemporaneous and cannot be found elsewhere. For the complete story on Dean's capture and imprisonment, see William F. Dean, General Dean's Story. New York: Viking Press, 1954.

difference." He stayed in a decent cottage, was amply fed and was given medical attention.³¹

General Dean was a captive of the North Koreans and remained so throughout the war; the Chinese did not enter the conflict until three months after his capture. The North Koreans were vicious captors, and any former POW will say that he'd rather be held by the Chinese than the North Koreans. The North Koreans tortured the body, the Chinese the mind. However, in a period of just four months after the Chinese entered the war (which was in November 1950), they killed at least 3,000 American servicemen who were their prisoners; they starved them to death.

Several months before this starvation period even began (it ended on April 1, 1951), General Dean had already signed a couple of statements at the behest of his captors. He was being nagged to sign something saying that the United States and South Korea were the aggressors. Of course, the general

Lieutenant General Walton H. Walker, Commanding General, U.S. Eighth Army, with Major General William Dean. On September 12, 1950, upon the demand of his captors, General Dean wrote a letter to General Walker saying, "I urge that you impress upon the Air the necessity to confine our attacks to military targets" (official U.S. Army photograph).

refused, but said he would write a letter to Lt. Gen. Walton Walker, Eighth Army commander, and on September 12, 1950, the Koreans agreed. This is General Dean's letter:

> Dear General Walker:
> Unfortunately, I was captured on the 25th of August. It was a physical capture, I was overpowered on my attempt to get back through the lines. I did want both the general and my son to know I had not surrendered.
> I have been well treated, but I am anything but happy at being a prisoner of war. I urge that you impress upon the Air the necessity to confine our attacks to military targets.

What is General Dean doing? There's no torture, no really intense interrogation, and yet he writes this letter seriously implying that the United Nations command was bombing civilians.[32]

The next day, September 13, only a little over two weeks since his capture, he signed another document saying that South Koreans hated Americans. "Many South Koreans have outwardly manifested hostility toward Americans," he wrote and signed. But the general could have had another agenda. Actually, he was very angry with the South Koreans. During his month on the run, he received almost no help from the South Korean people he ran into. The general thought he would encounter friendly Koreans but for the most part he didn't, although geographically he was in South Korea. "The South Koreans had been more hostile to me, the people I thought loved me were more hostile to me than the people who had not liked me," he said. In fact, his capture came about because South Koreans reported seeing him to North Korean troops.[33]

The following day, September 14, 1950, the day before the Inchon landing, the tough interrogation began. It lasted about two weeks. General Dean was in Sunan, some 30 miles northwest of the North Korean capital, Pyongyang. His military interrogation took place in a Catholic church that had been turned into a barrack for troops and also a prison and interrogation center. Perhaps the North Koreans thought that since it was easy to get the general to sign a couple of statements, they would try to get more information of military value. After all, he was a general.[34]

The first stint lasted sixty-eight straight hours. He was ordered to sit at a small table across from his interrogator. The chair was homemade and General Dean described it as "the back almost slanting forward, you couldn't lean back. It was the wrong height from the floor. It was just a bad chair."[35]

General Dean held in his mind sensitive military information, including the defense plans for Japan. The North Koreans grilled him with a team of four interrogators for almost three days with no sleep. When his eyes did close, the interrogator on duty would shout at him to wake up while kicking him at the same time. One of the North Koreans (named Kim) at one time yelled at the general, "You are sleeping with your eyes open."[36]

As far as General Dean was concerned, they could go on with this military interrogation for as long as they wanted. He knew that they weren't going to break him down. He could hold on. After about 68 hours, there was a pause for several days and then another 44 hours, then a pause and another 32 hours. Sometime during this three-stage questioning period, the North Koreans switched from military matters and began to pressure him on propaganda: the United States was the aggressor in Korea and exploited South Korea—things of that nature which seemed to be very important to them. General Dean did not capitulate during these interrogations.[37]

But he was terribly frightened. He practically sweated fear. Why weren't the North Koreans physically torturing him? These thoughts were pushing him to the edge of suicide.[38]

> I was fearful of physical torture.... That I might under the stress of physical torture divulge information that I had.[39]
>
> I had information that I might tell under pain and I was scared of myself. I didn't know. I don't think anyone knows how much he can take in physical torture until he has been subjected to it, and I never have.[40]
>
> I was subjected to long periods of questioning. I was subjected to long periods of cold. I mean being stripped to a pair of trunks when my questioners wore overcoats. But I didn't have bamboo spears stuck in me and I knew that they were capable of it because I had seen Korean corpses who died from having little bamboo spears stuck in them until they died. I knew this was one of their favorite means of torture. So I wasn't tortured. I expected to be.[41]
>
> I was afraid they were going to torture me. I was hoping they would shoot me.... I was hoping they would, but I was afraid they would start puncturing me with these bamboo spears. I would have welcomed a fast shooting.[42]

During the two-week interrogation, he was constantly called a war criminal. Initially, one may think of this as just talk, but it is an extremely serious charge, especially if you're physically in the hands of the party pinning this label on you. But it's only a label. There could be a trial and proof (sometimes not) and there's never a jury of peers but a military tribunal, which has the authority to hang the criminal.

There's no precise definition of a war criminal. Of course we've all heard of "crimes against humanity" and the breaking of the rules of ground warfare (as if war were a baseball game), but what does all this mean? Books have been written about the definitions of both crime and humanity. A war criminal is one who dismisses (or loses sight of) his tactical (military) objective and maliciously, with power, seeks to gravely harm (if not absolutely destroy) the civilian population: men, women and children. The destruction of the World

Trade Center is a good example. Have no doubt about it, many war criminals are executed:

> I had a feeling — it was just a feeling — that they wanted to try me as a war criminal. I am still convinced that they did not want me to die because they wanted to try me; they wanted the world to have the spectacle of the communists conducting a war crimes case similar to those we have read about in the past.[43]

These first few months of captivity were no picnic for the general. Throughout his three-year imprisonment he constantly kept thinking about the interrogations resuming. He said, "I hoped [it] would never be renewed, but I constantly feared it would." And this led the general into 1951, the toughest year of his life.[44]

We are talking about a grown man in his fifties, a major general in the U.S. Army. Although a prisoner of war, he was entitled to certain privileges not ordinarily accorded to other POWs. Among civilized nations, this is standard. Generals, as POWs, have been known to have their own private homes or at least their own livable room, depending on grade. But, as General Dean relates, "[I] was a dog, that I must remember that I had lost my dignity and that if the guard ever complained [that] I tried to act like a General, they were going to see to it that I was never to be treated like a General, and I was no longer a General, that I was a dog and I must remember that."[45]

During 1951, there were rats everywhere; they dropped at night from the ceiling on top of him. Then there were the lice (the "seam squirrels" as the general called them), and fleas, and bedbugs, and anything else one can imagine. General Dean testified that the bedbugs were worst of all: "They bit more than the lice."[46]

A year is a very long time. Fortunately, the general can describe a year better than most. The year is 1951:

> During that particular period, I was not permitted to stand up. I was not permitted to have anything to read. I was not permitted to have a pencil. I was not permitted to whistle. I was not permitted to move my lips if I were counting, and it was not until ... the middle of May of that year that I was permitted to take a few minutes exercise.... The only [other] thing I was permitted to do that year, after May, I was permitted to kill flies if I didn't move after them; if they came to me.[47]

Can one imagine not having the right to stand straight for one year, continuously sitting on a bare, dirty floor? Because of all this sitting, General Dean started seeing his guards and interrogators practically as giants. He tells the story of "one guard there who I thought would make a good basketball center back home. I didn't know that Koreans came that tall. I thought he must be about six feet six." In December 1951, when he was first permitted to stand (with the exception of going to the latrine and possibly washing up), the general said, "I found that I was taller than he was. That is the illusion you get sitting on the floor, just seeing them, never comparing your own height with them."[48]

Soon after being permitted to stand and just four days before Christmas in 1951, the general received a visitor. Wilfred Burchett was a correspondent for the French left-wing newspaper *Ce Soir*. "I have come to get your story of how you were captured," said Burchett. Dean asked if he were American and Burchett replied, "No, I am Australian." They took an immediate liking to each other and Burchett brought the general up-to-date, very accurately, on how the war was going. He also told him, "I think your wife said that your son is at the military academy [and] they know that you are alive." They stayed together about two hours, discussing Dean's month-long evasion before capture. Said the general, "It was just the personal experiences of being harried through the hills and being shot at by these South Koreans."[49]

Less than four months later, Alan Winnington showed up for an interview. Winnington was a correspondent for the *London Daily Worker*. He stayed a very short time because of a severe bout of dysentery and the general recalled, "the only question he asked me was what I did with my spare time; how I amused myself." As Winnington ran to the nearest latrine, he left General Dean a full bottle of bourbon. But Dean didn't drink it alone:

Wilfred Burchett. As a correspondent for the French left-wing newspaper *Ce Soir*, he met with General Dean shortly after Dean was taken prisoner and said to him, "I have come to get your story of how you were captured."

I invited this [North Korean] officer to have a drink. I thought maybe I'd make it last and have a drink before my evening meals for maybe a month, but they don't do things that way. He came and we had to drink it real fast, one after the other.[50]

So on one day in April 1952, Gen. William Dean got drunk with a North Korean officer.

Burchett and Winnington were the only two white men the general had seen during his three years of captivity, and this includes other POWs. Who were these men? Winnington is a shadow; Burchett, another ball game. A staunch communist (as was Winnington), he was well hated among the POWs. He seemed to be everywhere. Pick up a book on the Korean War and you'll probably find his name. But were he and Winnington actually reporters? The United States thought not. On October 22, 1953, three months after the war ended, Dr. Charles W. Mayo told the General Assembly of the United Nations:

> It may be of interest to note that Winnington and Burchett played a greater role in this [germ warfare propaganda] operation than merely acting as journalists. The statement in our possession indicate[s] that they actually participated in the interrogation of five of [our] flyers.[51]

The three phases of POW life in North Korea were quite distinguishable. Phase 1 began with the four-month period between December 1950 and April 1, 1951. This can be labeled the starvation period. Once the Chinese crossed the Yalu in November 1950 and attacked southward, the United Nations forces were outnumbered and outgunned; men were surrendering in droves to the

Group of Captured American Soldiers. From an official Soviet source: "1/30/51—Korea: A group of American soldiers is photographed after being captured by Chinese Communist forces fighting in Korea."

Chinese. The total number of American soldiers captured during the war (mostly by the Chinese) was a little over 7,000. During this four-month starvation period, 3,000 or more of them died at Chinese collection points and in permanent camps along the Yalu. Most of the dead were enlisted men. They starved to death.

On April Fools' Day 1951, the Chinese indoctrinators swarmed into the camps, hundreds of them, and the lectures began: forced indoctrination in communist doctrine, philosophy, and theory. It was either learn or starve. This is phase 2; it lasted until the end of December 1951. Phase 1 lasted four months, phase 2 nine months, and phase 3 for years to come.

The new year (1952) began with germ warfare fireworks. This was phase 3. The Chinese had finished with the 4,000 surviving GIs (who had learned their subjects well) and now they went after the officers, specifically pilots and aircrew. If you fell from the sky and landed in North Korea in 1952, you jumped into the germ warfare phase. To substantiate the claim of germ warfare, the Chinese needed confessions, and they eventually got so many they couldn't use them all. In fact, Colonel Schwable's was all they required.

In May 1952, two months prior to the capture of Colonel Schwable, one of General Dean's interrogators excitedly approached him. "I know you won't believe it, you will deny it. Even though you deny it, it is true. Your forces are engaging in bacteriological warfare." From this point on, his captors continually badgered the general about germ warfare, bringing him English language newspapers that had printed the confessions of two air force officers, photographs of dropped germ bombs, and any other documentation they could find to convince Dean. He, however, viewed this entire phase as "a bunch of applesauce."[52]

At one point, General Dean told the North Koreans that they would have to cut his tongue out before he would ever confess to anything — but confess to what? The general was totally useless to anyone when it came to germ warfare. What he knew about aerial tactics and ordnance wouldn't fill the head of a pin. No, North Korea's ally was holding someone of lesser rank but of much greater value than the general: They were holding the chief of staff of a marine aircraft wing and his co-pilot, Maj. Roy H. Bley, who just happened to be the wing ordnance officer, and who knew more about bombs than Major Bley?[53]

* * * *

The packed courtroom quietly watched as General Dean left the stand, walked to the front of the court, and crisply saluted. He then turned and went to Colonel Schwable's table, where he vigorously shook Colonel Schwable's hand and wished him well.[54]

Colonel Schwable looked skinny and nervous when he took the stand. When speaking, he used notes extensively because, as he explained, "A lot of these things happened a long time ago." For six tension-filled hours, Frank Schwable attempted to explain how it came about that he had completely lost his free will, his ability to choose. Not to choose the difference between right and wrong, good and bad, or best and right, but the inability to choose, period. How one's mind can become the slave to another mind's thoughts and desires; this is what Frank Schwable was attempting to tell the court and the world. His Marine Corps career was on the line.[55]

In summation, Col. Paul Sherman told the court:

> It seems inconceivable that things like what you have heard could be taking place in a civilized world. But they are true. It is high time America woke up to them, and above all it is high time that we should do something to protect ourselves and our posterity from the impact of a vile and dangerous plot against all mankind.[56]

"The inquiry is finished."[57]

2

The Wing

I remember the sensations of taxiing, taking off, flying, landing, and I was an aviator from then on. I was sold.
— Col. Frank Schwable, USMC Oral History, 6

The First Marine Aircraft Wing was huge, consisting of thousands of men and hundreds of planes. Without getting bogged down in organizational structure, for our purposes it's quite sufficient to split the wing into two primary divisions, or groups. They are Marine Aircraft Group-12 (MAG-12) and Marine Aircraft Group-33 (MAG-33). There was also a support group and various independent squadrons not attached to either one of these major operational entities. In the summer of 1952, MAG-12 was composed of six squadrons of aircraft and MAG-33 had seven. These group squadrons comprised mostly fighter and attack aircraft. Standing alone, this marine wing would qualify as one of the larger air forces in the world.[1]

The commander of the wing was Brig. Gen. Clayton C. Jerome, who had flown from Washington. He arrived in Korea on Friday, April 11, 1952. The next day he relieved Maj. Gen. Christian Schilt.* Neither General Schilt, General Jerome, nor any other officer or man from the wing, in their wildest dreams, could possibly have imagined that in less than two years from this change of command, they would all be together again in a courtroom at Headquarters, Marine Corps, with General Schilt as a member of the court and General Jerome as a witness.[2]

On the same plane with Jerome was his future chief of staff, Colonel Schwable. He had worked at the Pentagon with the general, and prior to that they were in combat together in the South Pacific. Once General Jerome was informed that he was getting a wing to command, Colonel Schwable was

---

This was a slot for a major general. A little over three months after arriving, General Jerome received his second star.

2. The Wing

Major General Clayton C. Jerome, Commanding General, First Marine Aircraft Wing. On speaking of Colonel Schwable as his new chief of staff, the general said, "I particularly desire to have this officer with me" (official U.S. Marine Corps photograph).

automatically going to Korea. General Jerome said, "I particularly desire to have this officer with me." When a general desires something, consider it an order. Jerome wanted Frank Schwable over anyone because he thought of him as "loyal, capable and energetic. I can't say anything better of an officer."[3]

General Jerome took command the day after landing, but Colonel Schwable had time to familiarize himself with his upcoming duties and therefore spent over two weeks with Col. Arthur Binney, the chief he was relieving. On May 1, Colonel Schwable joined General Jerome, his friend of over 10 years, and became chief of staff of the First Marine Aircraft Wing.[4]

General Jerome always outranked the colonel because he was seven years older. When he graduated from the naval academy in 1922, Colonel Schwable was still in high school. The general had a very high regard for his senior colonel, considering "him one of the brightest, finest, most conscientious, and during the war one of the bravest officers I have ever known."[5]

* * * *

Frank Schwable hunted and killed at night. He formed and commanded the first night fighter squadron in the military history of the United States; the marines were the first to do it.

During the Battle of Britain, the British had rapidly advanced in night air operations. It was in 1941 that then Major Schwable was sent on a world tour to examine and study Royal Air Force night fighters. He was duly impressed, and his recommendation to the navy's Bureau of Aeronautics, for which he worked at the time, was that such a fighter squadron be formed. Research and testing of radar and various required ground support units took time, however, so it wasn't until November 1942, with the war going into its second year, that VMF(N)-531 was activated. Lt. Col. Frank Schwable was its first commanding officer.

In July 1943, the squadron went to war. Beginning in September, they conducted night air operations over New Georgia, Bougainville, the Bismarck Archipelago, and the Northern Solomons. This air unit set the pattern for night fighters in the Pacific. Colonel Schwable himself flew more than 65 missions and was in the sky four to six hours every night. From his normal 145 pounds, he was down to 125 and still losing. General (then Colonel) Jerome, his commanding officer at the time, had to ground him and put him on the next afternoon flight to Australia. He needed rest desperately. The colonel was heart-broken, and Jerome observed that "It takes a strong man to cry; there were deep tears in his eyes because he was being pulled out of combat to go back and get a little rest. He wanted to stay right in there and fight."[6]

And that's what night fighters do best. Imagine this black, almost invisible streak in the dark Pacific night, radar locked on, and all four 20mm cannon blazing, lighting up the sky. What chance would one have as this ebony devil streaked by you at 400 miles per hour, its two Pratt and Whitneys generating over 2,000 horsepower per engine? None of this happened — at least not while Frank Schwable was there. The brief description is of a P-61 "Black Widow," and the colonel was pretty much on his way back to the Pentagon in 1944 when this night fighter entered the theater.

The night fighter in the Pacific during most of World War II was a Lockheed PV-1 Vega "Ventura" aircraft equipped with British Mark IV–type radar. On a very good day it did 300 miles per hour. The plane carried up to six people, had twin engines and could be loaded with one torpedo, 1,600 pounds of bombs, depth charges, or anything else a big plane can lift. It also carried guns that averaged out to six .50 caliber and one .30 caliber. If Frank Schwable had ever met up with a superior Japanese "Zero" fighter, this book would not have been written; the colonel would be dead.

People in the Pacific weren't ready for PV-1s to be night fighters and at first the squadron had a tough time landing, as Colonel Schwable described:

> I had trouble, I would say, for the first couple of months when we would come in at night. The antiaircraft people around the place would shoot at us — small caliber stuff—.50 caliber machine guns, things like that, but that's not very comfortable when you are tired; it's late at night coming in for a landing and have them start shooting at you.... But finally we were able to get the word around that there was such a thing as night fighters here and they were going to be flying at night.[7]

These planes obviously never went after fighters but targeted floatplanes, bombers, and transports. The colonel describes the environment:

2. The Wing

PV-1 Ventura. This was the "night fighter" flown by Colonel Schwable in the Pacific and in which he shot down four Japanese aircraft.

No, it wasn't fighter plane to fighter plane, but all those planes had a rear gunner that ... as you slowly climbed up behind them, they had just as good a chance to shoot back at us as we did to shoot them except that we knew where they were and by moving slowly rather than — like that — I guess most of them never even saw us.[8]

During one four-week period between January and February 1944, Colonel Schwable shot down four Japanese aircraft, a combination of bombers and transports; the times were 9 P.M., 10 P.M., 2 A.M., and 5 A.M. Frank Schwable killed some people that month.*[9]

Advancements are very rapid in war. While commander of the squadron, he was promoted, swapping his silver oak leaves for the eagle of a full marine colonel. It was time for him to go. In November 1944, he was transferred back to the Pentagon.[10]

* * * *

It's extremely important to realize how highly placed the colonel was in the Marine Corps. Not all colonels spend time in the Pentagon. Frank Schwable

---

*General Jerome believed that the colonel should have been credited for five kills (which he wasn't), as that would have made him an "ace."

held positions during the transition period between two wars that were steps on the way up to general. Following is a chronological list (dates omitted) of the responsibilities Colonel Schwable had. They mandated that he never go into combat again, because it would be a disaster if he were ever captured:

> Assistant Air Plans Officer, Strategic Plans Section, Operations Division, Offices of the Commander-in-Chief, United States Fleet and Chief of Naval Operations at the Pentagon.
> Commanding Officer, Marine Aircraft Group-12.
> Member of the Joint Plans and Operations Division, Joint Staff, Commander-in-Chief, Pacific.
> Head of Plans Section, Operations and Training Branch, Division of Aviation (later advanced to head the entire branch).

The Division of Aviation was lodged at the Pentagon, where Colonel Schwable had an office. Before being captured only months later, he held the position of Deputy Assistant Director and Executive Officer of the Division of Aviation, responsible to the commandant and the chief of Naval Operations. No, you definitely did not want this man in the hands of an enemy of the United States.[11]

* * * *

Everyone has an air force. The navy has an air force, the marines have three wings, the army has its own (albeit mostly helicopters), and the coast guard has a fairly large air contingent. Air forces are everywhere, but there was only one air force in charge in Korea and that was the U.S. Air Force. For marines, certainly not everyone is inferior to them but surely there is no one above; they're sort of an independent lot and reporting to the U.S. Air Force irked them a bit.

Tokyo was the headquarters of Far East Air Force (FEAF), the American air power responsible for that side of the world. One of the air forces under the command of FEAF was Fifth Air Force, which was in control of air operations in Korea and the wing reported directly to Fifth Air Force. The only deviation from this control was when a squadron was detached from the wing and assigned to a carrier, in which case that unit reported to the navy. Operation order 1-52 states that "Specific authority for operational control of Marine land based aircraft when not in execution of naval missions has been delegated to CG, FEAF."[12]

Although the air force had responsibility for the "assignment of tasks, designation of objectives, and authoritative direction necessary to accomplish the mission," the marines were in charge of their own administration, such as internal organization, discipline, logistic support, training, and maintenance of aircraft and airfields. In these matters, they reported directly to Commanding General, Aircraft, Fleet Marine Force (FMF), Pacific. The air force didn't care nor needed to hear about these things; they handled operations and the wing handled administration.[13]

* * * *

As chief of the general's staff, Frank Schwable was responsible for thousands of marines and, in fact, had four senior colonels (who had their own large staffs) accountable to him. These colonels each had a specific responsibility. They were G-1 (Personnel and Administration), G-2 (Intelligence), G-3 (Operations and Training), and G-4 (Logistics). Because the air force handled operations, Colonel Schwable did not have to concern himself with this aspect of the wing's many functions, but he had to make certain that the orders issued by the air force were carried out.

Once a month, Fifth Air Force issued an operation order to the wing and on a daily basis sent "frag orders," which were target assignments for the following day. These "frag orders" went to the wing and also were flown daily by courier plane to the two groups, MAG-12 and MAG-33.[14]

The air force owned 55 airfields and bases in Korea, designated K-1 through K-55. These "K" designations were used in lieu of place-names because the spelling of names on maps of Korea varied greatly. To avoid confusion, they were simply numbered.*

The marines were given use of K-3 and K-6. K-3, which was wing headquarters and home to MAG-33, was located on the east coast of South

Lieutenant Colonel Schwable, the first commanding officer of a U.S. night fighter squadron (official U.S. Marine Corps photograph).

---

*K-3: Pohang—also spelled P'ohang, Pohangdong, and P'ohang-dong. K-6: Pyongtaek—also spelled P'yongt'aek and Pyongt'aek.

Korea near the city of Pohang and about 70 miles north of Pusan. K-6, on the far west coast, was headquarters of MAG-12 and near Pyongtaek, 35 miles south of Seoul. As the crow flies, the distance between K-3 on the east coast and K-6 to the northwest across the waist of Korea was approximately 140 miles; the peninsula of Korea split the wing in two.[15]

On Colonel Schwable's sixth day as chief of staff, when he was just beginning to get his feet wet, the wing lost a pilot.

* * * *

Major Walter Harris arrived in Korea on Saturday, April 26, 1952, and was assigned to MAG-12 flying out of K-6 on the west coast. His tenure was short-lived, however. Ten days after coming to Korea, the 31-year-old major was gently floating to earth, swaying easily under the billowing white canopy of his parachute. The earth was North Korea and the eyes of the Chinese army were watching and waiting. It was 1:30, Tuesday afternoon, May 6, 1952, when they grabbed him.[16]

As was customary, his initial interrogation was of a military nature and it lasted three days. These were long, grueling days but, the major said, "Usually, sometime during the night, they would knock off and I would get some sleep. They never went after midnight."[17]

After these 72 hours near the front lines, he was moved north to an interrogation center and the germ warfare phase of his imprisonment began. For the first two weeks, the Chinese kept "trying to make me admit that the [germ warfare] program was being put into effect by the United States and the United Nations." He was thrown into a small grain storage hut and wasn't permitted to lie down, not even to sleep. If he did attempt to lie down, the guards forcefully made him sit up. Washing was not allowed, and the only time he left the hut was when they would suddenly pull him out and take him for questioning. Then they would "jump on you," according to Harris, and hammer and hammer for hours and hours at a time while he was forced to stand rigidly at attention.[18]

When he bailed out of his damaged fighter, he had badly injured his back, and the Chinese knew it—and used it. Harris said, "Finally, about the worst day I had in that particular camp, they kept me at attention all day long." Major Harris, like every pilot captured, was physically tortured in one way or another. Standing at attention in mind-numbing pain was horrible, and to add to this was the "infernal, ever present Chinese guard, with his burp gun pointing at your back," recalls Major Harris. "I don't mind having a gun pointed at me if the man behind it knows what he is doing. I had serious doubts that the people knew what they were doing. It shakes you up considerably."[19]

Navy and air force pilots received the same treatment but just a little extra effort was directed at marines. A Chinese officer said to Harris:

> We do not like marines. They are professional fighters, professional killers. They do not fight because they have to; they fight because they love to.... Furthermore, we do not like field grade [officers]. The junior officers and the enlisted men we can forgive because they have been ordered to do these things, but you and the other field officers, you tell them to do these crimes.*[20]

Walter Harris was a liar. Whenever his interrogator asked him any question that even remotely touched on something he thought they shouldn't know, he lied to them and then memorized the lie. He also tried to change the subject whenever he could. For example, he would explain the duties of a chaplain (they thought he was a political commissar), or discuss *Life* and *Esquire* magazines. Major Harris held their attention for a bit with these publications and said, "They were extremely interested in Esquire magazine because it had pictures of half nude women in it and American soldiers liked Esquire, so, therefore, American soldiers had the wrong ideas."[21]

Members of the armed forces are not instructed when they enter the service never to lie if captured — but they should be. In the vast majority of cases, the captors will discover the falsehood and when that happens, the most extreme penalty can and will be imposed. There was a Lieutenant Williams from Marine Fighter Squadron-212 (VMF-212), which was also part of MAG-12. During Lieutenant Williams's interrogation, the Chinese began comparing his honest answers to those of Major Harris (of whom the same questions had been asked). They were entirely different. After further investigation, the captors knew they were being conned, and the major was now in deep trouble.[22]

Walter Harris prayed hard, feeling he had a one-way ticket to death: "I was convinced they were going to kill me." The Chinese had already killed 43 percent of all Americans they held (during the starvation period, phase 1) and one more certainly wouldn't matter. For all intents and purposes prisoners of war have no rights. Unless they serve a purpose (military information, labor, or propaganda), captives in the hand of the enemy are useless. The death of Major Harris alone would be a tragedy, but coupled with 3,000 others it would be (to the Chinese, at least), just another statistic.[23]

The major was moved from the interrogation center to a second one, just on the outskirts of Pyongyang, named Coal Town. He was put in a dugout and stayed in that hole for 11 days. Because the door was always closed, inside it was pitch black 24 hours a day. An armed guard remained outside at all

---

*Company Grade: Second Lieutenant, First Lieutenant, Captain. Field Grade: Major, Lieutenant Colonel, Colonel. General ("Flag") Grade: Brigadier General, Major General, Lieutenant General, General.

times. The dirt floor was wet from the seepage of water, and even though summer was just around the corner, Harris said, "I was cold, I was filthy, I was sick with dysentery. I couldn't get out." And he was sure he was going to die. The thought of death was constantly on his mind.[24]

During those 11 days, he went to the latrine where he slept; he had no choice. It should be known that he did not speak with, or hear, another person except when some daily food was thrown at him. He was alone, somewhere in North Korea, in silent blackness. On the 11th day, an interrogator came to take a look and asked the major what the matter was. "I said, 'You know what is wrong with me; I am dying from dysentery.'" For the first time Walter Harris told the truth. He was believed, and within five minutes he was out of there.[25]

During his remaining year as a POW, the Chinese bothered him but it was half-hearted. Somehow they knew the major wasn't going to sign anything and they more or less gave up. Of his experiences, Major Harris said:

> They are masters at mental torture. They don't have to lay a hand on you to make you the most miserable person in the world. I would rather take a beating any day than be subjected to their type of questioning and treatment.... I hope I am never captured again but if I am, I think I would rather they shot me than put me through those paces again. If I am captured again, unless I am instructed otherwise, I am going to tell them name, rank and serial number, and I am going to stick to it. They might as well kill me then, as kill me slowly.[26]

Why didn't he sign a germ warfare confession? Mostly junior air force officers had already executed many confessions, and Harris knew this because the Chinese were very fond of displaying them. He didn't sign because he had his own personal convictions:

> My own particular case I think boils down to extreme stubbornness. I didn't want to admit to it. The thought was repulsive to me, of having my name attached to it.[27]

* * * *

Frank Schwable simply did not want his job. It was an important billet for him, however, since he was being groomed for that first silver star on his shoulder; the major drawback for the colonel was that he wasn't permitted to fly. He could get in a staff plane and fly over South Korea all he wanted but he wasn't empowered to cross (or even go near) the front lines. The custom in Korea, however, was for the very rapid rotation of key personnel, and General Jerome told him to just sit tight for a few months. Then, the general said, he would give him command of MAG-12 on the west coast. Although no specific date was set, this was music to the colonel's ears since he was going to get to do what he was trained to do—fight.[28]

Col. William Wendt was Schwable's G-3 (Operations) and had in his custody certain secret and top secret plans of the wing. As chief of staff, Colonel Schwable was authorized to read them, but he didn't. Colonel Wendt knew that his chief would be flying again within the next several months, and a few days prior to Colonel Schwable officially taking over as chief, Wendt approached him and said, "Are you aware that there is a restrictive clause that will prevent you, or anyone else who knows these plans, from thereafter being hazarded to capture?" He asked to see the order and after reading it, Schwable told his G-3 that he did not want to look at one single document that was in his possession. "Bill Wendt," replied Colonel Schwable, "if you think you are going to get me to read top secret plans which will thereafter prevent me from flying in combat, then let me assure you now that you are not." When classified data did occasionally cross his desk, the colonel passed it directly on to his G-2 (Intelligence) without looking at it. General Jerome noted, "I do not think he studied all of the long range plans the same way he would have had he expected to stay as chief of staff for the entire period he was in Korea."[29]

Frank Schwable was more than a nudge. One can just picture General Jerome going into hiding every time his senior colonel approached. Colonel Wendt said that "night after night in the mess and at every opportunity that he could buttonhole the Wing Commander, he reavowed his determination to fly in combat in Korea." His chief, he said, "wanted to fly more than any other thing in the world." Colonel Wendt continues:

> From the minute Colonel Schwable became Chief of Staff until the day I saw him leave to take the flight resulting in his capture, he haunted the Commanding General about wanting to fly, and went into the mess and out of the mess and up the streets and into the offices. It never ceased.[30]

Nine days after Major Harris was captured and only two weeks after the colonel took command of the general's staff, the wing lost another pilot.

* * * *

The Chinese captured Captain John Patrick Flynn, Jr., USMC, 29 years old, a staunch Irish American Catholic football player from South Dakota, on May 15, 1952. Prior to coming to Korea, he was a flight instructor at Pensacola. When shot down, he was piloting an F7F Tigercat from a night fighter squadron (VMF[N]-513) attached to MAG-12.[31]

Within a very few hours after being seized, he was shown the germ warfare confessions of two junior air force officers and then moved north, away from the front lines. Now we will have a short digression.[32]

No one knew where they were. You may notice that most of the time no mention is made of where these men are. That's because they don't know where they are. The interrogation center known as Pike's Peak is a classic example. There are more Pike's Peaks in Korea than anywhere else in the world. It seems that everyone had been at Pike's Peak, but they weren't.

There were four types of retention areas for prisoners of war in Korea:

Collection Points: These served as gathering facilities for recently captured men prior to shipment to a camp. Many, many men died at these points which, for the most part, were former Japanese mining camps. The usual stay (if one lived) was about two months.

Interrogation Centers: A temporary spot before prisoners were (usually) moved to a permanent camp. They were sprinkled all over Korea and at times had as few as two or three POWs in them for questioning. Most men in this book, including Colonel Schwable, were at interrogation centers.

Prison Camps: Located along the Yalu River, they were permanent facilities where men were shipped after collection and/or interrogation. These are the places one thinks of with searchlights, barbed wire, towers, and guards.

Propaganda Camps: There was only one major camp to speak of and that was Camp 12 outside Pyongyang. At its maximum capacity, it held a little over 70 prisoners.

Captain Flynn was imprisoned at one of many interrogation centers. A 21st-century example of an interrogation center is Guantánamo Bay, Cuba. It is not a prison camp.

So, wherever John Patrick Flynn was in North Korea, it didn't matter because he was just pounded and pounded on germ warfare. He wouldn't give them the right time of day, and after about four weeks of this and then being moved several different times, in early July 1952 he was placed in solitary confinement. They wanted his confession and they would use every method available to them to get it. When Flynn was thrown into isolation, Colonel Schwable had been a POW for two days.[33]

It was a bunker (or cave) of sorts and it measured 14 feet long and 10 feet wide. To a pilot, at an interrogation center in North Korea, it was immense. To Captain Flynn, who was a big guy, it was tiny. He recalled, "The ceiling, I couldn't stand straight up in it until I stood between the beams that ran crossways, the logs, the supporting cross beams. To stand straight, I stood between them."[34]

It was very dark inside but he could get a rough idea of what time of day it was by the shadows near the guarded entranceway. The hole was empty except for a straw mat and a blanket. The temperature during the summer was comfortable and the weather generally clear, but when it rained, the flooding caused problems. One day there was so much rain and flooding that the front of the bunker caved in and the Chinese had to dig him out.[35]

For his bodily needs, he was allowed out twice every 24 hours for very brief periods. As soon as he was brought back to the hole, interrogation began again. It just never let up. He was questioned from the moment he was shoved into the cave. During these periods, he was forced to stand at attention, the longest time being for eight hours. There was always a sentry at the entrance, and during those brief intervals when there was no questioning, Flynn was forced to sit at attention. During this "rest" time, his eyes would close "and the guard would watch me to see I didn't go to sleep and when I dozed off, he would usually wake me up by hitting me with a rifle butt."[36]

This wasn't exactly the smartest thing to do to this marine captain because all it did was annoy him. Flynn had played football for most of his adult life, including being on the Pensacola team in 1949, so these shots were nothing compared to what he took on the field. But they did cause "extreme anger and it brought out a very uncooperative frame of mind. I just felt like I absolutely wouldn't cooperate with them when they did that."[37]

One tactic the Chinese used drove Captain Flynn (and every other pilot at an interrogation center in North Korea) virtually insane. The Chinese officer would finish his questioning for the moment and, upon leaving, would inform the captain that he would be back in a few hours. Then he wouldn't return, sometimes for days. To all pilots, this waiting for the unknown was pure torture. Captain Flynn remained in the hole for four weeks undergoing this on and off again interrogation.[38]

By this time, the end of July 1952, the Chinese had an idea who they had in Colonel Schwable and they needed Flynn more than ever. Putting Major Bley aside for the moment, the captain would be a natural third-party collaborator to the confession of MAG-12 night fighters being the initial carriers of these weapons.

They had to torture him more. Captain Flynn was not permitted to talk — not a word. "I couldn't sing or talk to myself or make any sound," he recalled. It was a very stern silence:

> It had an effect on my morale because I had too much time to think and [the] silence bothered me a great deal. In my interrogation, I had a hard time talking. It was difficult to speak. My vocal cords would draw up or something. I noticed my voice was very hoarse and it was difficult to talk.[39]

If the Chinese wanted silence, John Patrick Flynn, Jr., was going to give them a silence they hadn't bargained for. Whenever an interrogator came in and asked if he had anything to say, the reply was a curt "No!" The officer would sometimes say to Flynn, "Let's get to the point," and Flynn would retort "There is no point," and then he would refuse to say another word.[40]

The F3D, a twin-engine night fighter, was expected to be deployed to Korea within the very near future. Chinese intelligence knew this and they needed some answers. Captain Flynn knew about the F3D. During one four-day period of his long, isolated confinement, he was taken for interrogation to Pyongyang, the capital of North Korea. The Chinese had to know about this new plane, and Flynn lied:

> Then they threw at me some information that just about floored me; the first information they told me, they wanted to know the exact date of the arrival of the F3Ds in Korea. I didn't think anyone knew about that. Then they brought out some books on the F3D, some manuals on it, with all the classified information in it. That took a lot out of me.

In the understatement of the year, the captain said, "I got to thinking then that the people are going to be pretty hard to deal with."[41]

This sort of thing happened to Flynn (and other POWs) more than once. He was asked if the plane had radar and he told them the truth, that it did. Breaking the name, rank, and serial number rule in this case was necessary because, Flynn noted, "They had a manual in front of them. When I told them a story, they would open the manual and verify it."[42]

After Pyongyang, he was taken back to his hole at the interrogation center and they started again. This time Flynn decided to pull religion on them. He told the Chinese that if he ever signed a germ warfare confession:

> that to my religion, being a Catholic, that if I gave him this, I would be guilty of grievous sin in that I would be aiding a godless cause and turning my back to my Christian faith. I went to great length to tell him that in the event I died before I got to a priest, which I thought there was a good chance of, I would forfeit my hope for eternal happiness.[43]

On a more secular note, although his spirituality was alive and well, his faith in America was faltering. John Flynn believed that things could have turned out differently had it not been for religion because "my patriotic sense of values became distorted due to their propaganda and everything else they kept throwing at me. I am ashamed to think right now what my patriotic values were because they weren't very good. At that time, that was not sufficient, patriotic reasons; I was losing them."[44]

Flynn's refusal to admit to germ warfare and his obstinacy in not even talking to his captors ("There was nothing to talk about. That was it.") signed his death warrant. It was about the first week in August 1952 when an interrogator opened the hatch to his hole and told him that because he wouldn't speak or sign, a military tribunal had been held in his absence and he was found guilty of being a war criminal and sentenced to death. His execution would be carried out in a few days. He said:

> It was a shock to me. I sincerely say that I believed them, that they were going to carry it out, but I actually was prepared for it and I told them to go ahead with it, that they had their alternative and it was their show, that they were holding the gun, so to speak, and to carry out their threat. At that stage of the game, I was feeling — my resistance seemed to be getting very weak. I thought, "This is as good a way as any." Having read the lives of the Saints, so on and so forth, "well, it isn't everyone that could be a martyr," and I felt along those lines at that time. So I actually was in favor of something like that, of their going ahead with it.[45]

Somewhere within this time frame, Colonel Schwable had been a captive for two to three weeks and, like all POWs, he was lying to his captors. One day a Chinese officer came into Flynn's hole and began questioning the captain about the organization of the First Marine Aircraft Wing. Flynn remained silent. The officer kept trying and got down to a specific; who was the commanding general of the wing? Who was the chief of staff? This fishing expedition ended with wanting to know the name of the wing ordnance officer. The captain honestly didn't know, but that was Major Roy Bley.[46]

Interrogation centers were not killing centers. Killing was done at a collection point or at one of the permanent retention areas along the Yalu. In 1952, there weren't many collection points left in North Korea. On August 13, 1952, John Patrick Flynn was transferred to a main camp on the river separating North Korea from Manchuria. He was to meet his executioners.[47]

* * * *

The front line is where the troops are, but in front of the fighting line, sometimes only a few thousand yards and at times miles, is the imaginary bomb line. This is an air force term. If the front line is stable, so is the bomb line, but if the front is fluid, the bomb line moves with it. It acts as a buffer zone to protect the troops from accidental friendly aircraft fire. Col. William Wendt (G-3) said that "in advance of [the bomb line] unrestricted bombing could take place and in the rear of it and forward of our front lines, controlled bombing was necessary."[48]

The bomb line was very important to Colonel Schwable and he had refused to look at any classified material anyone in the wing had concerning it. When a sensitive document needed to be signed, he would ask Colonel Wendt, for example, to point out the signature line and then sign without reading. The chief of staff gave Colonel Wendt a direct order when he told him, "You will keep the knowledge that would restrict me from flying across the bomb line to yourself." Even though Colonel Schwable would be taking over a combat group (MAG-12) within a few months, if he knew any current classified information, he would continue to be prevented from flying combat operations.

General Jerome pointed out that "Colonel Schwable, to the best of my knowledge and belief, never had access to material which would thereby have mitigated against his flying across the bomb line."[49]

Although Colonel Schwable enjoyed flying, it would not be incorrect to state that he was addicted to combat. Addiction is not healthy, physically or mentally. His desires, however, motivated his comrades. Colonel Wendt remarked:

> I found it a very inspiring thing to witness the fact that a man who was the Chief of Staff and who could well hide behind the regulation that said if he had any knowledge about top level theatre plans, he wouldn't hazard himself or be hazarded to crossing the bomb line ... [it was] a very inspirational thing and I think in keeping with the highest traditions of the Marine Corps, and the finest leadership qualities.[50]

3

The Preparation

> *Our past apathetic acceptance of the blessings of freedom and the old military routine of giving the enemy, when captured, only name, rank and serial number obviously are not a sufficient answer to murderers, torturers and immoralists who believe the ends justify any means.*
> — Hanson W. Baldwin *New York Times* January 28, 1954, 4

Gen. Clayton C. Jerome signed this order:

> Personnel with access to highly classified matter or broad knowledge of theatre plans or operations are not to be placed in a position where risk of capture by the enemy conceivably exists.

This was a "long-standing" mandate and the general went on to explain, "I know in my own case, I was the G-3 [Operations] for Comairnorsols [Commander, Air, Northern Solomons] in Bougainville when we were hitting Rabaul every day and I was not permitted to fly up there because I knew future operations.... No such long-range plans existed in Korea because we weren't going any place."[1]

It's somewhat adventurous for a person to disobey his own regulation but apparently Frank Schwable did just that. His signature was attached to, and therefore his responsibility rested in obeying, the following order:

> Commands are directed to assure that all personnel flying over or traveling within *or adjacent to* [emphasis added] enemy territory shall be briefed only on items essential to accomplishment of their mission.[2]

He then went on to say, as General Jerome did, that if it was even envisioned that capture could take place by getting too close to the lines and one had broad knowledge of operations and plans, present or future, you couldn't go.

An excuse was needed to disobey, and that excuse was reconnaissance. Colonel Schwable was taking over MAG-12, so as commanding officer, shouldn't he at least know what the front lines looked like other than from a map? But he wasn't getting command for another couple of months and the lines could change, so what was the rush? It was very premature.

General Jerome not only permitted but also encouraged reconnaissance flights over the lines, but that was for active duty aviators. He felt it was a good way to have new pilots, for example, gain experience by seeing and feeling what it was like to fly over enemy-held territory. He did not permit his staff, however, just to get in a plane and fly. There always had to be a reason. The general said, "I didn't send purely administrative planes over the lines." The question continues to linger concerning the final flight of Frank Schwable; was it a legitimate reconnaissance or was it "administrative"? We should remember, though, that he was a senior marine colonel, chief of staff of one of the largest air wings in the world, and not too many people were going to step up to the plate and question what he did.[3]

It was beautiful out, one of the best flying days ever during the entire war, and the last time that General Jerome saw his colonel until they met again 19 months later in a courtroom half a world away. It was early Tuesday morning, July 8, 1952, when Colonel Schwable and Major Bley took off in an SNB staff plane and flew directly northwest across the peninsula to K-6. An SNB is basically a small, twin-engine Beechcraft like the planes one sees at a local airport. As a matter of fact, Beechcraft manufactured the SNB.[4]

The co-pilot was not a lucky marine. Roy Bley wasn't assigned as number two man but was simply hitching a "ride in the airplane because I had to go to K-6 on business." Since he was an aviator, however, he offered to take the right side cockpit seat to assist the colonel during the morning flight to the west coast and back. Actually, this aircraft did not require a co-pilot when flying during the day in good weather; a second pilot was necessary only if instruments were being used. Major Bley simply picked the wrong plane in which to hitch a ride.[5]

At about 10 on the fateful morning, they landed at K-6. Major Bley left the colonel and went about his business while Schwable met up with Col. Robert Galer, commanding officer of MAG-12. Colonel Galer was a holder of the Medal of Honor for heroism during World War II, having shot down more than 10 Japanese planes during a period of 29 days in late 1942, thereby making him a "Double Ace." During his almost three-month tenure with MAG-12, the colonel made 24 flights over the bomb line and was once shot down. He evaded capture for over two hours before being picked up by a navy helicopter, which had to travel 75 miles northward, over enemy territory, to get him.[6]

Shortly after landing, the two colonels made an inspection tour of the base. Schwable informed the commander that he was going to relieve him in

Beechcraft SNB. This is the type of aircraft Colonel Schwable was piloting when he was shot down (courtesy Raytheon Aircraft).

about eight weeks and they discussed the future plans of the group, details on engineering and building projects at the base, and other miscellaneous subjects concerning the command. During their tour, Galer recalls Frank Schwable saying to him "that this was the first day with completely clear weather that he had flown in Korea and that he was interested in the terrain over which we were operating." Colonel Schwable did not want to fly directly back to K-3, which was southeast of them (and away from the front). He asked Galer for the best way back to wing headquarters going along the front lines.[7]

When flying behind the lines, an aviator's checkpoints in South Korea were the air force "K" bases. Galer suggested to Colonel Schwable that, after takeoff, he fly north about 35 miles to K-16 (Seoul, the capital of South Korea), make a right-hand turn and essentially go east; then over his left shoulder were the front lines. There were a few other midway checks but the final checkpoint was K-18. Kangnung (K-18) is a small city on the eastern shore of South Korea and about 125 miles north of Pohang (K-3). It was wing headquarters, home of MAG-33, and the final destination of Colonel Schwable and Major Bley. At Kangnung, they were to make another right and head due south for landing. Marine intelligence disagreed with this flight plan and analyzed that his first east coast checkpoint was not K-18 but some 35 miles further north at Sokcho (K-50). This would have added a further drift north, but it really doesn't matter because the colonel never got close to the east coast of South Korea.[8]

* * * *

There was absolutely no reason for Frank Schwable to make this flight. In support of the colonel, many officers vouched that he did not have knowledge of classified data (which may be debatable) and that his flight was authorized. Let's assume that both are true; knowledge of nothing and the required authorization in place, which it was. Not a single person, however, mentions either the senior staff positions Colonel Schwable occupied during the transition years or the last position he held at the Pentagon just months before his capture. If, as we recall, he was the executive officer of the Division of Aviation, USMC, then Frank Schwable had no business heading north.

This was not the first flight Colonel Schwable made while in Korea. During his nine weeks as chief of staff, he had flown four or five other times but never near the lines. One of the reasons the colonel flew this particular mission was that he needed his four hours in the air every month in order to qualify for flight pay. As chief of staff, he found it difficult to squeeze in the hours, and this trip was as good a time as any to add to the required monthly four.[9]

Even though the transfer was at least another two months away (at a minimum), the colonel was determined to go north because, he said, "I was then preparing myself to fly combat missions against the enemy." He further stated, "I wanted to obtain my first look at the general area of operations in which I was soon to fly active combat close support missions."[10]

In addition to wanting to see the supposed future ground he would be flying over, there was what some would consider a valid reason to make the flight, not wearing the hat of the future commander of MAG-12, but wearing the cover of chief of staff. Reports had recently passed over his desk of accidental bombings of UN troops by marine pilots because of confusion in locating front line positions. The colonel said, "I believed sincerely that I would be in a better position to act on that type of investigation if I could see for myself the type of terrain, front line markings, etc. that could lead to such confusion and mistaken identity of positions."[11]

Whatever the reasons, valid or invalid, it really is a moot point because the colonel was determined:

Well, naturally, if I'm going to be flying up and down the lines, I had better at least know what they look like. So it was my first opportunity to fly up where the business was going on, and that is what I did.¹²

* * * *

Replacement pilots came into the two groups approximately once a month, and for the first few days they were given an orientation briefing on the operations of the group and the wing. During this overview, they were told the guiding principal was that if captured, they were to furnish only name, rank, and serial number. According to Maj. Leroy Frey, operations officer for MAG-12, "That was always of interest to the people and there were questions asked of it." Later on, all customary preflight briefings were on "the latest escape and evasion tactics and location of position[s] of enemy antiaircraft." After the code of name, rank, and serial number was initially mentioned it was totally ignored. Not one single surviving American POW captured in Korea, enlisted or officer, ever adhered to it.¹³

During their hitch with the group, however, and contrary to the formal orientation, when the question of name, rank, and serial number came up, no one ever told the pilots, "Stop! That's it! You can't go any further." However noble, it would be imbecilic to even think of spouting out only name, rank, and serial number with the open end of a gun barrel resting between their eyes and life dangling by a thread. According to Major Frey, in discussions about this code of silence with the pilots, "It usually came out [that] you would probably do as an individual holds up, some probably could, and some couldn't. It was on an individual basis." This was obviously quite a bit of latitude vis-à-vis the doctrine in place. Major Frey continued by saying that they needn't come to a grinding halt after furnishing the required three pieces of personal information. In fact, "We didn't tell him now this is the ultimate here.... That was a decision they would make themselves." The problem with this philosophy is that although it offers the POW an opportunity to remove himself from strict, rigid guidance, in return it leaves absolutely no guidance at all.¹⁴

The governing authorities concerning silence while a prisoner are Article 1223 of Navy Regulations, which dictates strictly name, rank, and serial number, and Section 0919 of the United States Navy Security Manual, which adds date of birth, place of birth, and home address. Therefore, in the naval service, there are six things one can tell a captor, not three. To violate this code of silence is a court-martial offense. After the war, for two years the army conducted 14 courts-martial across the United States against soldiers (officers and enlisted, including two lieutenant colonels) who broke the rule. The charge was collaboration with the enemy, and depending on the attitude of the convening authority, it could carry the death penalty. Collaboration and treason are the same thing; a military distinction without a difference. Some of the court-martialed soldiers received severe prison terms.[15]

Fifth Air Force was the mother hen over the wing and many preflight briefings were provided by air force officers to the marines. The wing itself had its own intelligence-gathering apparatus, including Naval Forces, Far East. All information during briefings was culled from various operations and intelligence documents and these briefings did not consist of opinions by the briefers except in one arena: "What do you do if captured?"[16]

It's common for researchers in this specific area to know that the air force told all of its pilots to go far beyond the code of silence, and some of these men, when captured, essentially gave away the farm. They reached a point of being practically ruthless in furnishing information to the Chinese. They were told to make up stories (lie) before taking off in the event of being shot down. Of course, the question is why make up stories if one can only furnish name, rank, and serial number?[17]

Why did the air force blatantly ignore the code of silence? Because it was running out of pilots! It was not that there was a pilot shortage, per se, but many of the men just plainly refused to fly in Korea; they wouldn't go. When the navy and marines encountered this problem, which they occasionally did, those men were administratively processed out of aviation and they either left the service or were transferred to non-flying duties. The deputy commander of Fifth Air Force, according to Col. William Wendt (G-3), was barraged with "various applications to be relieved from flying duty from Air Force personnel.... I would suggest that the problem of getting pilots was a fairly acute one." The air force had to ease up and therefore, one way to possibly furnish a comfort level to men flying in combat and to get more men to do so, was to instruct them (which they did) to ignore the rule of name, rank, and serial number. Colonel Wendt said, "I believe they may be interrelated."[18]

No one had a clue what to replace the strict code of silence with but everyone, almost without exception, said that undiluted silence wasn't enough guidance. The court of inquiry investigating the conduct of Colonel Schwable was almost unconsciously also investigating the value (or lack thereof) of the rule of name, rank, and serial number. One of the opinions of the court was "That there exist, and existed at the time of Colonel Schwable's capture, contradictory and confusing doctrines and instructions within the various services of the Armed Forces of the United States as to what information or misinformation a prisoner of war may, or may not, give his captors."[19] Following are some examples of the variations.

Col. Joseph W. Keane, Jr., USMC: He was briefed that giving only name, rank, and serial number "was currently considered an antiquated, not practical concept, and we were briefed on what I considered to be a more lenient procedure." He was told that he could discuss "inconsequential matters with the enemy." Colonel Keane's personal thought on the subject was that if people stuck with pure silence, they "wouldn't live very long."[20]

Col. Nathan G. Post, USMC: During World War II, the colonel was based on Okinawa, the Japanese were on the run, and he was briefed that the "regulations of name, rank and serial number would be overlooked and the situation was such that whatever you told the captors would be of no consequence, that you could tell them anything."[21]

Col. Robert Galer, USMC: He never saw anything in writing but just knew "the local session of rumors the people had, were that both SAC [Strategic Air Command] and Air Force units had [been] briefed on a different approach than name, rank, and serial number, but these were never verified or brought up as official correspondence, but I heard it in my officer's club at K-6."[22]

Col. William Wendt, USMC: MAG-33 was planning a major attack and the colonel, as assistant chief of staff (G-3), decided to go to the briefing. He received "an indication that more than name, rank, and serial number could be given in the Korean War." Colonel Wendt said that if captured, the pilots and aircrews "were certainly told to have a definite story to give the communists." As far as marine intelligence officers briefing their fellow marines, they followed Fifth Air Force policy. Colonel Wendt noticed that Marine Corps briefing officers themselves "typified Fifth Air Force thinking on this subject, and in that light their view would appear to be that something more than name, rank and serial number was what a captured pilot would be required to give."[23]

Col. Arthur Binney, USMC: "Whenever a plane was lost, which was frequently, unfortunately, the boys would surmise what they might be up against and discuss what they would do under the circumstances," said the colonel, the chief of staff whom Colonel Schwable relieved. This was a very stressful topic to the marine pilots and it was addressed every night in the officer's mess. While commanding MAG-33 some time prior to his assignment as chief of staff, Colonel Binney told his men "to divulge nothing of military value; that they should use their own judgment and certainly not sacrifice their lives to prevent something that was known to everyone, I mean that was printed in the magazines, that were available." Obviously, this advice, no matter how well intentioned, was against navy regulations but the colonel thought that "with the enemy we were fighting, I felt that it was sound judgment."[24]

Col. Frank Schwable, USMC: Regulations say one thing and briefings another. The colonel noted, "Those are your confusing and conflicting directives that a man sits over there all by himself and tries to figure out in his mind and he can't figure them out. So he grasps, I think, apparently, at what maybe he himself subconsciously wants; he sort of says, 'Well, that is the best conclusion I can reach from what I think.'" Totally frustrated, Frank Schwable asked:

> What were my military instructions if caught as a POW? Give name, rank and serial number only, or at most confine your answers to publicly known material! But what about propaganda? What are the instructions about false confessions for propaganda purposes where the issue can be finally reduced to [the] question of whether to "confess" or die — a question that now must be solved by each individual, not on the basis of heroics but in the light of cold, factual, inevitabilities.[25]

Maj. Walter Harris, USMC: When he arrived at El Toro, California, as part of the 20th aviation replacement draft, the major was required to attend school for a week. During one lecture, a marine captain told the replacements that since they had been instructed on how to escape and evade, "Now, we are going to tell you what to do in case you cannot escape and evade and get captured. It is not a pleasant thought.... Name, rank and serial number is out, gentlemen. They are going to find out anything they want to find out, anyway. Go ahead and tell them the truth right off." Unfortunately Major Harris didn't follow this dictate. His reaction to the statement was "I almost fell through the chair when I heard that." He was rather cocky: "I knew at the time that 'Red Hot Fighter Pilot Harris' would never get captured, so I never did pay too much attention to it."[26]

When he was released from captivity in 1953, the major reflected on his experiences as a POW and most particularly on the code of silence:

> If you are instructed and warned that you must stick to name, rank and serial number, when the going gets tough, when they are putting that pressure on you and you are trying to keep from rationalizing, saying, "Well, maybe it is all right to tell them this, maybe it is all right to tell them that," you don't have to depend on your own discretion, your own judgment, because in the back of your mind you can hear your commanding officer saying, "name, rank, and serial number," and it is that last little straw that a drowning man can hang on to keep from sinking. There is a time when every prisoner needs that straw, that little piece of driftwood, to keep from drowning. So I would like to see the next time I got into battle for my country a definite, strong policy that tells me exactly what to do and does not leave it up to my own poor judgment which, when the going gets rough, as I said before, tends to make me rationalize.[27]

General Lemuel Shepherd, USMC: "If the Geneva concept is unworkable in waging war along the red front, it should be replaced by something better."[28]

* * * *

It was just a little after 2 on this beautiful Tuesday afternoon when it was time to return to K-3. Colonel Galer, who signed the plan for the return trip and therefore was the "clearing authority," accompanied Colonel Schwable to the airfield. When they reached the operations building, Major Bley was already there waiting for them with the flight plan in his hand. Leaving Galer and Bley on the front steps of the building for a few minutes, Colonel Schwable went into the operations office to "check the weather in respect to going up near K-18" on the northern part of the far east coast of South Korea. Upon returning, he announced that they were ready to go.[29]

Strapping themselves into their seats (Schwable on the left, Bley on the right), the two marines brought the twin engines to full power, raced down the runway and were airborne. They climbed on a northerly heading and, according to Major Bley, "pulled up over the city of Seoul on the north, around the general area of Kaesong, flying an altitude of somewhere between five and six thousand feet." Panmunjom was in the distance and the colonel pointed out to the major the balloons tethered over the area where the armistice negotiations were taking place.[30]

After leaving Kaesong, they took an approximate heading of 55 degrees magnetic at 6,000 feet. They stayed on this course for about 25 minutes, circled a few areas to get a better picture of what was below, and then continued in a northeasterly direction. Major Bley knew they were okay because he could see friendly identification panels on the ground. Then, according to the major, "We evidently got behind enemy lines."[31]

Somewhere near the Hwachon Reservoir, which is about 70 miles northeast of Seoul and some 60 miles from the east coast, there was a "tongue," an appendage sticking out. (Whoever said the front lines had to be straight?) Occupying this area was the Chinese army. Unfortunately, Colonel Schwable's instructions were to basically fly a straight line; there was never any mention of this salient. The following is Colonel Schwable's opinion about the spur. He describes what happened:

[We] went up to the lines and went flying east, right along the front lines so I could see — what was the terrain like? Could you spot the troops from up there? Jungles, or was it open plains? I wanted to see for myself beforehand. I thought I was flying just behind our lines, and I was, but apparently there was one place where there was a little salient, like a finger down south — pointing south — and I didn't know it, so I flew across it.... But I was low, you see, so that I could try to see the [friendly] troops and their installations and things like that and flying across this salient. I actually flew across a little bit of their territory — Bongo — that was it.[32]

Two days before, on Sunday, July 6, 1952, Colonel Schwable wrote what would be his last letter to Beverly for a long time. Obviously, she was glad to hear from her husband and to know that he was happy to be in action and "thoroughly enjoyed" his work.[33]

4

The Capture

I was born a marine, and I knew I was going to be a marine and there was never any question of it.
— Col. Frank Schwable, USMC, Oral History, 3

Certain things in life happen suddenly, and suddenly Frank Schwable saw 40mm tracer shells passing close to his starboard wing. Roy Bley also saw them directly ahead. The colonel applied full throttle coupled with propeller pitch control, hard turned to the right, and climbed. During this southward loop, they were fatally hit.[1]

For a few seconds, everything seemed to be okay and then both engines abruptly "stopped at once, without a sputter." Schwable looked over at Bley's controls and they were all out — the wobble pump, the cross-feed and engine fuel suction pump, and the selector valve. He next glanced at the instruments but couldn't see much because they were covered in blood. Major Bley was in very bad shape.[2]

Roy Bley seemed to have been the target of every Chinese gunner on the ground. All of the shells came up through the co-pilot's seat and "right between my legs, through my legs." He wasn't even aware that the engines had stopped "because I was hit in so many places [that] I didn't have my full wits about me." There were 12 wounds on the body of the major, eight of them very large and four smaller ones, which were caused by shrapnel from the plane. "I had a hole through my right wrist, through [the instep of] my right foot..., a hole through my right thigh, a large piece of shrapnel in my right shinbone, one wound in the right side of my chest, one under my right arm." Due to the immense physical shock of the moment, coupled with an enormous adrenaline rush, Roy Bley felt absolutely no pain.[3]

One of the main fuel lines was under the right cockpit seat and when it was shattered and the engines quit, they began sinking. There were two thoughts in each man's mind, which were to put on their parachutes and try to restart the engines. While Colonel Schwable was harnessing up, the major noted that some of the instruments were working; he could see they were normal except for the air speed, which was very low, and the fuel pressure, which was zero. He switched tanks and wobbled the fuel pressure pump, but no dice. He then trimmed the plane and nosed forward to pick up air speed in order to maintain stability. While all this was going on, the distance between the ground and the belly of the turning plane was getting narrower and narrower. At about 1,700 feet above the North Korean mountain ranges, they both knew they had to jump.[4]

Frank Schwable helped Bley toward the rear of the now pilotless plane and opened the door. The colonel was a little concerned with the two of them in the rear because with no pilot, this particular type of aircraft had a tendency to climb a little with the rearward weight and then go into a spin. That didn't happen.[5]

The SNB was going dangerously slow, turning at 80 miles per hour, and they had to get out. With both marines standing at the open door, the colonel ordered Major Bley to jump. Watching Bley's wounded body fall from the plane, he waited until he saw the white canopy of the major's parachute open and then the colonel bailed out. While the men were floating downward, the staff plane continued on its circle and flew directly into a mountain. Frank Schwable was floating south of and above Roy Bley and the major could hear Colonel Schwable yelling that as soon as he hit the ground, he'd come and get him and not to move. The landings were not very pretty.[6]

* * * *

Gen. Clayton Jerome was notified about the shoot-down of his chief of staff a little more than two hours after the incident. He ordered his legal officer, a Major Hearn, to investigate the matter.[7]

It was immediately discovered that both men got out of the aircraft. They bailed out between three and five miles behind the front lines but there were forward observers out there who saw the entire thing. It didn't take much skill to figure out whose plane it was; there weren't too many SNBs flying along the front lines in Korea. These observers also saw both parachutes open and drift downward. The commandant of the Marine Corps was immediately notified and General Shepherd called Beverly Schwable, whose family he knew, and told her of the incident and that her husband had escaped the plane safely.[8]

The investigation at wing headquarters also found that the flight may have had faulty navigation, but this was uncertain. In Korea, there is a 7-degree compass variation, and it's important that a flight plan take into consideration this difference. If one didn't do it, it was quite possible that one would go off course. The general said, "The fact is that the variation had been neglected many, many times when people did not draw actual flight lines on the map."⁹

Another consideration was the wind. At K-3 that day, the upper air was from the southeast at 50–60 miles per hour. The question arose whether this was taken into navigational calculations?¹⁰

The last thing that this quick investigation claimed was that the plane must have been on autopilot. There was just no way a two-engine Beechcraft could not go into a spin with all the weight in the rear and no one driving. Being on autopilot creates a drift, but on autopilot one doesn't notice it as much. Major Bley insisted that at the time they saw the tracers, they were flying manually. But that's the last time either of these men remember anything about autopilot. It's certainly conceivable that one of them may have instinctively switched it on prior to bailing out.¹¹

* * * *

Colonel Schwable got snagged in a tree. Somehow he unbuckled his harness and climbed down. Roy Bley was about 150 yards north of him and Schwable headed in that direction. This was extremely rugged country, as most of North Korea is, and it wasn't easy for a soon-to-be 44-year-old man, who was basically out of shape compared to, say, a 19-year-old marine, to traverse this territory. He had to climb the side of a ridge to get to Major Bley and it was almost straight up. "I felt like a side hill goat where one leg is this short and the other one is that long, trying to walk along the side of a hill."¹²

While Colonel Schwable was trying to reach him, Roy Bley had been knocked out cold. Just before he hit the ground, his parachute canopy got hung up in a large tree, slamming him into it backwards and knocking out the major. When he came to, he found himself helplessly dangling from his harness about nine feet off the ground. Knowing he was behind enemy lines, he had to get out of there and head south. He said, "So I jerked open my parachute harness and fell out." When he hit the ground, he knocked himself out once more. Coming to again and aware that his chute probably attracted quite a bit of attention, he started crawling south and up a nearby ridge. Close to the top, he saw Colonel Schwable climbing north toward him.*¹³

Schwable reached the peak and began making his way toward Major Bley, whom he could see. As soon as they met, the colonel took a knife from

---

**Some say that Frank Schwable should have immediately headed south and attempted to sneak through the front lines to safety on his own; he was just too valuable to be going in the wrong direction in order to assist his wounded co-pilot. Although it would have been the prudent thing to do, it just wasn't the colonel's (nor any other marine's) style to leave a fallen comrade behind.*

Bley's pocket and told him he was going to climb up the tree and cut up shrouds "to tie up some of my wounds."[14]

"Lying there in a stupor," as he recalled, Major Bley watched the colonel reach the tree, climb it, and begin slashing away at the parachute. Schwable and Bley heard the shots at the same time. The major saw the colonel fall from the tree and thought he had been shot, but it was Frank Schwable hustling down as fast as he could. Then Bley heard "jabbering" soldiers running up toward him. The colonel was looking at his co-pilot, who was sitting on the crest of the sharp ridge, and watched as the major pushed himself off the top and disappeared down the other side. Roy Bley rolled onto the feet of approaching Chinese soldiers.[15]

The two marines were on the ground for only 10 minutes before they were separately caught, Schwable on one side of the ridge and Bley on the other. Colonel Schwable was an easy capture (as was Major Bley) and about a squad size unit of Chinese soldiers approached him with weapons at the ready. The unarmed chief of staff gave up. There were about 10 of them, the time was 3:30 in the afternoon. Schwable said, "It was obvious to me the minute I got my feet on the ground and had not broken my neck, there I was, a Colonel, and I had some pretty good experience and pretty good background, and there I was in the Chinaman's hands."[16]

"We were so close to the front lines that they were just all over the place — all over the place," remembers the colonel. Alone, he was taken to the bottom of the hill to what appeared to be a squad area, given a drink of water, and searched. He was wearing the Marines' summer khaki uniform, with no decorations except for the silver eagles on his collar and the gold wings of a naval aviator pinned above his left breast pocket.[17] "I was caught flat-footed. Not having anticipated flying across the enemy lines, I had the works on me," said the colonel. At this point, as with most recently captured men, "the works" went way beyond name, rank, and serial number. In Colonel Schwable's case, they snatched his wallet, which contained his Marine Corps identification card and Virginia driver's license, which furnished the captors his date of birth and home address. The wallet also contained photos of his wife and two children, David and Susan. They took his flight instrument ticket that was issued on March 31, 1952, at Naval Air Station Anacostia, and mess cards for Bethesda and Anacostia. The searchers also found his flight clearance ticket, which stated that his home station was the First Marine Aircraft Wing and gave K-3 as his point of departure and K-6 as the destination.[18]

Soldiers are never instructed not to lie if captured but they are also never ordered (and they should be ordered) that, if possible, throw everything away except money; money is important in a POW camp and one should hide it. Colonel Schwable supported this simple logic when he said, "When you get shot down things happen awfully fast, too fast, much too fast. If I had sense enough to be able to think, I would have thrown my wallet away. It never occurred to me."[19]

After gathering the colonel's personal belongings in a handkerchief, the Chinese tied his hands behind his back and marched him southward, up a 2,500-foot mountain, toward their positions. At the top, Colonel Schwable met his first English-speaking Chinese official. The officer demanded his name, rank, and serial number and then asked, "First Wing?" There was no sense in lying; the officer was staring at his outward-bound flight clearance ticket. Frank Schwable answered yes.[20]

At about 5 that afternoon, the front line officer was finished with Schwable and obviously communicated to his superiors that he was holding a colonel from the First Marine Aircraft Wing. This communication was probably forwarded to Chinese intelligence. One hour later, with his hands still tied, Frank Schwable started to hike in a northwesterly direction. In Korea, no one simply walks, they climb. Up mountains and down mountains they went until they reached what Colonel Schwable describes as a regimental headquarters of the Chinese army. It was 1 in the morning, July 9, 1952.[21]

* * * *

Anytime you go to war with a nation of different color, it's a race war. There have been many of them in the 20th century, but two of the largest race wars were the Pacific Theatre during World War II, and Korea. The key word in a race war is "inferiority." Most have seen posters of the buck-toothed, thick-spectacled Japanese soldier, half slouched over, looking like the biggest idiot that ever walked the face of the earth. This is supposedly the typical "Jap," representing those who planned and successfully executed one of the greatest surprise attacks in history; the conquerors of southeast Asia; the designers and builders of the practically invincible Zero fighter plane and the naval architecture which begot *Yamato*, the greatest, most powerful battleship the world had ever seen. Never underestimate your enemy, especially in a race war, and yet we do it every day.

Many Chinese interrogators were educated in England and America. The two schools in the United States most often mentioned are the University of Chicago and the University of California. Roy Bley was extremely angry at the education of his interrogators; he mentions it several times. Bley talks indignantly about their master's degrees, saying they "were well educated, college graduates, not only in their own country but college graduates here in our own country, people who had Masters Degrees in economics and sociology."[22]

One year before the Korean War, the Chinese nationalist government under Chiang Kai-shek was booted out of China and sent on its way to Formosa (Taiwan). The Chinese army went with him — or did it? Many officers of the nationalist army refused to go; they had their wives, children, traditions, roots, everything in China. It was their home. These are the men who stayed behind. Many became officers in the Chinese communist army.

Certain officers who remained on the mainland had their infantry training at Fort Bragg, North Carolina, and artillery training at Fort Sill, Oklahoma. All manuals were translated into Chinese for their convenience.[23]

These are the people whom Korean War POWs were confronting. They had no idea that these extremely intelligent captors had already conceived a propaganda campaign that, in itself, was well worth a master's degree if not a Ph.D.

Shortly after capture, Colonel Schwable was questioned about the command structure and organization of the wing. He told them. At this time, they still didn't know what his position was except that he was a marine colonel. However, he offered the truth:

> I am pretty sure that the Chinese know that the Joint Chiefs of Staff control the military functions. I know from the various questions they asked me that they knew CINCFE was the Unified Commander in the Far East, and that the Fifth Air Force came under CINCFE, through FEAF. I know that. They told me that. I knew it. So on those sorts of levels of command relationships, I talked to them about it. But I am convinced in my own mind that I didn't give them anything that they didn't know, because they know an awful lot.[24]

* * * *

For the next two weeks, time and place had no meaning; dates, days, and hours were wrong and minutes did not exist. But there had to be a center of reality and that reality was what Frank Schwable knew; what he had in his mind. He had in his memory the future code plans of the U.S. Navy and Marines, the tactical employment of new weapons and, according to Col. Paul Sherman, "the strategic concepts under which the United States was and is basing its defense."[25]

Frank Schwable was allowed a few hours sleep. On the morning of July 9, he was taken about five miles away to a battalion or regimental headquarters. For the remainder of the day, he underwent military interrogation. His initial interrogators were officers of the Chinese army and all they wanted to know is what was in front of them; these were soldiers and they were not concerned about anything else. The colonel honestly didn't know too much about the operations of front line troops anyway, so he really couldn't supply the Chinese with any valuable real-time tactical intelligence.[26]

4. The Capture

The troops he was with were facing a South Korean (ROK) division and most of the Chinese soldiers had never seen a white man before. The colonel observed that for the most part they were "just a bunch of kids," and were like "curiosity ridden little monkeys." During the day-long interrogation, soldiers would gather around and, according to Schwable, "They would look at me, the guards would smile and laugh and chatter, they are just like a bunch of monkeys all gathering around and chattering, squatting on the deck, looking at me. They would point at me."[27]

The colonel claims that it was on this second day of captivity that he began his isolation:

> I started then and there what turned out to be fourteen months of solitary confinement, never saying one single word to another American until the morning I left the Yalu River for repatriation with the exception of several comments to Major Bley, in the presence of an interpreter during three subsequent moves, and several whispered words to a few other POWs during transit.[28]

After capture, Roy Bley was moved and thrown into a cave. He wasn't interrogated. He just lay there in the darkness and in pain. About 6 P.M. on this second day, he was placed onto a stretcher and carried out of the hole in the side of the mountain. He saw Colonel Schwable, of course accompanied by guards, walking toward him, his hands tied with three-quarter-inch rope. They were marched into a valley where a jeep was waiting for them. Bley was removed from the stretcher and because of the wound in his right thigh, he was dumped into the right corner of the rear seat; a guard was in the rear left corner. The colonel sat in the middle and saw nothing but bandages covering the major's body; Frank Schwable thought he looked "half doped up." Up front were the driver, an interpreter, and a second guard. With six people, it was crowded, and in passing, Colonel Schwable remarked, "The Chinese get a great many people in a jeep."[29]

They traveled for about six hours north, "through river bottoms, trails, and very poor roads," as the colonel described it. When they got to where they were going, they were taken out of the jeep and split up. Roy Bley was put into a "mud hut cell" which was six feet wide, eight feet long, and seven feet high. Here he remained alone, mending his wounds, for five days.[30]

Removed from the jeep, Colonel Schwable was put into a Korean hut. A couple of days later, he was moved to another one. At this point, it should be kept in mind that the colonel is still dealing with Chinese soldiers and not interrogators. They would come later. But these troops needed information, and during this five-day stay, the colonel recalled, "I was interrogated by a great variety of people." The enemy would constantly enter his tiny hut and question him about what was going on at the front and, more importantly, "What are you doing here?" Colonel Schwable told his first lie:

> I said I was brand new in Korea, I had just come there; I was as yet unassigned, had no job, and that was the very thing I was doing that day, taking my first look around Korea along the front lines. Therefore, I didn't know anything of the ground situation; I didn't know anything of the organization; I was just brand new; I didn't know anything.[31]

Frank Schwable had "the works" on him, and one of the papers was his flight instrument ticket issued on March 31, 1952. The colonel arrived in Korea with General Jerome only 11 days later. In trying to convince his captors that he was new to the area, he said to them, "Look at this particular card here, my instrument ticket. That proved at least on the first of April, I wasn't out here." He stayed with this story and continually got away with it, at least with the troops. Actually, they couldn't have cared less; they were primarily concerned about what was ahead of them. This does not mean that they weren't communicating with their superiors; they were, and while all this was going on with the army, Chinese intelligence and political people were conducting their own investigations in order to find out who this man was.[32]

During the fifth day at this location (Monday, July 14, 1952), Bley and Schwable were moved. Late at night, a truck with a canvas top covering the bed pulled up to the major's mud hut and carried Bley out on a stretcher. They slid him into the back of the truck. He traveled in the darkness for only a few minutes when they stopped and picked up Colonel Schwable. At this time, Bley was removed from the stretcher and was ordered to sit on a narrow bench, which ran along both sides of the back of the truck. They traveled northwest about 45 miles. Both marines remained awake in the truck for the entire night and listened to a hard rain falling on the canvas cover tied over the back.[33]

In the truck were the usual guards and an interpreter, who sternly forbade them to speak. During this four-hour ride, a few short stops were made, and when the interpreter did leave the vehicle, the two officers had an opportunity to whisper a few words. Major Bley recalls the colonel apologizing to him "for putting me in this compromising position." They both expressed their deep concern to each other about whether anyone had seen them bail out (or spotted the chutes) and also spoke about their families and, as Bley said, "How we hoped we would be able to contact them."[34]

It was dawn when they reached their new area, which was a small North Korean village. By this time, the two men were going into their seventh day as prisoners under the control of the Chinese army. They had not yet been in a prison camp, an interrogation center, or a collection point, just various locations occupied by the army. This was to be their last army location and

4. The Capture

they remained here for one week. There was much happening behind the scenes, and until higher levels figured out who they were and what to do with them, they remained guarded by the army. On the fourth day, July 18, 1952, if he were anywhere else Colonel Schwable would have been celebrating his 44th birthday.[35]

The pilot and co-pilot were split up again, each placed in a small bunker in an obscure ravine. The colonel underwent military interrogation for several days, each session lasting from dawn to dusk. According to Schwable, this questioning was "conducted by a more mature officer" and it "emphasized current plans and organization." The captors had also picked up bits and pieces of the SNB from the side of the mountain where the plane crashed and compared various identification numbers from the aircraft with the colonel's flight clearance ticket.[36]

It was nearing the last day of Colonel Schwable's week in this area when his back began to bother him. It became pure torture during his 14-month confinement. His back had never bothered him before and he didn't know the cause, but the colder it got, the more unbearable the pain became. The colonel remarked, "I can tell you that of all the actual things I think I went through, I would say that the thing that bothered me the most, was a continuous [un]relenting backache that got worse and worse as time went on."*[37]

It was about 4 P.M. on Monday, July 21, 1952, and Frank Schwable was undergoing a military interrogation when suddenly everything stopped and the colonel was removed from the room. He had already surmised that his army captors were communicating with higher authorities (probably the Political Department) and he had a funny feeling that he was going to be moved shortly. "I got the impression that by that time, they had made up their minds and plans as to what they wanted to do with us; they had sent a telegram or runner, or something, and said get us up to this interrogation camp." From the evidence available, it was at about this time that senior authorities either in Pyongyang or Peking knew who Frank Schwable was.[38]

This was the first time in seven days that Colonel Schwable had seen Roy Bley — Bley's custodians had received the same order to move. Initially, they were split up, the colonel in a jeep and Bley in a truck. During the trip, several changes were made and they were sometimes together and sometimes alone. At one point they were in a convoy of a truck and two jeeps with 12

---

*Upon his return to the United States in September 1953, one of his first stops was Bethesda Naval Hospital. X rays were taken of his back and it turned out that for several years prior to being captured, he had had an arthritic condition in the lower three vertebrae but it never bothered him. It was at this time that it initially flared up and just got increasingly worse throughout his captivity.

guards and an interpreter. They moved northwest for 21 hours. The interpreter told both marines that they were being taken to an interrogation center named Pick-up Camp.[39]

They reached camp on the afternoon of Tuesday, July 22, 1952. Roy Bley was whisked off into a valley and Schwable didn't see him again for two months. The colonel was now alone.[40]

5

The Camp

Everything that was done was accomplished with a specific purpose in mind, that it was planned ahead of time, and that it fitted into a definite pattern designed to break me down, in all ways to utterly confuse and stupefy my mind and then to give me the coup de grace — the choice of a false "confession" or death. I had not been in this camp five minutes before the process began.

— Col. Frank Schwable, USMC, Court of Inquiry, Vol. 3, Exhibit 10 (6)

Except that it was in northern North Korea, no one knew where this place actually was. It isn't noted on any officially disseminated prison camp lists — not by any of its names. This large interrogation center was known as Mining Camp, Labor Camp, Work Camp, Mountain Camp, Valley Camp, Pike's Peak, and finally Pak's Palace (which it definitely wasn't). Marine Sgt. R.A. Strachan said, "I heard it referred to as Mountain Camp, Mining Camp, and just about everything else." Some also called it Pick-up Camp (PUC), and this name will be used.[1]

It was at a rather high elevation. Colonel Schwable said, "Quite often the clouds, early in the morning, would be right down on the mountains and everything would be dripping wet." One prisoner stated that it was northwest of Pyongyang while another said northeast. It was a 21-hour trip to take after capture, but another POW from the same camp might claim they were 10 hours from the lines. It obviously couldn't take 21 hours to get there traveling at an average speed of 10–15 miles per hour with frequent stops and only 10 hours to return.[2]

PUC had no barbed wire fences, guard towers, or anything of the sort. Armed guards were all over, however, and it seems that there was a company-size detachment present. That was sufficient because where was one to go? To the north was Manchuria, to the east the Sea of Japan, west the Yellow Sea, and to the south a long, long hike through North Korea. There was never one person from any of the services to successfully escape from a collection point, interrogation center, or POW camp in North Korea.

The interrogation center was separated right down the middle by a very high, long ridge. On each side was a small, deep valley and in each valley was a Korean village. These two valleys housed the prisoners, who were kept in a Korean home or village structure of one sort or another. Some POWs never knew there was an extension of the camp on the other side, while some did, because they had been transferred there, had climbed the ridge in winter to gather wood, or had run into people from the opposite valley. There doesn't seem to be any tactical, propaganda, or psychological reason for having the camp split, except for housing.

Not only was PUC a very large interrogation center but it was also a collection point. This camp housed enlisted personnel, mostly infantry (as well as aviators to be interrogated), and the captors ran out of room. If there was a small North Korean village on the other side and the Chinese needed it, they went in and took it. Throughout the Korean War, there was never any love lost between the Chinese and North Koreans.

When he was walked into one of the valleys, the colonel was ordered to address all Chinese, no matter what rank, as his superiors. He was given some rice and soggy vegetables to eat but no water; it was the heat of summer and he had no water during the truck ride up and wouldn't receive any for another day.[3]

The colonel was going to be in this place, on one side of the ridge or the other, for a little over four months. During this period, he was in six different locations but only three of importance (the other three were temporary). They were "the House" (two weeks), "the Tent" (two weeks), and "the Lean-to" (13 weeks). The house was for thinking, the tent for practicing, and the lean-to for execution.

Frank Schwable was temporarily thrown into a hutch late on a Tuesday afternoon, July 22, 1952.* In this context, a hutch is a hole that is dug, generally at an angle, into the side of a hill. Colonel Schwable couldn't stand up in it. It was three feet wide and seven long. The entrance had a ridgepole that was perched atop two supporting vertical poles and then covered with twigs, leaves, grass, straw, and anything else the Chinese could find. The floor was mud. As the colonel remembers, "The minute it rains — and it rains a lot in North Korea in the summertime — the minute it rains water comes down through this grass and leaves and twigs, it seeps in from all sides. There is nothing to stop the water from running down the hill right on into your hutch."[4]

---

*Various documents have this date as between July 22 and July 25. Exercise caution in trusting POWs with dates. Hopefully the first one is correct. A person can be asked on what day of the week an event took place and he'd probably know; the date is another thing. Thankfully, many of the POWs spoke of time in days, not dates.

5. The Camp

Next morning, an interrogator started asking questions that aroused more than the curiosity of this marine colonel; he was becoming suspicious. "I got the impression they were all set for us. They knew exactly what they were going to do. They knew exactly who we were." Colonel Schwable had never been more right in his life.[5]

* * * *

When the Chinese officer called Schwable to the entrance of the hutch and began the usual questioning, almost by rote the colonel again claimed total innocence because he had only recently been assigned to Korea. It was at this moment, two weeks and a day after his capture, that Colonel Schwable's collapse actually began. He described one of the greatest shocks in his life: "The Chinaman leaned back a little — he had a piece of paper in his hands — he said, 'You are the Chief of Staff of the First Marine Aircraft Wing. You came to Korea in April.' I am perfectly frank, I gave [him] a little smile and just nodded my head. That is all there was to it.... I didn't argue about it; I just nodded. I felt I was caught short."[6]

Intelligence-gathering agencies utilize a number of avenues, and a very important approach is to read everything that the enemy (or potential enemy) publishes: newspapers, magazines, obscure trade journals, technical manuals, and the like. A wealth of good intelligence is always accumulated in this manner. Some of the time, through human error, small amounts of classified data are also released publicly. The reader just has to know what he's looking for. Sometimes, however, hard intelligence is published because of pure stupidity and that's what happened in Colonel Schwable's case.

No one ever claimed that bureaucrats, especially middle-level, think for themselves. For the most part, bureaucrats are not decision makers but manual readers. The manual is the decision-making device for them. Could there be some manual somewhere that states that the public should be notified when a senior officer is missing in action?

It was on July 12, 1952, four days after the colonel's capture, while he was still in the custody of front line troops, that the following was jointly issued by the Department of Defense and the U.S. Marine Corps. This is what the Chinese officer was holding in his hand:

DEPARTMENT OF DEFENSE
OFFICE OF PUBLIC INFORMATION
WASHINGTON, D.C.

IMMEDIATE RELEASE   12 JULY 1952   L15-6700 EXT 53177

Marine Corps Headquarters announced today that Colonel Frank H. Schwable, chief of staff of the 1st Marine Aircraft Wing in Korea, was missing in action.

Missing with him, from a flight over enemy lines in a twin-engine aircraft, was Major Roy H. Bley, his co-pilot and a veteran aviator.

Both flyers were presumed to have been shot down by enemy anti-aircraft fire. Ground observers reported two parachutes opening, and aircraft in the area reported seeing signal flashes from enemy territory near burning wreckage of a plane. An all-night storm in the area prevented serial rescue efforts, but they were reported continuing.

Colonel Schwable, a Naval Academy graduate of 1929, is the highest ranking Marine aviator to be reported missing in action in Korea. His wife, Beverly, and children, David C., 14, and Susan M., 5, reside at 2620 Fort Scott Drive, Arlington, Virginia. His mother is Mrs. Maude T. Schwable, 2245 Marilouise Way, Presidio Hills, San Diego.

Major Bley's wife, Margaret, resides at 1333 Orange Avenue, Santa Ana, California. His parents are Mr. and Mrs. William M. Bley, Route 2, Box 15, Cabool, Missouri.

Both flyers went to Korea last April with Brigadier General Clayton C. Jerome, present commander of the 1st Wing.

— USMC —

This notice was plastered in virtually every major newspaper in the United States, in original or slightly condensed form, but either way, it gave away the farm. The *New York Times* printed the news on page two of the Sunday, July 13, 1952, edition: "MARINE AIR WING LEADER MISSING IN KOREA." Beneath this bold headline, they published a formal photograph of the colonel's weathered face. He wore a "pisscutter" cover and an open-necked tropical uniform shirt. The Associated Press supplied this photo to the paper. Beneath the photo was a condensed version of the press release.[7]

Since this announcement was brought to the attention of the public four days after his capture, in just 11 days, a week and a half, it was in a hutch somewhere in the upper part of North Korea and in the hands of a vicious enemy who wouldn't mind killing Schwable and, if he weren't so valuable, probably would have.

Frank Schwable needed time and he didn't get it. Would the Chinese have eventually discovered who he really was? Of course. The question is when. It has already been seen that the most intense, ferocious interrogations lasted a relatively short time; 10 days seems to be the average. Some have gone on for, at most, a couple of months. The colonel's was continuous, the month of August being a training month for the next 13 weeks in the lean-to; weeks of absolute torture of the body and mind. And what if Colonel Schwable had another month's reprieve; would he have worn out the Chinese? Would what they wanted have become stale as the new year rolled in? They couldn't have known that the war would be over in six months, but other POWs did wear them out and in a much narrower period of time.

It was just a few short days earlier when the colonel was thinking, "Name, rank and serial number [and] you begin to wonder, what are they going to release on you?" After he saw the paper, he said, "To me, the most damning thing is that it said I was the senior Marine aviator caught to date." Frank Schwable had been a colonel for eight years and not only was he the most senior marine, he was the most senior colonel captured throughout the United Nations command, including the armed forces of the United States. Since General Dean was isolated by and captive of the North Koreans, Colonel Schwable was the senior officer present (SOP) to represent all United Nations prisoners under Chinese jurisdiction.[8]

Former marine John Pratt, Colonel Schwable's attorney, said, "It is a little bit ridiculous when this kind of thing can take place and people can be charged with violating regulations which these press releases themselves violate." But this press release was a cause and the commandant, General Shepherd, can best describe the eventual effect:

> ... the chain of events leading to the collapse of Colonel Schwable's moral resistance began when he was confronted with proof of the falsity of his original account. From then on he was continually on the defensive and successfully deprived of any element of moral ascendancy which might otherwise have assisted him in resisting his captors.[9]

* * * *

It began in "the house" during the first two weeks of August 1952, where Schwable "encountered organized, methodical, high level, preplanned interrogation, political indoctrination and torment to accomplish the foul propaganda objectives the Chinese had in store for me." The plan was to keep Frank Schwable in this house for two weeks of silence and meditation; to begin the process, this is required.[10]

The small house was U-shaped and occupied by a Korean family; all houses in the two valleys were inhabited homes. At one end of the U was the kitchen, then a combination living room/bedroom, and at the other end of the U was a small storage shed. During the summer, the Chinese stored their winter clothing in it, and in winter, it became a woodbin. It was in this room that Colonel Schwable was thrown for the next two weeks. When he had the opportunity to lie down, his head would touch the clothing and his feet would touch the rice paper that covered the wood-framed door. It was high enough for Frank Schwable to stand in at his five feet, eight inches, but only wide enough to lay out a one-man blanket with each edge touching a wall. There was a window, and when Schwable looked out, he could see another house on a hill above his; at a straight line of sight, the ground of the quadrangle-shaped residence was level with his eyes. Colonel Schwable refers to this building, the only one he could see, as Pak's Palace, "because it was very fancy ... the front of it had much grill work." It wasn't a palace; Pak's Palace was a place, an interrogation center as a matter of fact, not a freestanding house.[11]

The room was extremely small, much smaller than a walk-in closet, and very hot; to make matters worse, twice a day smoke would fill the storage room from cooking in the kitchen at the other end. Schwable did nothing in this room but think. There were no interrogations. The Chinese told the colonel when they moved him, "This is a period of thinking things over." It was a time for "thought and reflection." Colonel Schwable describes it as "a period of just sitting stupidly like an animal in a cage to think and think, to reflect, to become bitter at my own misfortunes, to delve into the uncertainties of the future, to let my fears, worries, and imagination run rampant." He continues by saying:

> You are sitting there all alone; you don't understand anybody. There is no distraction. You sit there and you just think. You reflect. You analyze. You grasp at anything that your mind can concoct, anything, and anything you flash back [on] as you go along is exaggerated more and more. Your judgment becomes warped.[12]

Wherever Frank Schwable was for the following months at PUC—the house, the tent, or the lean-to—he constantly tried to get out of his confinement through any pretext he could think of, but all were useless except for the latrine. As a general rule, whenever he needed to make a head call, permission was granted. "Latrine" is inaccurate, however, because there was no such facility. The latrine was the ground of North Korea for the entire time: summer, fall, and the dead of winter. When he used the excuse of a head call, an armed guard always accompanied him and the colonel walked as far as he could from the house until the guard forced him to stop—and go.[13]

His back hurt from the constant mandatory sitting but it was still the middle of summer. The severe pain really wouldn't kick in until the colder weather came on. The colonel, however, ran into another physical problem during these two weeks: He broke a tooth. To prepare rice for cooking (and rice is basically all the colonel ate), it was threshed on the open ground. Inevitably, a few small stones would be in the cooked rice; it was like eating fish while watching for bones. A few days after Colonel Schwable got to the house, he shattered one of his molars when he bit into a stone. He said, "I chipped off a great big three-quarters part of my tooth. The edges were so sharp that it rubbed my tongue all the time." Thankfully, apparently no nerve was exposed and it was more of an annoyance than a bad toothache. He complained to the Chinese but they did nothing about it.*[14]

---

*Upon his repatriation, Frank Schwable had quite a few dental appointments at Bethesda Naval Hospital before the molar was finally repaired.

Guards were everywhere and there was never a moment at PUC when the colonel, awake or asleep, was not without an armed guard who was specifically assigned to him. He was watched 24 hours a day at this interrogation center. Colonel Schwable couldn't stand them and in frustration, he remarked, "I couldn't even speak the language of the guards. You talk about solitary confinement here at home, or any kind of confinement in a jail, the guy in the jail can at least understand the guard."[15]

Because it was summer, the door of the shed was left open, but then a guard was posted just outside the doorway to watch him. The colonel "felt like a specimen in a zoo, being stared at constantly either by grinning, curiosity ridden Chinese troops or by grunting, growling guards." But two could play the same game, and Colonel Schwable stared right back, noticing that "I found I could outstare any Chinaman in all of China, or, rather, any Chinaman in North Korea." These contests sometimes went on for hours and Colonel Schwable would get some satisfaction in watching "the son of a gun squirm." There wasn't any place for Frank Schwable to run, so he just sat and stared until the guard became so uncomfortable that he'd slam the door closed in Schwable's face.[16]

The colonel described the mostly "young kids" who continually watched him: "Guards, as people, naturally varied in their personal characteristics but by and large they were cold, stern, suspicious, extremely alert to anything I did besides sitting perfectly still, extremely demanding and apparently only too happy to exert their authority over a white man." Not only a white man but, as Frank Schwable quickly realized, also over a senior U.S. Marine Corps colonel. By the time this two-week thinking period was complete, the colonel's inherent pride in being one of the elite — a marine — was basically smashed. He said, "A Marine officer among a bunch of Chinamen certainly has a feeling of superiority right off the bat, you can't help it; they broke that down, they did everything to just make you feel as little and as insignificant as they possibly could."[17]

* * * *

It was during the third week in August 1952, that Frank Schwable was moved to the tent. It was time for him to practice before the torture really started. When the germ warfare interrogators began their work, they didn't want to be bothered with training him to write what they told him to write. They moved him to somewhat larger quarters for training, and the trainers were given two weeks to complete their mission inside the tent.

Two interrogators came to his storage shed in the middle of the night and told Colonel Schwable to get his gear together. They marched him a short way up the valley to a place some POWs referred to as the "air force area." There they threw him into a tent. The Chinese needed larger space because two interrogators would be with him at all times. These two men were officers in the Chinese Air Force. "This is it, this is where you are going to [stay] now," they told him. "You are staying right here."[18]

These two airmen were not pilots but professional interrogators, and Colonel Schwable remarked that neither officer "knew one end of an airplane from the other." Maybe not, but evidence points to the fact that these two officers (in addition to most of the interrogators Colonel Schwable was to meet), spoke fluent English and Russian, had a formal college education, and spent 18 months at a special school in Peking for interrogators with courses conducted mostly by Soviet personnel.[19]

The tent was just large enough for three people and there was nothing in it except for a "little child's school desk" on a dirt floor. Colonel Schwable slept in the dirt for a little over a week. Then the rains came and "the whole place inside was like a quagmire of mud," remembered the colonel. "Water just came on through; every time you put your foot down, you were ankle deep in mud." The Chinese brought in two empty ammunition cans and laid a board across them. This was Frank Schwable's bed for the next week.[20]

All daily interrogations in this smelly tent were conducted by the two air force officers from 7 A.M. until 6 P.M., with one short break for food in the middle and the other meal given after they left. There was no exercise (and never would be), no washing and, the colonel said, "It was just go, go, go." Colonel Schwable developed dysentery and trips outside the tent were permitted in order to relieve himself. Once he was too late and soiled his marine uniform.[21]

Frank Schwable was losing weight and so it wasn't difficult for him to slip into the small chair with the desktop attached, pick up the "post office type pen," and begin to write. He was forced to write for 11 hours per day for 14 straight days. He said that it was done "purely to tire me out and it did tire me out." The colonel can best describe the two weeks of practice[22]:

> I was there only a couple of weeks but I was writing every damned minute I was there during those couple of weeks. I still feel it was just to wear me out.[23]
>
> I was kept writing for weeks till my eyes, fingers and back ached to the point where I could hardly sleep at night.[24]
>
> [The purpose] was to teach me to lie readily, to break down my inherent repugnance for deceit, and to adjust my mind to creative writing.[25]
>
> Cramped over a child's school desk in a dark, damp, mildewy, leaky tent, my eyes and back ached painfully the entire time and without exercise and limited to two meager, unsavory Chinese meals a day, I soon developed diarrhea and became thoroughly exhausted and run down physically; I became mentally dull, unresponsive and stupid in my reactions. At the same time it became habitual and easy to

lie and as natural to write false or purely creative materials as it is to speak and honor the truth in a free land."26

The colonel summarizes this time in the tent as being a period of "degradation, humiliation, intimidations, mental poisoning, and physical, mental, moral and spiritual oppression." The court of inquiry found that "he was conditioned to creative and imaginative writing by being required to write extensively concerning his flight training twenty-one (21) years previously, and the U.S. system of awards and decorations."27

On the first day, as soon as the sun came up, the air force officers came into the tent and began questioning him about his flight training at Pensacola two decades earlier. Colonel Schwable tried to convince them that things had drastically changed since then and that the information would be totally useless (which they obviously knew). During the questioning, Frank Schwable finally got annoyed and told them, "I am not going to tell you any more." At around noon, he found his food ration cut.28

"Now, don't you tell us any lies, you just write it down," ordered one of the officers. Because he really didn't remember very much about the training in Florida, he said, "I can't write it down without lying." The interrogator then ordered him to do the impossible: "Don't you lie but write it all down." Therefore, he recalled, "I sat down and drew up a created flight training schedule based on 1931 conditions that may have looked like a workable system to that non-pilot interrogator but I hope I never have to fly with a pilot who takes that training."29

Writing about Pensacola wasn't intensive. The bulk of the two-week-long "creative writing program" was on medals. The two interrogators wanted him to write about the awards and decorations issued to American servicemen.

It's quite certain that Frank Schwable had military information that Chinese intelligence didn't have. Except, however, for the front line troops who needed current tactical data on their enemy, Colonel Schwable was never asked for, nor interrogated, on military subjects. Like General Dean, he worried about this line of questioning and expected to be physically tortured for it. So he thought, "All right, here is a subject I can stall them off on for some time and it is not going to hurt anybody or anything." He also wrote because of "the constant, constant nagging. They questioned here and they questioned there, and back to this, here, there, and back to that."30

He felt he had to delay them from entering into any sensitive areas. He said, "I thought of all the harmless things I can tell these monkeys, that is it." The colonel dragged it out as long as he could; there were quite a few medals to go through. Whenever one of the Chinese was present, Schwable could be seen diligently writing away, but as soon as the Chinese left, the colonel brought everything "to a standstill until I heard him coming, as long as I had done one extra page between the time he had left and came back." After his first composition on military decorations was complete, the interrogator took it, went back to his quarters, and read it. When he returned, he tore the entire thing up in Colonel Schwable's face, threw it onto the mud floor, and said, "You have missed several medals. Now do it right."[31]

There was nothing nice about these two air force officers nor, for that matter, any of the interrogators and other Chinese Frank Schwable encountered during his 14 months of solitary confinement. There were never any pleasantries, smiles, or warm greetings; nothing but screaming, badgering, harassing, tormenting, and, in the tent, writing. He said it went "on and on. It is over and over." Harassment was constant: "How are you doing? Count each page." There were never enough pages, so one or the other of the officers would scream at the colonel: "Get going on this...; you are stalling. You will never get anywhere." Day after day was spent just "writing and rewriting," said Colonel Schwable, and then "explaining verbally what medals and decorations are awarded by our services, what the requirements were to receive each award, how citations were worded for each, and how, in detail, the recommendations were handled — I could not then convince myself ... that the Chinese were seriously seeking such militarily insignificant information." They weren't.[32]

There are only two gifts, no strings attached, that each of us is blessed with and one of them is free will.* The ability to choose is precious. It was during the first day or two of September 1952, when his training was over and Colonel Schwable was moved again. He was now about to enter the three-month period when the Chinese actually robbed him of his free will; they removed it from his mind. By the time the freezing winter was half over, this marine officer had completely lost his ability to choose. Others made all the choices, and it was Colonel Schwable's function to execute them.

* * * *

There were a number of eminent men, military and civilian and for the most part psychologists and psychiatrists, who took the stand during the court of inquiry and attempted to explain to the four members menticide — "killing of the mind." Two of these men stood out, however, as having a little deeper background, experience, and knowledge about menticide than any of the others. Both of these doctors had been in World War II, one as a spy and the other as a colonel in the Dutch army.

The other is personality; there's only one of you.

Alan M.G. Little, Ph.D.: He received both his bachelor (1924) and graduate (1927) degrees from Cambridge University and then returned to the United States where, in 1933, he earned his doctorate from Yale. After receiving his master's and while working on his advanced degree, he taught at Yale. He then spent another six years teaching at Harvard after obtaining his Ph.D. When war broke out, he went into government service and in 1944 transferred to the Office of Strategic Services (OSS), the forerunner to the CIA. For two years, beginning in January 1947, he was a spy stationed at the U.S. Embassy in Moscow with the pretended function of being a press attaché. All of his work, both before and after his embassy duty, was on the USSR: its philosophy, economics, political organization, and subversion techniques. He read and spoke fluent Russian and said he "learned it in order to equip myself for the work in the Office of Strategic Services." At the time of the inquiry in February 1954, Dr. Little was with the Foreign Service Institute at the Department of State, where he studied and analyzed "Russian propaganda, its purpose, the methods and techniques."[33]

Alan Little was neither a psychologist nor a psychiatrist. He said, "I was an archaeologist and my early training was in the humanities, namely Greek and Latin. I was a professor of Greek and Latin. I was also a student of political science and now I am a student of semantics and of propaganda. One thing leads to the other."*[34]

Dr. Little furnishes his definition of menticide:

Menticide is the annihilation of the individuality and social responsibility of the individual. It is the destruction of the individuality of the person to whom these techniques are applied.... The point is to bring a certain point of malleability where the thing can be molded, like the potter and the clay, but the clay is still there.†[35]

The foundation of menticide is the implementation of the studies and theories of Ivan Pavlov. It is through these investigations, experiments, and analysis that the Russians began to understand the conditioning of the mind. The best person to explain Pavlov is Dr. Little. In the following excerpt, he extemporaneously describes this man and his work:

Ivan Petrovich Pavlov was a very great Russian physiologist. There is no doubt about his greatness. He was a great man. He was not at all sympathetic to the

---

*At the time of the inquiry, Dr. Little was a member of the American Archaeological Association.
† ... The published works of Alan Little were not consulted, nor were those of the other academicians and scholars who testified at the investigation after the Korean War. They made their remarks and analysis of menticide spontaneously, with no written notes or other promptings, and they did it instantly, without hesitation, and eloquently. Their testimony is refreshing and inspiring to read.

regime in Russia. In fact, he fought the regime during most of his life and only became reconciled at the end of his life.

He was the son of a priest and when the children of priests were excluded from the educational system on that ground of their being the sons of a priest, he resigned his professorship and was only with great difficulty prevailed upon to return to his work.

He made a great study, starting with the digestive tract and the digestive juices, of the processes of the reaction of the digestive system to emotional stimuli. He used for his experiments dogs primarily, and his work was largely with animals.

During the period of the revolution, Lenin himself invited Pavlov to come to the Kremlin to start work on the human animal, to find out what made that tick, and at the end of three months Pavlov, who had protested against this, came out with a three hundred page book on the operation of the emotional forces on human beings.

> According to Dr. Little, Pavlov said "that just as an animal can be conditioned, just as a dog can be conditioned to respond to a set signal, the dog is the prototype of the human being on a similar scale."[36]
>
> There's not much of a gray area in the mind of a dog. There's not much free will in the life of a dog. A dog's life is generally black and white. A dog will leap before it looks; it doesn't have the brainpower to look before it leaps. Humans, however, have a tremendous gray area between black and white and it is within this gray area that choices must always be made (black or white doesn't require much choosing). The Chinese, through menticide, attempted to wipe out the gray area. Dr. Little labels this cleansing the "Semantics of Confusion." All this means is to place a human in the frame of mind where there's only black and white. Dr. Little said that they "deliberately force him into saying either you are for or against us, this point of view is either right or wrong, this is black or white, when in reality in life, there are many individual shades of gray in between black and white." Adding reality to the "Semantics of Confusion" concept, Colonel Schwable said, "They say black is white and you try in every way you can to show that black isn't white, but there is no use because you end up [believing] black is white."[37]
>
> The treatment of Colonel Schwable did not reconcile very well with Dr. Little's spirituality. He said, "The Russians do not believe in anything that we in Christian parlance would refer to as the soul. They believe in the human being as being as a mass of material having life, emotion, but his brain also being subject to the same laws as the rest of matter, namely, a purely mechanistic process." As Dr. Little is saying, and what the Chinese were working on with the colonel, was the elimination of free will, a gift from Dr. Little's God. The doctor also said, "It makes a whale of

a difference in your treatment of people whether you regard them as God's children or a recording machine."³⁸

Joost Abraham Maurits Meerloo, M.D., Ph.D. Since World War II began, Dr. Little observed that Dr. Meerloo had been "trying to popularize the idea of menticide being a crime worthy of being dealt with by the United Nations." When Meerloo was questioned at the inquiry about the origin of the word "menticide," he immediately replied, "I coined the word myself." In addition, Dr. Meerloo wrote the definition for several dictionaries and verbally stated that "I define menticide by saying that [it is] an organized system of psychological intervention and judicial perversion by which a powerful tyrant synthetically injects his own thoughts and words into the minds and mouths of the victims he plans to destroy by a trial [which] may well be called menticide."³⁹

Born in 1903 in The Hague, Netherlands, he graduated from Leiden University in 1927 with his doctor of medicine degree and received his Ph.D. in psychological medicine five years later from Utrecht University. Despite the Netherlands' neutrality since the beginning of World War II in 1939, the Nazis invaded the country in May 1940 and disbanded the Dutch army in which Dr. Meerloo was a captain in the medical corps.⁴⁰

After separation from the army, he returned to his private psychiatry practice and at the same time joined the Dutch underground. He wrote for underground papers, furnishing advice on how to cope with the German occupiers of their nation. In the middle of July 1942, he said, "I was warned by my patients 'that you are wanted by the Nazis.' My name was mentioned." On July 22, 1942, he left his

J.A.M. Meerloo, M.D., Ph.D. One of the very few experts in the world on the torture called menticide. As he proudly explained to the Court of Inquiry, "I coined the word myself."

practice of two years and darted for the Dutch frontier where he decided to travel through Belgium and France to Switzerland. He didn't get very far. At the Belgium border he was stopped by the Germans and imprisoned, first in Antwerp and then Brussels. Dr. Meerloo was interrogated several times about the underground and the Germans also wanted to know his reasons for running.[41]

Not satisfied with any answers Dr. Meerloo gave them, his captors put him on a train for Germany, but one night he escaped. He recalled, "Then I had to find my way alone, without any organization, through France. Then I walked through France." He reached Vichy France and then entered Switzerland where the Swiss caught, imprisoned, and then returned him to Vichy France. Put into a concentration camp, he escaped six weeks later. His options as to where to run were quickly diminishing and this time he opted for Spain. He said, "It was difficult in wartime. I worked there with peasants and they showed me the way over the Spanish border." It was now early October 1942. In Spain, he located official representatives of the Dutch government in exile and in a short time, he was promoted to the rank of major (and shortly thereafter lieutenant colonel) in the Dutch army. He said, "my pay was put back into my rank."[42]

For the next three years, Colonel Meerloo was head of the Department of Psychological Warfare of the temporarily exiled Dutch government headquartered in London. In this position, he made a short trip to the United States, where he met with President Roosevelt and discussed with him and his senior military advisors his views on mind warfare. In March 1943 and until his discharge in October 1945 as a full colonel, Dr. Meerloo said, "I was working on psychological warfare."[43]

Shortly after the end of the war, Meerloo was invited to the United States to lecture at various universities and organizations on psychological and biological warfare but, according to the doctor, biological warfare "had a different meaning at that time. It was not germ warfare. It was more the German explanation of the term 'biological warfare.' That means warfare against a race, diminishing the power of the people by sending them to other countries. There was a complete plan worked out; the Dutch have to live in Siberia, the people in Siberia have to live in Holland, in order to destroy their powers for good." In January 1946, Meerloo made his permanent residence in New York, and in 1950 he became an American citizen. At the time of the inquiry in February 1954, J.A.M. Meerloo was teaching at Columbia University and at the New School for Social Research in New York City.[44]

"I wish to emphasize at the very outset," said Colonel Schwable, "that my personal experience is not of the blood and thunder type, it is not spectacular, I have no broken bones or loss of teeth, etc. to demonstrate that I suffered horrible physical torture — which I did not — it is, rather, an account of slow, quiet, methodical and diabolically persistent contamination of the mind, body and soul preparing me to accept the 'only way out.'" Nicely said, but the last part is true and the first part false. The fact that the colonel claims he didn't undergo physical torture can possibly be chalked up to marine bravado. He talks about not undergoing physical torture repeatedly, and repeatedly he's wrong. At one point, he does admit that it was so cold in winter that he was frostbitten and also admits that he was on the edge of insanity because of the horrible pain in his back. He said, "That kind of physical torture I feel I suffered at the hands of the Chinaman and he did it willfully, maliciously, and knowingly. That kind I had."[45]

Torture works. Physical torture in conjunction with the torture of the mind works better. Concerning physical torture, Dr. Meerloo said that "when you are hungry and when you have to stand all the time, being tired, staring into the lights, looking at what we call a certain kind of paternal figure, that already gives you the tendency to give in. Of course, not the first time, but when it is repeated and repeated." And in the case of Frank Schwable, repeated and repeated for months on end. Psychiatrist Winfred Overholser, a graduate of Harvard and of Boston University, noted that sometimes physical torture could have an opposite effect because it has a proclivity "to make a person so angry at the moment that it would add a bit to his resolve." Major Harris and Captain Flynn testified to this, and it will be seen even more so with others.[46]

In an unpublished manuscript with a working title of "Pavlovian Strategy as a Weapon of Menticide," J.A.M. Meerloo said, "The technique of ... menticide makes use of simple Pavlovian conditions such as is [sic] used with dogs. The totalitarian wants first the required response from the nerve cells, then control of the individual, finally the control of the masses." The system of menticide always begins with conditioning and training by combining positive and negative stimuli. Some of the negative motivations are pain, hunger, threat of death, and the like, but there's only one positive stimulus — reward. The former Dutch army colonel said, "Such are the general experiences told by our soldiers who were prisoners of war in Korea. Hunger and food were the most frequently used as negative and positive stimuli."[47]

Let's go back to late 1950 when the Chinese entered the war and into early 1951. The strategy, tactics, logistics, firepower, and masses of the Chinese army overpowered — in fact, overwhelmed — UN forces and over 7,000 Americans were captured. They began dying like flies from pre-planned hunger and in a period of four months, there were only 4,000 left. From April 1, 1951, these prisoners had seen enough of negative stimulus to last a lifetime (in this case, shortened by hunger) and they only wanted one reward — food. After April 1, few POWs died, and few POWs stuck with name, rank, and serial number. This was not menticide; it was only the training and practicing. As Dr. Meerloo said, "Hunger [alone] is able to put people into submission." That's all that was needed for the survivors to comply with all the desires of the Chinese, but they were not being forced to sign a germ warfare confession that would disgrace the colonel and the corps and put the United States and the United Nations in an aggressively defensive posture. Menticide, per se, was reserved for a select few, and primarily for one man during the entire Korean War.[48]

Pavlovian strategy brings about a "confusion neurosis," which is a sense of unreality. One is so confused that one cannot choose what is real and what isn't. Because of this, Meerloo believes that "it gradually leads to complete mental submission and willingness to play any role." He talked about "special grades" of bringing people to submission and pointed out that "by the use of Pavlovian [methods], everybody can, in the end, be brought into submission." Dr. Meerloo takes it one step further by saying, "The question is always that we never know [when] somebody will break down. There are people who break down, we

Charles W. Mayo, M.D., Alternate Representative of the United States to the United Nations. "The question before us — the charge that the United States forces engaged in bacteriological warfare in Korea — plainly involves the honor and integrity not only of my country and her soldiers but also of the United Nations itself, under whose banner sixteen member nations fought in Korea" (courtesy the Mayo Clinic).

know, only after six hours of interrogation. There are other people who will break down after days of interrogation." He suggested that it really was quite academic, however, because "we all break down. I still think for us it is not a question of when somebody will break down, but will he break down [and] the answer is yes."[49]

At the United Nations, Dr. Charles Mayo, an alternate representative to the United Nations from the United States, said that the confessions signed by POWs in Korea:

> were not simply a sudden bright idea on the part of the Communists, but were an integral part of a tremendous and calculated campaign of lies; and that in this campaign of lies, the Communists used carefully worked out techniques and a considerable body of trained personnel in order to break the bodies and souls of men and thus fulfill their plan.[50]

Col. Paul Sherman, counsel to Colonel Schwable, agreed that the Chinese did not have to beat anyone because "they have a more effective means in the scientific application of modern methods of using an age old system of perversion of the mind of man." He went on to ask rhetorically:

> What American could have suspected the kind of torture to which our officers and men were subjected by their communist captors? We could not even have dreamed of the kind of horror which would make strong men turn livid, shake with anger, and the tears to flow at the very thought of the indignities which were inflicted upon them as a result of the misfortunes of war and in the pursuit of their profession.[51]

6

The Menticide (Part I)

> *At the outset we should notice that the tortures used in these cases, although they include many brutal physical injuries, are not like the medieval tortures of the rack and the thumbscrew. They are subtler, more prolonged, and intended to be more terrible in their effect. They are calculated to disintegrate the mind of an intelligent victim, to distort his sense of values, to a point where he will not simply cry out "I did it!" but will become a seemingly willing accomplice to the complete destruction of his integrity and the production of an elaborate fiction.*
> — Dr. Charles W. Mayo, Alternate Representative
> of the United States to the United Nations,
> Court of Inquiry, Vol. 3, Exhibit 21 (8)

It was the first Monday of September — Labor Day —1952, when Colonel Schwable was moved over the high ridge to the opposite valley and put into a small lean-to attached to the southwest side of an occupied Korean house. The shed had two seven-foot-long wooden posts attached to the roof overhang with a three-foot separation between them and vertical stakes were stuck into the ground. Two other shorter posts were dug six feet out from the house. The slanting roof and straight sides were framed and the entire framework was then covered with sticks and twigs. Only sticks and twigs were to protect the colonel from the upcoming harsh North Korean winter. The closet-size six-foot-long, three-foot-wide shack was a part of the house before Frank Schwable got there and, upon initially seeing where he was to be kept, the colonel referred to it as a "little stick-in-the-mud lean-to." At its height it was seven feet and then the roof gently sloped down to five feet, eight inches, at the entrance; it wasn't necessary for Frank Schwable to stoop upon entering or leaving the confined space. Surrounding the house was a stone walkway, and the floor of the lean-to had small stones scattered about. The colonel noted that his universe for the next three months was "tucked away back in a deep, obscure, isolated valley in the North Korean wilderness where I could easily be disposed of without attracting attention or notice."[1]

After his two weeks of creative writing exercises in the tent, the colonel did not put another word to paper for 90 days. This was not because the Chinese didn't want him to furnish a written account of his participation in germ warfare, it was because the colonel refused. He was okay with scribbling about insignificant subjects such as medals, but when it came down to composing a lengthy germ warfare confession, that was completely out of the question. It took 90 days of mental and physical torture to break him.

During this period various interrogators and army political officers would come to question Frank Schwable, but he was not barraged by swarms of questioners and lecturers. There was only one lead interrogator and according to Schwable, "That guy stayed with me until the whole problem was cleared. He was the political man, the interrogator, the everything." This Chinese officer was in his early to mid–30s, and the colonel described him as "a pretty intelligent guy; spoke wonderful English. I think he graduated or at least went to the university up there in Washington, either Seattle or someplace like that." He went on to say that this lead interrogator "had a excellent background in economics and communist political theory and I took a very poor second place every time I argued with him on these subjects."[2]

Frank Schwable had known about the Chinese push on germ warfare prior to his capture. In fact, shortly after he was in custody, one of the front line officers asked him, "What about the bacteriological warfare?" The colonel's reply was, "It is the silliest thing I ever heard of." The Chinese didn't think so, however, and for the remainder of his time as a POW, he was never asked a question about anything of military significance; every effort, instead, was made to break him down to the status of a puppet for the cause of germ warfare and to admit his major participation in planning and controlling the attacks as chief of staff.[3]

After a certain period of time, a prisoner tends to become familiar with his captors and this leads to discovering certain commonalities, but not so in the rough North Korean mountains. The colonel never knew the name or rank of the senior interrogator nor those of any subordinate interrogators or political officers who either questioned or lectured him. This personal isolation even drifted down to the continuous guard detail assigned to him. Each detail had a shift of 72 hours and then was relieved by another 72-hour group of sentries. This isolation continued for months on end.[4]

A specific pattern was never established as to when the interrogator would arrive at the lean-to to badger and harass Colonel Schwable into writing. It should be noted at this juncture that, except for possibly a very small handful of Korean War POWs (if any), practically all 4,000 repatriates signed something while American prisoners that harmed, at least in the propaganda arena, the United States, but they never personally wrote what they signed; it was written for them by the captors. Colonel Schwable, however, was being forced, with guidance, to create, organize, compose, and handwrite his own confession and propaganda. After that was done, his signature per se would be a fait accompli. Therefore, the torture of the colonel's mind was the primary objective of the Chinese and one of the many methods used was lack of pattern or predictability. Sometimes harassment would be a full morning or afternoon and sometimes it would last from the moment he woke up until midnight with only two very short breaks for food. Food was brought to Schwable twice a day by a Chinese soldier who had a pole balanced horizontally across his shoulders with a wooden bucket at each end.[5]

Colonel Schwable describes his days:

> In 14 months in Korea, there were never two days that were alike. They are the most inconsistent people that you can imagine. I don't know whether they do it on purpose or whether it is inadvertent. This morning the ... interrogator might come up and be with you all morning long, and you would not see him again until tomorrow. Tomorrow he might be with you in the afternoon. The next time he would be with you morning, noon, and night. I tell you this. If they put it on an hourly basis, they put in their working hours in the morning and afternoon. They would put in at least a couple of hours most mornings, most afternoons, and every now and then they would not show up at all. Frankly, that is the worst day. Later on that was the worst day that came along because all day long you are sitting there holding on, dreading that guy coming and you don't know when he is coming, so you worry about it all day long.[6]

In comparing himself and his circumstances with others, the colonel thought that other POWs, for example, got a break once in a while during interrogations, either a rest break or a change in subject, but not him; for Schwable the primary focus was germ warfare and it hardly changed. He noted, "When they start on you with one idea, to get one thing out of you, then there isn't any break. That is where it goes on and on and on." One other comparison the colonel was fond of making was with an actor. He observed, "While the actor attains this desirable degree of perfection through study, skill, and practice, the POW is submerged into this detrimental state of mind through exhaustion, intimidation and utter despair."[7]

The Chinese wouldn't require much convincing that Frank Schwable didn't fly in combat. As the colonel said, "I flew no missions that could, in any conceivable way, be construed as being germ warfare raids. As a matter of interest, the Chinese Communists did accept this one fact and charged me not with participating directly in the delivery of bombs on the target but rather with planning such operations and conducting normal staff functions in connection with bacteriological warfare." This was much more serious than flying a plane and dropping a bomb; he was the cause.[8]

Frank Schwable knew this was the avenue they were going to take almost immediately upon arriving at PUC. When not being interrogated about germ warfare operations, he was required to sit, never stand, in his dark space and think. He thought about treason but he never had "treasonable feelings" because "you can't feel that way when you do something that you don't do on your own." Although the colonel claimed, "Suicide never entered my mind," it certainly crossed it several times. He thought about how he would do it and determined that the best way was to just get up, run, and let the guards shoot him: "You can get them to do it."[9]

A major thought in the mind of Frank Schwable during his periods of silence was name, rank, and serial number and his emerging anger toward the regulation and its drafters. His initial thinking on the subject was very positive and that it was necessary. He said that navy regulations are "our guide, our Bible. That is fine. It is a good regulation. It is a safe regulation." But as the days turned into weeks and the thinking process became more chaotic, he began losing respect for the code of silence and started imagining the people in Washington who wrote and signed it; had any of them ever been a POW? Had they ever gone through what he was going through? The colonel asked himself, "Did they look at it from the point of view of its possible implications — possible I say?" And then his mind replied, "No, they didn't." He now began to hate the people who wrote it. The next obvious step was to ignore the regulation. The colonel sorrowfully added, "You can't help it when you are sitting over there thinking about these things all by yourself. You can't help it, perhaps it is not right, but I guess what you do in your own mind is that you begin to condemn."[10]

* * * *

"Brainwashing" is a misused word and has lost any meaning it ever did have. It was over a half-century ago when it was coined. Menticide is brainwashing; actually "mindwashing" since mind is a function of the brain. Colonel Schwable underwent true menticide: the temporary loss of choice (and reality). It is the "washing" of the mind or, if you prefer, the brain. On the other hand, brainwashing, as commonly used, is actually indoctrination and doesn't take anything away but has the opposite effect. Menticide subtracts from the mind while brainwashing (indoctrination) adds to it.

Brainwashing, as we're accustomed to using the word, is actually a teaching tool. No enlisted POW in Korea ever underwent brainwashing, as in menticide, which is true washing, getting it clean. The Chinese referred to POWs as "students." Some of the subjects taught them by professionally educated,

English-speaking instructors (educators) were the causes of the Korean War, the ruling rich families in America such as DuPont, Morgan, Ford, and Rockefeller, and general studies in capitalism, imperialism, the construction of a new China, and so forth. This was very intense study (eight to ten hours a day for over six months) that introduced knowledge of the previously unknown and thereby made the arena of choice much wider. Hence it caused total confusion, especially for the uneducated enlisted troops, who were in the majority. Colonel Schwable never once had to undergo any of these courses of study. That was "brainwashing." With Frank Schwable, brainwashing actually took place, it was enormously successful, and the event, when the mind is finally completely void of free will, is called menticide.

* * * *

Not on a daily basis but once or twice a week a Chinese officer would come in and begin to harass the colonel with propaganda. According to Schwable, he began getting "heavy doses of political indoctrination." It was in September 1952 when, during one of his lectures, this officer told the former chief of staff that he had been branded a war criminal for his participation in biological warfare. The officer continued and told him that from this point forward, "Geneva Convention rules don't apply to you; you are not a POW." Now Frank Schwable had to contend with what he called a "war-guilt" trip.[11]

In frustration, the colonel remarked:

> Now, you have some monkey sit there and tell you day after day after day, "You can advance the cause of peace. You can hurry this thing along, you can help. You want peace, your people want peace," and they grind that out and grind it out, and grind it out, and that is why people like Colonel McLaughlin, a good strong sensible man, signs a peace appeal. That is why hundreds of them signed peace appeals.[12]

Lt. Col. John McLaughlin, USMC, was one of the senior officers at Camp 5, the largest Chinese-administered POW camp in Korea. It was located on a peninsula jutting out into the Yalu River; across the river was Manchuria. By June 1951, the POWs, both officers and men, were well on their way to being indoctrinated in communist political and economic ideas (studies began in April) and every POW in the camp was being harassed, badgered, and threatened to sign an appeal for peace, which was drafted by the Chinese. Just a simple signature was required on this anti–American propaganda document. There were three days of debate and then everyone signed — the entire camp, including Colonel McLaughlin. Colonel Schwable said "hundreds of them signed" but in February 1954, when the colonel said this, no one in the United States had any real idea of what went on in the prison camps in North

Korea. The last person to sign the peace appeal at Camp 5 was one of the camp's doctors, Capt. William Shadish, and his signature was number 1,671.*[13]

During the entire 14 months of captivity, Frank Schwable was in virtual solitary confinement. With the exception of certain circumstances (such as a transfer), he was alone and isolated, hardly ever seeing and never speaking with another person unless they were Chinese. Some prisoners can cope with isolation better than others. A good example of this is a writer who actually volunteers for (in fact, demands) seclusion. J.A.M. Meerloo said, "Those people who are used to thinking for themselves and to be alone, those people don't suffer so much." Nevertheless, segregation as a prisoner involves things that voluntary solitude in a comfortable location with pen in hand does not, and one of them is dirt. It's important to keep a prisoner dirty, and Colonel Schwable was so filthy he looked like a pig. Once a person is covered in dirt, feces, and urine, with long straggly hair and a beard infested with vermin, and remains that way for months, according to Dr. Meerloo, "All our childhood memories are in revolt because we are not allowed to be dirty as a child." The captive starts to feel as if he is being treated like a child and then, observes the doctor, "You give in as a child."[14]

Generally, Colonel Schwable was never deprived of sleep but the colonel's mind wouldn't allow him to sleep. His sleep was regulated, however, and he simply couldn't lie down any time he wanted but only when the guard told him to, and then it was done immediately and not before. Various guards would order him to lie down on the ground at different times and it's fairly safe to assume that these jailers were given the time to furnish the order by their superiors. Colonel Schwable said, "You sit there. When he tells you to lie down, you lie down. There is no argument about that."[15]

There was never a feeling of security or relaxation in the sleep of the colonel and he described it as "an apprehensive, restless rolling around, I guess, with your eyes closed," waking up the next morning as tired as you were the night before. And during this sleep there was one primary thought in the mind of Frank Schwable. Over and over he would keep thinking, "My God, he is coming pretty soon; I wonder when he is coming to wake me up." Beside restlessness in the colonel's sleep, there was an absolute fear.[16]

While sleeping, according to Dr. Meerloo, "part of our ego builds up again. So when we don't get the opportunity to build our own forces up again, and especially our self-confidence, that means we become more and more exhausted and exhausted." Meerloo added, "Through lack of sleep, it is pos-

---

*This was only in one camp and doesn't include many of the other smaller camps spread out along the Yalu east and west of Camp 5. The peace appeal was also distributed for signatures in all these other camps, so it wouldn't be going overboard to estimate that at least 3,900 signatures were obtained (and probably more) out of a total POW population throughout North Korea of approximately 4,000.

sible to bring people into complete submission, but it takes a long time," and that is exactly what the Chinese had. Every senior prisoner undergoing a major interrogation was told by their captors to take their time in cooperating. Take a month, take a year, for all they cared take 10 years, but the prisoner was also informed that he was not to be moved from the spot he was in until he did exactly what he was told. In the case of the colonel, he conceivably could remain in a shed the size of a closet for the rest of his life.[17]

On the other hand, they could kill him and this was on Frank Schwable's mind all the time. Killing a POW is quite easy; sickness is a classical excuse and if the other side doesn't even know that one of their own is a prisoner (for example, no name lists had been exchanged), no excuse at all is necessary. The colonel recognized that "no accounting for me would ever be needed except possibly 'Died.'"[18]

* * * *

He was 38 when captured and one of the few Marine Corps "mustang" officers held by the Chinese. Major Bley was without a formal college education and achieved the rank of major not because of his academic credentials but because of his experience and leadership abilities. A mustang is a rare breed, admired and at times idolized as a man who made it.

A mustang is a commissioned officer who was once an enlisted man and worked his way up from private to officer. Roy Bley, for example, went to Marine Corps boot camp at Parris Island, which is reserved for enlisted recruits. An ordinary person can spot a mustang officer without speaking to him by one or both of two identifying badges. The first are tattoos. With very rare exceptions, officers are not permitted to have tattoos; if you see one with a tattoo, you can safely bet he's a former enlisted man. The second badge is the Good Conduct Medal. If an officer is wearing this award on his left breast, he was definitely enlisted. This medal on his chest is publicly advertising that he's a mustang because the Good Conduct Medal is specifically reserved for the men; officers are expected to maintain good conduct at all times and thus don't receive a personal decoration for that. Major Bley had one other rarity in that he was a Marine Corps pilot as an enlisted man. He was actually designated a naval aviator in January 1938, almost five years before he received his commission as a second lieutenant of marines.[19]

The events surrounding the torture of Maj. Roy Bley cannot be measured in time or place because time had no meaning to him and he didn't know where he was except that it was someplace in North Korea. It is a fact, however, that he was in PUC, sometimes in the same valley as the colonel and at times over the ridge in the opposite valley. Furthermore, in addition to arriving with Schwable, Bley once saw him. Upon entering the camp, the major was put into a mud hut where his wounds were bandaged and where he remained for weeks. One day during middle afternoon, Bley had just completed removing a bandage from his wounded foot when a guard came in and motioned the major to follow; he was being moved. He was taken over the ridge and during the hike walked past a tent. From 30 yards away, the major glanced toward it. He recalled, "Inside the tent I saw the colonel." Roy Bley thought that this took place in the middle of September 1952, but he was three or four weeks off because Schwable's creative exercises took place in this shelter during the last two weeks of August.[20]

The Chinese found out who Bley was or, more accurately, what his job was, at precisely the same time they discovered Schwable's, thanks to the press release. Therefore, the pressure placed upon him to sign a germ warfare confession as chief ordnance officer of the wing was immense but not the same type of pressure as was placed on his colonel. Bley did not undergo menticide; his was more physical pressure. The major underwent beatings and other tortures that Colonel Schwable never went through. Schwable had the pressure of the mind; Bley the body. Why this 180-degree turn in torture tactics is not clear except that the Chinese may not have had the trained personnel in that isolated hideaway to perform menticide on two people at the same time. On the other hand, they may have figured that he simply wasn't worth the effort of going through the thinking, practicing, and execution periods and they would have been correct. Therefore, menticide was reserved for Colonel Schwable alone.

Wherever he was located, usually a cave or mud hut, he was interrogated on germ warfare, but this very tough Marine Corps major wouldn't give them the right time of day. He wasn't signing anything; in fact, he just annoyed the hell out of them. Finally they put him in a "punishment cave" somewhere in the mountains and there he stayed. The cave was about five feet wide and six feet long, but only four and a half feet tall; it was truly a cave. The floor was pure mud due to the constant seepage of water. Day after day he was required to sit at attention in the mud and when he was allowed to sleep, he lay down in it, like a hog wallowing. His only companions were mosquitoes, lice, and rats, which roamed freely in the confined, very dark space. Dysentery caught up with him and he had to urinate and defecate all the time. During the day they took him outside for bodily relief but at night, these movements were done in the cave; Major Bley lived, sat, and lay down in his own waste. Although his wounds were slowly healing of their own accord, this natural process was painfully prolonged. The major said, "They either didn't have medicine up there or if they did have it they didn't offer much of it to the POWs, at least not to me." The only medical treatment Major Bley received, other than bandages, was iodine, but all that did was cauterize the less serious wounds on his beaten body.[21]

There were only two things Roy Bley was permitted to do in the punishment cave from morning, when he was kicked awake, until night, when he was ordered to lie down. They were either to sit at attention or, when an interrogator stooped to enter, stand at attention. That was it. On sitting, the major noted, "Even though my leg was infected, I still had to sit at attention in cross-legged fashion for long periods of time." When the dreaded interrogator came to harass, Bley had to immediately stand and continuously maintain a position of attention, albeit a bent-over one since the ceiling of the dank, smelly cave wasn't even five feet high. "I had to stand in a stooped over fashion," recalled Bley, and this position of stooped-over attention had to be held for up to eight hours a day. Not too many people in excellent physical condition can do this; it was practically impossible for the severely wounded major, and he would simply collapse into the mud from pure exhaustion. He didn't want to do that because it brought about a severe beating. Many times, this marine resisted standing again, preferring to just lie in the mud but, he said, "If I refused to get up, or I couldn't get up, they kicked me or used rifle butts on me until I did get up." Either one or both of his 24-hour-a-day guards would then proceed to kick and beat him, not just once or twice but according to Major Bley, 40 to 50 blows every time. Bley reflected, "They had no scruples about any form of punishment that they thought would assist their brain washing method in order to get something out of a POW."*22

The guards and interrogators, according to Bley, "were very strict" and if he didn't answer questions correctly, they took his meager rice food ration away. And they would tease him. The major was a cigarette smoker and when an interrogator stooped into his cave, most of the time he would have a cigarette in his hand. After taking a puff without inhaling, he would blow the unfiltered smoke in Roy Bley's face. At times, he would even be offered one, he recalled, "but if I reached for it, he would hold it back and [say], 'After you cooperate with us you can have all the cigarettes you want.'"23

Sometime during mid–November 1952, Major Bley was removed from PUC and trucked north to Camp 5. This regular POW camp held on average 1,500 prisoners, mostly American enlisted men. Interrogations and tortures didn't normally take place within the camp proper, however, and those POWs designated for this treatment (mostly officers) were kept in caves and shacks just outside the camp's main gate and southern-facing barbed wire. (There was no wire on the other three water sides of Camp 5.)

Tossed into a six-foot-wide, eight-foot-long, and seven-foot-high mud

---

*Practically none of the 4,000 repatriated Korean War POWs ever heard the term "brainwashing" while prisoners; it was introduced to most of them when they returned to the United States.

shack, he would remain there for five weeks, or until about Christmas 1952. There obviously were no toilet facilities and there wasn't even a dirty mat on the floor to lie down on; it was barren.[24]

For a couple of days the major was guarded, fed, and left alone. Soon a strange Camp 5 interrogator came in and, without saying a word, simply walked up to Bley and gave him a tremendous punch in the mouth, knocking him across the shack and onto the ground. His mind immediately shifted into an instinct/reaction mode and Roy Bley surprisingly leaped to his feet, rushed his attacker, and started swinging. The major was in such bad shape he couldn't fight his way out of a paper bag but he did get in two punches before he was overpowered by the pair of guards on duty. They twisted his hands behind his back and tied him by the wrists. He was forced into a corner and shoved to his knees, where he remained for six straight hours while the Chinese officer verbally tormented him. From that moment on, whenever anyone came into the shack, Bley was tied and on his knees.[25]

During his five weeks of looking and feeling like a pig in mud, his interrogations were infrequent, possibly once a week, for this time was reserved for reflection and thought. According to the major, he was "required to sit quietly in the corner when the guard was at the door, but if the guard didn't stand at the door, I would stand up and try to get some form of calisthenics in order to keep in shape the best I could." Major Bley said the Chinese looked at this muddy, solitary existence as "what they call [a] thinking period, with the warning that whenever they came back, I was to cooperate."[26]

When, after days of being alone, an interrogator did come in, Bley said, "I told them I would give them nothing but my name, rank, and serial number." The first time, his punishment for doing this was two days without food. It gradually got worse until the last time, when he was starved for six days. On occasion when he would receive his scheduled two meals a day, it would be a bowl of rice mixed with some cabbage or turnips. Once in a great while he'd also receive a small bowl of onions; there was never any meat.[27]

Sometimes the major could see out when the guard left the entrance cover open. In the distance he noticed caves, other mud huts and, once in a while, POWs. There were huts closer to his that he couldn't see, however, but he could hear. Frequently, the silence would be broken by the shrieking of an interrogator followed by the screams of an American captive.[28]

Frank Schwable capitulated during the last days of November 1952, but at the end of December, Roy Bley continued to hold on. It was at this time that he was moved again. There was a special cell they wanted to take him to; it was a box covered in ice. Inside, chunks of ice were on the floor and around the walls. Needless to say, there was no heat; the temperature was well below zero. Bley testified that "My fingers and feet became frostbitten; I was never allowed out of that cell; I would be yanked up any time during the night for interrogation." Physically, he was a mess. In this icebox, he developed some sort of nervous affliction which caused tremendous pain in his back, legs and feet. He said, "It got so bad for a while I couldn't walk, I couldn't put on my shoes; they were all puffed up."[29]

By the end of January 1953 (Colonel Schwable had agreed to a confession two months before), the Chinese had had it with the obstinate marine and he was either going to sign or die; it was getting down to that. Around midnight during the last week in January, a guard woke Major Bley and ordered him to follow; they were going to the camp commander's office. When they arrived, in addition to the commander, other Chinese officers were in attendance and to Bley it "appeared to be a formal military tribunal." Without a trial, witnesses, or the major having the right to defend himself, "There I was, pronounced a war criminal." He was shown Colonel Schwable's signed confession and essentially named a co-conspirator in the effort to anoint the civilian population of North Korea with disease. He was then informed "that I was to stand by for deportation to China where I was to be executed. While I was standing by, I was to go without food and remain awake." There was one little way out of his execution, however, because his "standby" period was 48 hours and during that time of grace, he had one last chance to change his mind.[30]

The 48-hour ultimatum was actually in writing, in perfect English, and signed by a Chinese general, probably a General Wang who was the senior North Korean officer responsible for all Chinese-administered camps in country and whose headquarters were at Camp 5.[31]

After the midnight terror, Major Bley was taken back to his icy cell. He wasn't required to sit or stand at attention, but he was deprived of food, water, and sleep for the next two days. At this point, the major didn't much care because, he recalled, "I had to walk in [the] cell as long [as] I could, or I would have frozen. I couldn't have slept in the cell anyway, without being frozen." And while he paced to keep alive, his colonel's signature on a confession was gnawing at him and he began questioning if this, an execution, was all worth it. After two days, the major said, "I was pretty well mentally and physically broken." At the duly appointed hour, the interrogator walked in. When asked of his decision, Major Bley told him he would "go along with the lie."[32]

The officer had with him a draft of the confession Bley was to sign; no creative writing was required of the major as had been of his colonel. He was ordered to rewrite it in his own hand and sign, which he did over a period of a few hours. It was taken away, edited, brought back, and then rewritten by hand and signed again "on smooth paper." However, that wasn't the end; another indignity was forthcoming.[33]

6. The Menticide (Part I)

Sometime after signing, probably within a few weeks at most, the major was taken to a room in Camp 5 and on a table was a microphone and tape recorder; he had to read his confession. A month after signing, on Wednesday, February 25, 1953, to be precise, his statement was broadcast over Radio Peking because Radio Pyongyang was too weak. According to the *New York Times*, the broadcast was in perfect English (but translated for target audiences) and since Bley was the senior weapons man of the wing, it "included elaborate details concerning storage, loading and security measures." Composed by the Chinese, it had no excess propaganda; it concentrated on the storage, security, and delivery of the weapons "rather than [on] emotional appeals."[34]

From the time of capture in early July 1952, Frank Schwable capitulated at the end of five months and Roy Bley, seven. Numbers are deceiving, however, since the Chinese didn't get into really hard interrogation with Bley until Colonel Schwable had been in the lean-to for a month. Before that, he had been in the house and the tent, so the colonel had a few months' head start on the major. In either case, they both underwent terrible hardship and Colonel Schwable describes his co-pilot as a marine that had "an extra share of guts."[35]

* * * *

During his four months at PUC, Colonel Schwable noted that he saw only two other American POWs (which is inaccurate) but at least a score of Americans, mostly enlisted marines, were watching him, especially during the months of October and November 1952.

The camp was also a collection point and housed between 32 and 35 GIs in addition to 10–15 officers being held for interrogation. The population of Pick-up Camp probably never exceeded 50 prisoners. Of the 221 marines captured during the war (190 ground troops and 31 aviators — some who never returned), over 10 percent were being held at PUC for shipment north to a regular camp. The vast majority of collected marines at PUC were captured either during the middle of April or the first week in October 1952.[36]

William Shockley, USMC*: Practically every enlisted marine held at PUC was with the First Marine Division when taken prisoner and Shockley was no exception. About three weeks after his capture in early October, he arrived at the camp and like everyone else, had no idea where he was. He was thrown into a rag-covered windowed cell. Looking through the opening, he could see the lean-to about thirty yards away over a

---

**When he testified at the investigation 16 months later, Shockley was a civilian and no rank is given but it's safe to assume that he was a corporal or a sergeant. This also applies to other former POWs who were discharged after repatriation and were witnesses at the inquiry.*

cleared space. Shockley described it as "a temporary sort of deal, just thrown up next to the Korean house under the eaves." When he first saw the shack (he couldn't see the colonel inside), there was an interrogator standing in front, actually pulling on his own hair, jumping up and down as if he were on a pogo stick. Shockley heard him screaming, "You confess, you will tell." The next day, Shockley noticed the interrogator had returned. Shockley saw him stand in front of the entrance and from the darkness he heard a voice say, "Go to hell." Shockley's view was unobstructed and, he said, "If I stood back in my cell, I could observe very nicely the colonel's cell." Schwable confirmed the marine's sighting and said "I think he had me fairly accurate[ly] spotted because he said he was in a lower house and could just look through the window and see me. I think he had me definitely spotted."[37]

For 15 days, William Shockley spied on the colonel. It wasn't a constant surveillance but, he said, "I tried to see him every day, if possible, at different times, I would watch. Of course, I was closely guarded and wasn't supposed to look out of the small window that was there, but on several occasions I did see him." Because he was isolated, this marine was thrilled to know that another American was in the area but he quickly noticed Schwable's appearance and "considered him very thin. He seemed thin, too thin, to me." Colonel Schwable himself was aware of his loss of weight from his normal 145 pounds because "my pants wouldn't stay up." When Shockley was asked to describe Frank Schwable upon initially seeing him in October, he said:

The first time I really noticed his features, sir, was that I noticed he looked something like a little mouse. I hate to say this about the Colonel, but his features were so drawn he reminded me of a little mouse. That was the main thing that I noticed, his jowls were sunk in and his eyes seemed to be very droopy. He moved very slow as if he was tired and drowsy.[38]

Even from a distance of 30 yards, the marine could see very dark circles under Schwable's eyes and not what one can really call a beard but long, dirty, stringy whiskers coupled with hair to match. He hadn't washed himself for over two months and the colonel commented that when "your hair is coming down all over you, [you get to] feel pretty horrible." He summed up the total absence of personal hygiene by lamenting, "I wallowed in filth and dirt; I was purposely kept unshaven and denied haircuts to the point that I was as filthy as a tramp; I had been kept in little hovels on the ground, in tiny Korean rooms, dark, mildewy leaky tents and now in this cold, open lean-to."[39]

Sgt. James L. Hale, USMC: A cement block building was the home to Sergeant Hale and about 20 other enlisted prisoners. The remaining 15 or so enlisted were scattered around the valley in huts and caves. The house was a football field away from the lean-to and across a draw that had steep grades on both sides. The quarters had some heat and Sergeant Hale said, "We had what they call a kong running under the house. You built a fire on one side and the smoke comes out on the other. It is a complete hole running through the house."[40]

As a group, the officers who were POWs during the Korean War did not do their duty; they did not perform as responsible leaders of men. There's one thing, however, that stands out in all POW camps throughout North Korea and which the officers took almost immediate charge of. That was the gathering and secreting away of names, especially of those in solitary. This was sort of an insurance policy; if the Chinese knew that others knew you were alive, they wouldn't be so quick to kill you. All camps required that officers and men be separated but they always found ways to communicate. According to Sergeant Hale, prior to Colonel Schwable arriving at PUC, "We had one washing point where we were washing our dishes.... We would pass notes through this wash point, like our group would go down to wash our dishes and one man would slip a note on the rock or under the rock and later the officers would come down and wash their dishes and they would get the note." They were caught, the practice stopped, and it's doubtful whether Frank Schwable's name was ever known to anyone at Pick-up Camp. When the colonel's name is mentioned, it would only be after they were transferred to a permanent camp in early December and saw and read the confession that had Schwable's photograph attached to it. Then it would click. In any event, the sergeant said, "Every man that came in the camp, we would watch and see him."[41]

As a general rule, the collected enlisted prisoners were not interrogated on germ warfare; after all, they were infantry. This didn't stop the Chinese from constantly lecturing on the subject, however. "They showed us pictures of these bombs that were supposed to have been broken open," observed Hale, "but you could tell they were fake pictures and they [i.e., the bomb casings] weren't even bent, and if they were dropped from a height, you know they would have been all bent up."[42]

September remained warm but the harsh North Korean winter was coming upon everyone, captor and captive alike. By December, the temperature hovered around zero and there was snow on the ground. Winter clothing was issued, eventually also to Colonel Schwable, consisting of blue, thickly padded trousers and jacket. This was very warm clothing, but the three accessories — shoes, mittens, and hat — were of inferior quality and essentially useless.[43]

Hale's line of sight to what he calls a "grass hut" was at a 45-degree angle. From his position, the lean-to looked to be on the side of a hill with a steep drop-off in front. At the bottom of the drop was a stream, and the water was within easy walking distance of the lean-to. Sergeant Hale could also see other huts around the shack but Colonel Schwable was not aware of them. The sergeant didn't see Frank Schwable that often. He said, "It was very seldom we got a chance to see him." Hale always uses "we" and that's because everyone in the concrete house was spying on Colonel Schwable. The group noticed there was always a guard and most often two of them, continually pacing outside the entrance to the hut. Interrogators were constantly coming and going and Sergeant Hale tells us:

One day they would probably come up and talk to him for an hour, or two hours. Then they would leave. Maybe [for] two or three days they would not come back. They probably let him think about what they told him quite a bit, then they would come back and try again. They just kept this up.[44]

The sergeant never saw the colonel physically beaten but he did see and hear mental abuse. Whenever interrogators came to the lean-to, according to Hale, "They would jump up and down and say, 'You will tell,' and then from what I understand, he would tell them he was not going to tell them anything. They would jump up and down and say, 'You will tell.'" Eventually, a reply would be voiced out of the darkness and, as only a sergeant of U.S. Marines could so eloquently say, the colonel "would just tell them [to] go fuck themselves."[45]

Cpl. Melvin Gaynor, USMC: The corporal entered camp in mid-October and was put into a bunker about 50 yards from the lean-to. Somehow he found out, while on wood gathering detail, that the man in the shack was a marine colonel. Gaynor saw Schwable four or five times and said, "He had a tired appearance. He wasn't very clean, he needed a shave." One day in late November, Gaynor was on detail again and passed within 35 yards of the lean-to. He glanced inside and saw Schwable, who he described as "shaggy, fatigued, eyes were bloodshot." On another trip at dusk, he passed again and looked but the colonel wasn't there and he saw only a "mud floor, and he didn't have no magazines, no smoking materials; there was none of that in there. Very small. It was easy to observe inside."[46]

Corporal Gaynor noticed that the only time they let Colonel Schwable out of his solitary closet was to go to the latrine and that was always between 5 and 6 in the evening. "They never let him out in the daytime," stated the corporal. Gaynor saw Schwable on his way to the makeshift latrine and noticed that he was not only filthy but "he more or less looked

6. The Menticide (Part I)

beat, and he was walking with a limp. They just let him go to the head right outside where they had him in solitary. There were Korean civilians there and it didn't make any difference. The guard motioned him to stop, and that was where he had to go to the head. He had no choice." When Gaynor hiked by the place where the colonel squatted, he saw that the feces were soaked in blood.[47]

Most POWs claimed that at one time or another they had dysentery but the colonel openly admitted that he didn't know the difference between dysentery and diarrhea so he simply stuck with diarrhea. It was like clockwork the way it came and went, noted the colonel, and "about every two weeks I got a ten day spell. When I did, to me it was terrific, it was a good, griping, aching kind of diarrhea. I would have it for about ten days and then it would seem to go away for a couple of weeks, then it would recur." The colonel used leaves to wipe himself and as fall, then winter, rolled along, he had to use leaves covered with frost. It was irritating physically but mentally he felt totally degraded and said, "I knew those monkeys had paper around there."[48]

That was on a good day; a bad day with diarrhea was when the guard wouldn't let him out. Whether it was on orders from the interrogator or just a mean guard, the colonel didn't know but during those totally isolated, solitary, dark times in a closet-like space, the colonel just sat there, "holding on for all I was worth, hour after hour." And he just sat there with this burning, aching, unbearable flame in his bowels, suffering, as he puts it, "the torture of the damned until somebody would let me go," which they oftentimes did not. Relief then came within the lean-to and Schwable said, "Your place of confinement is just small enough so that if you relieve yourself in a corner, you sleep in it. Your choices are awfully limited."[49]

It was 4 on a very cold winter morning, probably November sometime, when Frank Schwable awoke and had to urinate because, according to him, "I am a little older ... and I have to go a little more often." Nevertheless, the guard wouldn't let him out and in fact, blocked the entrance with branches, small stones, and logs, and went to sleep. In the shack was a tin can Schwable used for drinking and it was about half the size of a regular soup can or can of beans. The colonel peed in the can (with apparently some spillover, recognizing the size of the receptacle vis-à-vis the need to go). He went back to sleep and at 6 A.M. awoke and his pee was one solid block of yellowish ice. He found a small stone and for two days chipped away at his urine. He recalled, "Meanwhile, I didn't have anything to drink because there was nothing to put it in." After 48 hours he got most, not all of it, out, managed to get some water to pour into the can, and after a drink said, "Hot water and melted urine didn't taste very good, but I was thirsty."[50]

Frank Schwable wasn't the only animal around to consume bodily waste; there were also the dogs. In the house to which the lean-to was attached were children and, as seen by Colonel Schwable, "Those little kids would go out and relieve themselves right in front of the place and the dog is there to eat it because that is all the dog gets. I had that happen. The first couple of times I saw that I was trying to swallow my rice and I can tell you I vomited."[51]

The children who defecated in any permissible open space share a common thread with all children. It is a spiritual thread, and it rests in innocence. They don't know or understand birth, war, or death and it isn't until they're approximately six years old that children begin to realize the existence of a "higher power," someone higher than the father. Colonel Schwable perhaps became aware of the innocence of children while he was, at the same time, conceivably facing death, never to see his own children again.

Occupying the house to which the lean-to was attached was an older Korean woman, her daughter, and the daughter's three children, two girls and a boy. It was chestnut season and two of the school-age children would set off for classes each morning with their pockets filled with chestnuts. They had to walk near the colonel's shack to get to school. When they passed by, they'd sneak a look to make sure the guards weren't watching and then drop a chestnut to the ground. According to the colonel:

> ... and then they would go a little further and they would drop another chestnut. Usually the guards did not notice it, so when I would go out in the woods there to take a crap, I would go by where these chestnuts were, and I'd pick up a chestnut, and when I came back I would pick up another chestnut, and they were the best damn things I ever ate.[52]

> *Sgt. Pearson O. Porter, USA*: Captured in the middle of September 1952, army sergeant Porter was a forward observer with the 58th Armored Field Artillery, 65th Infantry Regiment, Third Infantry Division. He was tossed into one of several bunkers in the vicinity of the lean-to and it wasn't until about the middle of October that Porter first saw the occupant of the grass shack. As part of the collection point population (and not in solitary as the colonel was), prisoners could speak and interact with each other and they were always trying to figure out who was in the lean-to. Porter recalls, "He was too old to be an enlisted man. He didn't give the appearance of having been an enlisted man ... unless he was an old top sergeant, or something. I couldn't tell because of the Chinese [winter] uniform."[53]

All of the POWs talk of wood-gathering details and that's because all were involved; it wasn't forced labor but simply essential for survival. It isn't rare to read about temperatures of 30 degrees below zero in 1952, so fire was life. It's never explained what a "detail" was, but it's probably two to four men and possibly a few more, but not many. Each detail would make about four trips per day and each journey took about 30 minutes. Since they were mostly in a valley, on their way up into the hills they would pass isolated houses, bunkers, and caves. Sergeant Porter made two to four trips each day, which took most of the afternoon, and he would pass Schwable's shack and at times see him outside.[54]

There was a small rock near the entrance to the lean-to and sometimes, on a chilly morning with the sun shining, the colonel was permitted to go out and sit on the rock for about an hour. Most of the time, however, the interrogator used the rock while Frank Schwable remained in dark isolation. When he was on the rock and POWs did pass, whenever possible the colonel tried to give some sign; a wink, a nod, a tilting of the head, anything to show that he was alive and needed to be recognized. It was really a matter of life or death and any sort of communication could extend life. Porter relates that one day, "I was with a Negro Corporal. We passed by and he asked Colonel Schwable if he was a flyer at which he nodded. That was the only communication we had with him."[55]

There was hobnobbing between the 30-odd enlisted men in the camp because the majority were kept in the block house described by Sergeant Hale. They continually spoke with each other and exchanged information; when there was something to see, someone saw it. During his long periods of sitting, the colonel had somehow found a very small nail and over a period of time he whittled a rudimentary pipe from a tiny piece of wood. POW Robert Grover of the army's Second Infantry Division was heading into the hills on detail when he passed the lean-to and noticed Colonel Schwable "just sitting there. He had an old Korean pipe. I managed to get hold of one, too, along the way. That is what impressed it on my mind, because I smoked a pipe a lot before. He was sitting there smoking. As we went past, he winked."[56]

One of the things that none of the voyeurs saw was the colonel standing still; they either saw him walking under guard with a fixed bayonet at his back, or sitting. Because of all the sitting, when he had to stand and walk somewhere — which would be only one of two places, either the head or the camp commander's office — he was so stiff from sitting that walking was a strain. Every time he was forced to stand and walk, he did so stooped-over and limping until he worked the kinks out. Probably because of his age and poor physical condition, the Chinese did not insist that the colonel sit at attention and he could raise his knee and lean on it or even sometimes brace his back against the wall. Frank

Schwable recognized that "from guard to guard it was different. You never knew." But one thing the colonel was not permitted to do during daylight hours or without a guard's permission was to lie down or put his body into any position that even resembled lying down, such as putting his arm out to the side and using it as a prop. When he did try it, the guard would come in and prod the colonel with his gun. He stated, "When a Chinaman, who is pretty vicious looking when he wants to be, when he pokes a burp gun right in your nose, it is kind of convincing."[57]

The last time Sgt. Pearson Porter saw Schwable was sometime in November 1952, when there was an interrogator jumping up and down, screaming and shaking his finger in the colonel's face. The sergeant couldn't hear or understand too much until the end, when Porter distinctly heard the former chief of staff of one of the corps' three air wings tell the Chinese officer "to go fuck himself."[58]

Sidney Oehl, USMC: During the last week of October, Oehl and his group were heading into the hills when they passed within five feet of Colonel Schwable, who was wearing his winter uniform. According to Oehl, "He was very thin and very old looking, had a beard, mustache. He needed a haircut very badly." It shouldn't be taken for granted that the colonel was permitted to see other POWs, because he wasn't; he was generally in the dark and behind closed doors. When the guard saw Americans heading toward the shack and the colonel was outside, he would be shoved back in. It was uncommon, therefore, for Colonel Schwable to see others and to do so, according to him, he had to be outside at the time they were passing and, he recalled, "His guard and your guard both had to be looking [in] some other direction." When Sidney Oehl saw Schwable, for example, the colonel was outside sweeping.[59]

What there was to sweep on the stone walkway around the lean-to is unknown (probably leaves since it was late fall) but whatever it was, the colonel jumped at the chance to get out of his cramped space and move around. The colonel said, "I think they used to take a great deal of pleasure in exerting their authority as Orientals over a white man and they would tell me to go out and sweep."[60]

Airman First Class Franklin Hall, USAF: Airman Hall was a crewmember aboard a B-29 when he was shot down on November 8, 1952. Taken to Pick-up Camp, he saw Frank Schwable for about 10 days in a row. Hall remembered:

> He had what seemed to be a box of some kind, sort of like a cigar box, which he kept some papers in and tobacco and a pipe. He was sitting there with that box in his lap. Occasionally he would take out the papers and write briefly on the paper

and put the paper back in. Maybe just sit there for a long time and not do anything, just sit there, looking around.[61]

The box was old, made of cardboard, and about the size of a toothpaste container. Since it was worn, the colonel strengthened the sides by finding small scraps of paper and pasting them to the box with rice until they hardened. Every so often, the colonel would receive a cigarette and after smoking, he would put the butt into the reinforced box; it was used solely for cigarette butts.[62]

Since he was air force, for the first three days after his capture, Franklin Hall was intensely interrogated on germ warfare. For three midnights in a row, he was taken out of his "dog house," which was also a lean-to, brought to an isolated spot and forced to dig his own grave. All Hall ever said about these midnight journeys was, "3 walks, 3 graves." But Dr. Charles Mayo, at the United Nations, brought these walks to the attention of the world:

[One man] was sentenced to death 12 times, and he refused to yield. Another man was made to dig his own grave, was taken before a firing squad, heard the command to fire, and heard the click on empty chambers; and he refused to yield. Such testimony as this seems to teach us that the spirit of man can run deeper than the spirit of Pavlov.

Airman Hall was 19 years old.[63]

7

The Menticide (Part II)

Is this really happening to me in a modern civilized world, or am I merely living a nightmare that soon will be dispelled by common sense realism?

—Col. Frank Schwable, USMC, Court of Inquiry, Vol. 3, Exhibit 18 (2)

The month is November 1952. Frank Schwable capitulated this month. He almost saw the entire 30 days through but at the very end, he couldn't take any more. He had gone through July, August, September, and October but this was the worst month of all. To discover what went on in Frank Schwable's mind, one must get into it. To begin, he summarizes his experiences from capture up to this point:

> During the five months of continuous solitary confinement leading up to my capitulation, I was degraded, humiliated, intimidated and broken down physically, mentally, morally and spiritually; I was confused, bribed with false hopes, frustrated, deceived, influenced by constant poisonous propaganda and misleading statements, almost driven wild by a constant gnawing backache resulting from sitting on the floor, relatively immobile, for so long in confined spaces; I was discouraged, nearly frozen, sickened at times from the food, and finally was broken by dread of the results that would ensue on both sides of the line if I were forced to capitulate; worried sick about my family; assured in my mind that the Chinese were determined beyond all reason and logic to carry out their threats against me without hesitation; and imbued with a complete reaction of utter, total despair at the ultimate hopelessness and futility of the situation. Under the strain and deterioration of this treatment, my will to resist was finally destroyed. I made my evaluation of my worth to the U.S.—dead or alive—and I then capitulated to the Chinese in utter desperation [at] the end of November 1952.[1]

The colonel forced himself to forget about his immense physical pain because there was pain everywhere. Finally he said, "You convince yourself that there is no bodily pain, it is pain in the mind and pain in the mind you can't control." But the physical pain and humiliation were always present and the colonel asks us to "imagine having to sit on a dirt floor in cold weather with no support for one's back for hours on end with a throbbing backache, an excruciatingly full bladder, and the gripe of diarrhea unrelieved except in clothing." The Chinese knew precisely what was going on at all times and they also knew of, and prepared for, an upcoming torture that would have a major influence in breaking the colonel. They were going to freeze him.[2]

* * * *

The body can freeze and in the North Korean mountains, where the temperature quite often reached 30 degrees below zero, it can freeze fast. "Now, I think that is cold in any man's country, or any man's language," remarked Colonel Schwable. By this time, the colonel was wearing a blue Chinese winter-padded uniform, had a mat to lie down on and a heavy blanket. Later in the month, he was furnished with a second blanket. He said, "I put on everything I could put my hands on, including an old dirty towel I found one day [but] I was still cold [and] with no stimulation from exercise and with no warmth from within my heart or soul, I was miserably cold."[3]

When the cold got nasty, straw was brought into the lean-to and some was placed under his sleeping mat while the remainder was stuffed around the bottom three exposed sides of the shack to help keep the wind out. He wasn't happy about the straw, however, because it had small insects in it. Although Frank Schwable didn't know what they were and admits that he wouldn't know a louse if he saw one, he recalled that there were "lots of little tiny bugs that crawl all over you." Even with the straw, the place was still "no warmer than an ice box."[4]

All day he would sit in the lean-to, teeth chattering and body shivering. He was all but frozen to the bone and said, "I started to shiver and I never stopped shivering." The interrogator saw this suffering and once asked the colonel, "What is the matter, are you cold?" and although there was no need for a shivered reply, Schwable gave an affirmative one and the officer shot back, "We have given you an extra quilt. We can't do anything else."[5]

It wasn't just the cold but it was the type of cold; it was a constant, living, dynamic cold. The colonel said, "You just sit there week after week for a couple of months with each day and each night getting colder. I think you will know what I mean by cold, not just temperature." It was so "damn cold, awfully cold," that when he went to sleep, he'd put his canteen under his head and the next time he would look, there'd be a block of ice in the container. A small tin of warm water was brought to the marine with each of his two daily rice meals. Of this he said, "If it dropped on a stone, the minute it hit the stone it was frozen. I don't know how cold that is, but it was awfully cold as far as I am concerned."[6]

Night was the worst time because it got colder. Darkness came in late afternoon and the colonel sat in the frigid night and watched icicles drip, he recalled, "and I would just sit there and watch the water drip, drip, drip. Pretty soon it would be drip — drip — drip, and pretty soon it would quit dripping, and it was freezing and so was I. Oh, I used to dread that." During the day he prayed for night, and night brought pleas for day. When he was ordered to sleep, the colonel said, "The minute I would lie down, I would start praying for morning to come."[7]

* * * *

His November days were spent sitting:

> ... on the floor of a closet in a deserted house, in winter, being able to move about only several times a day to ... go to the latrine; to be watched incessantly and to hear an intelligible word only when one single person visited you sometimes daily and sometimes not for three or four days, always saying in effect when he did come, "You are a war criminal, you will never leave this valley until you confess, you know the U.S. forces are using germ warfare, we already have several pilots who have told us all about it, you are prolonging the war, winter will get colder and colder, confess, confess, confess."

The colonel described these interrogations: "Like the slow dripping of water working on the nerves; the Chinese kept repeating that the only course of action open to me was to confess, confess, CONFESS!!"[8]

Sometimes pure logic was used on Frank Schwable. The core of the Chinese argument can be labeled the "Futility of Resistance." They would keep saying to him, "We are in no hurry; you can do this tomorrow, next week, next year, twenty years from now, fifty years from now. We are in no hurry." The colonel had every reason to believe them — and did — because in his mind he was absolutely certain that he would never see his country or family again unless he gave in and surrendered.* "I don't know much about Chinese," remarked Colonel Schwable, "but I believe most Orientals are known as a very patient race. And they really make you feel that if you don't do it today, tomorrow is just as good, next year is just as good, twenty years from now is just as good, but you are going to do it." By November, Frank Schwable had reasoned that the Chinese were going to keep him for the rest of his life unless, at some point, he signed. It appears that the colonel began thinking and analyzing with a Chinese mind; what would he do if the roles were reversed and he was the captor, not captive? He'd do the same thing. The colonel admits that:

There were actually two stages of Colonel Schwable's captivity; capture in early July and surrender in late November.

7. The Menticide (Part II)

... there was absolutely no doubt in my mind for one second that they would keep me indefinitely because of the absolutely perfect setup they had [and] nobody could have given them a better one. They had a chief of staff, they had a colonel, they had an aviator, all in one place, and who should sit alongside of him but, among all people, the ordnance officer who knows all about bombs. You could not have had a more ideal setup and I recognized that as soon as they started on [germ warfare]. It was so ideal they did not dare to let up.[9]

In mid-November Roy Bley was moved north to Camp 5 but the remaining population of about 50 prisoners at PUC stayed where they were. Although the major didn't sign until two months after his colonel, Schwable naturally didn't know this and therefore the Chinese kept telling him that Major Bley was in a permanent POW camp (true) because he confessed (false). They worked Bley and Schwable the same way and the colonel said, "They played one of us against the other. I mean I was constantly told that 'Why, yes, you flew right along with this guy, here he is, Major Bley, we have him. He has already cleared this problem. He has gone up to the main camp.' They were doing that continuously." Almost every day the interrogator would say to his prisoner, "When you have cleared your ... problem, you will be taken up to a main camp, you will be taken out of solitary, you will be put with other people, you will be warmer, everything."[10]

The end of the colonel's resistance, in late November 1952, began with a head call. While returning to his shack after relieving himself in the woods, he passed out cold. This scared the daylights out of him because it was then that he knew he was simply falling apart. He said, "This thing is beginning to get a little bit close." Composing and signing the confession was becoming increasingly real in his jumbled thoughts. In Colonel Schwable's mind, the justification for doing so was, "If you don't [write], they will write up the stuff anyhow, like they do all their propaganda, and they will put your name to it, and who is to ever say that you didn't do it?" This is not true. The confession had to be so detailed that no one could have written it but Frank Schwable himself. The colonel didn't ask one question, however: If they could write it themselves, why didn't they do so months before?[11]

Thinking, thinking, and thinking: "I evaluated the situation, I tried to analyze everything that was going on.... I think I thought of everything there was to think of." The colonel could contemplate all he wanted but the more his mind worked, the more perplexed he became. He said, "I was damn confused, very confused." In this muddled intellectual existence, Colonel Schwable began to realize that it was only a matter of days, at most a week, when the time would arrive, as he put it, for "just complete collapse, collapse of any will or ability to resist any further."[12]

* * * *

It was only his second mission as a member of Air Group 102, which was assigned to an aircraft carrier attached to Task Force 77, when he was shot down during the first week in November 1952 near Woson Harbor. After he was captured, 24-year-old Lt. (j.g.) Andrew L. Riker III traveled for one week to a place he called Pike's Peak* and was immediately thrown into isolation. Lieutenant Riker said his solitary confinement space was "about two feet wide and six feet long, built on the side of a wall of a house, more or less resembled a doghouse. That is what we called them." The camp itself was fairly large and had several buildings in addition to shacks and bunkers.[13]

During his first few weeks in the doghouse, Lt. Riker was left alone to think but he was forced to endure this isolated thinking while sitting at extreme attention. Most of the time, the position was absolutely erect; back straight and legs out flat as a board. This navy pilot noted that "you were never allowed to lean back on your elbows or so much as hardly change your position. In other words, you had to sit up all day long in one position unless you had to go to the latrine." If the lieutenant did attempt to change his posture, one of his constant companions would come in, poke the lieutenant with his rifle until he got back into the proper position, and order him to stay still. On rare occasions, a lenient guard would allow him to bend his knees or, when not being watched, he would lean against the wall for support. A few times he was permitted to squat and the lieutenant said, "I found, for instance, in a squatting position like the orientals squat, I was able to stay at that three or four hours at a time without my legs going to sleep. It is because your muscles get so flabby there is no tension or anything in them. You would be surprised, after a while you can get to do it without any strain."[14]

It was during his last 10 days in the doghouse at Pike's Peak that the Chinese began their germ warfare interrogation of the lieutenant. The daily routine, as for every other POW being harassed to sign a confession, was that there *was* no routine. This drove them all to a maximum stress level. Riker points out that during his interrogation, at times the Chinese would badger him for 14 consecutive hours, "I would say from eight in the morning until ten at night, [then] sometimes you would go a day without it. Other times it would be all day. Sometimes only two hours a day. Then sometimes they would leave you alone for four days."[15]

His interrogator was a chain-smoker, who wore very thick glasses. There was something wrong with his hands, because his fingernails were raised off

---

*The POWs dubbed quite a few small collection points and interrogation centers Pike's Peak although there was one interrogation center formally named Pike's Peak. We don't know if Riker was in this center but since he constantly refers to it as such, the assumption is that it was indeed there.

his fingers. He would begin his talks with the lieutenant by commenting on how terrible war is, that everyone wants peace, and then, according to Riker:

> Slowly but surely, he would work into this germ warfare business before I even actually realized what he was talking about. Then it suddenly dawned on me that he wanted something that I knew nothing about at all. He would go on to say that "We know that this has been done, so it is not up to you to tell us how it is done or anything else. We know all about that. All we want you to do is say that you did it."[16]

Riker was a junior pilot off an aircraft carrier in the middle of the ocean and he knew nothing of germ warfare, but the thick-spectacled Chinese officer "just wouldn't take no for an answer," said Lieutenant Riker. He would simply sit and smirk at the naval officer and keep saying, "We know it. We know it." As with other aviators, Riker, too, was tossed the proverbial carrot of a permanent home but with a catch. The officer would say, "Your case is very simple and we have closed your records, but every man must confess to germ warfare before he goes to a prison camp."[17]

The lieutenant was slapped around a few times by the officer but endured nothing serious. Riker remarked, "They tried not to do it that way if they could help it. They were able to make you behave without doing it that way." He went on to say, "As far as I am concerned, they were pretty good on their psychology of the human mind. They knew how to work a man over so that he was more or less broken down to saying anything they wanted him to say."[18]

It was during the first week in December 1952 that the lieutenant felt he was beginning to fall apart; in his isolated doghouse he began crying. The aviator said, "I was at my wits' end. I didn't know what to do." In desperation, he said, "I told them they could shoot me." But the Chinese didn't need this junior officer since they already had enough confessions to fill a book, with Colonel Schwable as the principal character. Within a few days after telling his captors to kill him, Riker was moved to a permanent camp along the Yalu. During this move, Lt. (j.g.) Andrew Riker was to meet Col. Frank Schwable.[19]

* * * *

When he was captured in December 1951 (six months before Schwable's capture), Lt. Col. William G. Thrash, USMC, was assistant operations officer of the First Marine Aircraft Wing. In that capacity, he said, "I had access to Fifth Air Force plans in case of a failure of certain operations in Korea, retaliatory measures, and so forth." Once again, the Chinese attitude was "So what?" Something more important was brewing; it was in late 1951/ early 1952 that the opening phase of the germ warfare campaign began. At first, Colonel Thrash thought they were trying to teach him something and said, "The initial phase of the propaganda program of bacteriological warfare appeared to me to be one of convincing the prisoners of its truth. I didn't realize at the time that they were actually trying to get confessions."[20]

Colonel Thrash got involved with germ warfare when the Chinese confronted him with an accusation and this 36-year-old senior marine officer noted, "They never openly accused me of dropping bacteriological warfare, but they did think [that] with my rank, I must have participated in the program. They demanded to know what part I had taken in the program." All of this took place in December 1952 and into 1953, and at this juncture Colonel Schwable had already confessed. Thrash said that one day, "They had [something] for me to read and they would open the door, allow me to have light in order that I could read it, and I was presented with a copy of some communist publication, I don't recall the name now, in which a reported confession by Colonel Schwable was contained."[21]

Months after Frank Schwable signed (and only months before the war was over), the captors never let up on Colonel Thrash, who wouldn't sign. His torture was not menticide but simply harassment and threats, coupled with physical pain. Once during midwinter, the colonel was partially stripped and forced to stand at attention out in the open while guards packed ice around him up to his knees. In the same vein and also in freezing temperatures, Thrash said, "I was bound [and] placed out in subzero weather. There I suffered considerably." However, what was worse than the physical pain, according to the colonel, was "the mental duress, or constant confinement, poor food, negligence, continual harassment."[22]

Colonel Thrash describes the atmosphere of typical interrogations he went through:

> [On] numerous occasions ... I would be taken to a room with four or five interrogators. I would be forced to stand in the room. Sometimes they would bind your hands behind your back, strike you in the back, kick you, or shove you, throw small items, something on the table. But purely it appeared to me to be an effort to frighten me rather than actually torture me.[23]

The colonel took a fatalistic view of signing, reasoning that one was a dead man whether he signed or didn't sign. Thrash had to assume, since he was quite firm in not signing anything, that it was just a matter of time before he disappeared. The colonel said that his fatalism "stemmed more from a fear that the communists would take a man, accuse him, failing to break him, they would dispose of him; if they did break him, they would also dispose of him." After being shown the confession, Thrash had the feeling of "utmost sympathy for Colonel Schwable.... I felt that perhaps having forced such a confession from him, in all probability they would dispose of him."²⁴

Col. William Thrash did not sign and was eventually repatriated during Operation Big Switch. Upon reflection, he said, "My condition alternated between frustration, indignation, and sort of despair. Whether I ever felt I would break or not, I don't know. I always considered their demands too high and I always held out hope that somehow I would get out."²⁵

* * * *

Outside the lean-to was the surrounding walkway covered with small stones and splitting off from the path was a narrow dirt trail leading to the opposite end of the same valley. At the other end of this often muddy track was the administrative center of PUC that housed the interrogators, the kitchen, which fed both prisoners and garrison, and the camp commander's residence and offices. The commander was a Chinese army colonel (probably attached to the Political Department) and the distance between the two colonels, one in a freezing lean-to and the other in a warm house, was 1,000 yards. During his four months at PUC, Colonel Schwable was taken to the commander's office for a long "talking to" approximately once a week, five times during the day and 10 times during the middle of the night.²⁶

On Friday, November 28, 1952, Colonel Schwable was interrogated in the freezing cold all morning and, with a very short break for something to eat and drink, for the remainder of the afternoon. Darkness came early and the colonel ate his evening rice alone and then just sat, watched, and listened to icicles drip, then stop, teeth chattering and body shivering the entire time. At 10 on this Friday night, he was ordered by the guard to lie down and sleep. Frank Schwable slept scared and his mind raced: "Are they going to drag me out tonight down to the camp commander's office for another one of those vile political lectures?" The colonel's imagination would kick in and add to his ever increasing fear. He would think, "Here he comes, they are going to dig me up and march me down there; I am going to stand in front of that yellow monkey and listen to him yak at me." On this particular Friday night, the colonel's imagination, thoughts, and frightening dreams were to become real.²⁷

It was as close to midnight as one could get without going over when Colonel Schwable was awoken; it was time. The commander was waiting. Schwable walked the half-mile with the guard at his back and reached the colonel's office. For the next two and a half hours, the marine pilot was forced to stand at a rigid attention. Colonel Schwable did nothing but listen. He said, "I can remember that little guy sitting in there and giving me the most concentrated talking to that I had had in my whole experience over there."²⁸

The commander said, "You must confess; it is for the good of the world. It is the peace appeal. You must cleanse your soul, you know you did it; we have [people] who have said you have done it. We have an international scientific commission report; we know your night fighters started this thing." The commander continued and said, "Unless you clear this problem, you will never leave this valley—not even after the peace is signed." Frank Schwable was then reminded that he had been pronounced a war criminal several months before and therefore was not a prisoner of war and "rules" did not apply to him. Colonel Schwable emphatically noted, "I was considered a war criminal for my alleged connection with germ warfare and that I would not therefore be treated as an ordinary POW under the Geneva Conventions and would not be repatriated unless I confessed."[29]

This war criminal thing was starting to get the best of Schwable because he simply did not want to be one; he wanted to be a prisoner. War criminals are the lowest of the low, but as a POW, he'd be sent to a regular POW camp, the interrogations would be over (or so he thought), he'd be with other Americans who would know he was alive—and, therefore, it would be harder to kill him. "So," said the colonel, "you build up in your mind a feeling that it is an honest to God privilege to be a POW if you can only get out of this solitary confinement."[30]

How? Sign! "I [don't] know what to do. [I] can only say no to the guy so long." Frank Schwable simply couldn't relate to his environment on this early Saturday morning. "I couldn't believe I was there," he said. He admits that he was "pretty thoroughly whipped" and that he had to make "the most serious decision of my life." He was exhausted and weak, both mentally and physically, and felt that:

> ... resistance would be both futile and fatal; it was here that in utter confusion and depression, with a lost sense of values, and a bewilderment over the fantasy that this propaganda issue created that I finally concluded I could be of more value to my country alive than dead or as a prisoner of war and that I must therefore submit.

"The night fighters were the first ones, weren't they?" asked the camp commander.

"Yes," answered Colonel Schwable.[31]

Why? Menticide is insidious; it's crafty, cunning, and so very subtle that one doesn't know it's happening until it has happened and then there is pure collapse. Taking each incident of badgering, harassment, and threats in isolation, one might have the automatic reaction of "I could take that." However, when these tactics are grouped together over a period of four months, menticide truly reveals itself as an artful ambush. And, as with any ambush, one doesn't know it's happening until one is in it — and then it's too late.

Colonel Frank Schwable, USMC, speaks:

> When you have gotten to the point where you will make such a terrific concession to another man, as I did to that little Chinaman, then I did not have any resistance left. I did what that guy told me.[32]
>
> I know there are such things as heroics but if any man lost his life maintaining silence [on] this propaganda issue, he lost his life in vain.[33]
>
> Given sufficient time and determination by an oppressor, *any man can be broken down eventually*, one way or another, heroics notwithstanding.[34]
>
> I felt [that] sacrificing my life over a lost propaganda cause was not in the best interest of my government. That was my decision, made under the special circumstances existing at the end of November 1952.[35]
>
> Even in my torment and mental and physical anguish, I could see I was of little value to the U.S. if I were six feet under the ground.[36]
>
> In making my most difficult decision to seek the "only way out," my primary consideration was that I would be of greater value to my country in exposing this hideous means of slanderous propaganda than I would be by sacrificing my life through non-submission or remaining a prisoner of the Chinese Communists for life, a matter over which they left me no doubt.[37]
>
> I could resist to the bitter end or until I became mentally irresponsible — death or insanity — to gain what?[38]
>
> I knew I could be disposed of with no difficulty at a moment's notice; I knew they would stop at nothing; and therefore, it was only too apparent that the Chinese would accomplish their aim or I would either be killed or retained as a prisoner for life. There was no doubt about it.[39]
>
> My inherent pride as a Marine officer was submerged and with it my moral and spiritual outlook was contaminated.[40]

Write!: It was about 2:30, early Saturday morning, November 29, 1952, when Colonel Schwable was marched back to his lean-to and permitted to lie down on his mat, softened by straw. He rested for three to four hours. At first light, the interrogator came into the shack and said, "The colonel is so happy that you have decided to cleanse your soul and to confess and thus help the peace movement."[41]

The Chinese in getting started wasted no time. Paper and a pen were handed to the colonel and the creative juices began to flow, "for the most part," according to Frank Schwable, "while [I was] sitting on the floor trying to use a folded quilt for a table." The interrogator would furnish ideas on the flow and structure of the work, but it was only the colonel who could vividly take the reader into wing headquarters and into the minds of the personalities involved in the planning and execution of a germ warfare campaign over North Korea. A writer becomes attached to his work, if not to a character then attached through events and/or circumstances. To Colonel Schwable, the distortion of reality became real and reality itself practically ceased to exist. Frank Schwable eventually lost sight, according to him, of "where the truth ends and the lies begin [and] it was in this general frame of mind that I fought off the devil himself as long as I could; it was in this same frame of mind that I finally scribbled out the actual words of my statement."[42]

Colonel Schwable knew that the wing did not participate in germ warfare in Korea; he said so: "I knew we had not." Yet in writing the confession, he not only became engrossed in drafting but became obsessed with the subject matter and upon reflection said, "It was real to me, the conferences and how the planes would fly up there and how they would go about their missions, that was real." The colonel could not get the contradiction out of his mind. He knew that what he was writing was false, but at the same time it was true to him. This thought process can probably best be compared to that of a novelist; making fiction real. Once the creation began, the colonel said that he started "to live it, to sense it." He would sit on the mat with the folded heavy blanket on his lap and start to imagine the unique aerial tactics involved in dropping bacteriological weapons and he would think, "How did your squadron get from here up to there, and how did they drop these bombs?" Soon he would figure it out and then the offspring of his mind would be memorialized on paper.[43]

"I actually lived in my mind the plans and conferences I reported," the colonel reflected, "[and] in my stupefied and disordered mind's eye, I pictured myself in conference with General Jerome, for instance, and, mumbling aloud to myself, discussed the problems involved — it was realistic to me in detail." During his writing, Colonel Schwable felt that he "was living in a world of ungodly fantasy; it was impossible to believe that what was happening was real." Schwable called the entire menticide experience a "diabolical swindle" and simply couldn't believe that anyone who was civilized, "friends and foe alike," would do such a thing, would plan and direct such a swindle. But the real question is "Why not?" This is a U.S. Marine who believes that his "foe" shouldn't do this? Do what? Send out some of the best, if not the best, propaganda of the 20th century? The colonel is complaining about *how* they achieved the final outcome, but does it matter? One may say that the quarrel with the colonel at this point is that he's saying words to the effect that "it's not fair; they're not playing by the rules." What rules? Once rules are instituted, you have a game, not war. In a way, it appears that Colonel Schwable forgot he was still at war even though a POW, and his previous function prior to capture as chief of staff was to plan and direct the killing of people. As a marine, he was trained to kill — and he did. His enemy was just doing the same thing but with a different target — the mind.[44]

On December 2, 1952, Colonel Schwable was awoken from a restless sleep and in the bitter cold was marched down the snow-covered trail to the administrative area at the opposite end of the valley. At headquarters, in a large room were a group of Chinese officers awaiting him. It appeared to be on the order of a military tribunal but the commander wasn't there and instead, his executive officer was in charge. Colonel Schwable was forced to stand at attention in front of these officers, and he admitted that he was in a daze. Frank Schwable was sternly informed that whatever he had written over the past four days wasn't worth a damn and he was to start over. He was told that he had tactical operations "at the wrong place and at the wrong time"; he had to move operations back six months and cover a broader area of North Korea. The commander's second in charge was screaming and yelling at Schwable to go back and do it right. The officer was in such a rage that he grabbed his cover and rushed out of the room with the interpreter chasing after him in a vain effort, according to Colonel Schwable, "to translate his ravings into English."[45]

For the next few days, the physical task of writing was nearly impossible; the mind was willing to fabricate and compose, but the body and the instrument the body was employing would not comply. The colonel was using a fountain pen and on Wednesday, December 3, it quit, not for lack of ink but because it kept freezing. Frank Schwable would write only two or three words and then he would sit on the pen in an attempt to thaw the ink. After a few more words, he'd sit on it again for a couple of minutes, then write. More important, however, was that his writing hand became frostbitten; the frostbite began with several knuckles of his right hand.[46]

On Thursday, December 4, he was removed from his home of three months to a small, lightly heated room in a Korean house. The colonel said, "I was allowed the use of a partially warmed Chinese office so that neither my fingers nor the ink in the pen would freeze while I was writing.... [I] continued to write on the subject of germ warfare, submitting to the Chinese at this time a first near-complete statement on the subject."[47]

Colonel Schwable and his interrogator worked feverishly to get at least a rough draft of the confession in place; he was coached all along. "The night fighters started this out, didn't they?" the interrogator would say, and the colonel would reply to the question with a simple "Yes." "They would carry one bomb, wouldn't they?" and again "Yes" and this would go on and on. When Schwable passed over something that the Chinese thought important, they would prod him to expand on that particular fictional event and also to bring in more detail and personalities. The interrogator continually took bits and pieces of the confession with him and these sometimes unrelated scraps were organized and put into a coherent whole by the captors. On Saturday, December 6, a complete rough draft of the confession was shown to Colonel Schwable. "These are your words, look at them, there they are. They are your words. We have just edited them a little. Now you transcribe those in your own handwriting," they said. The colonel admitted that the words were his but said, "The thoughts were theirs."[48]

The actual published confession was dated when the rough draft was completed and this required Colonel Schwable copying in longhand, on legal size paper, the edited and organized typewritten admission the Chinese handed him. According to the colonel, "It was the first paper that had any completeness to it, any degree of completeness, that was the 6th of December." At that point, even though it was in draft stage, the colonel remarked that "it was a smooth piece of paper."[49]

It has never been mentioned in any of the several thousand pages of documents that the population of Pick-up Camp was being held hostage to the signature of Colonel Schwable, but it certainly is a coincidence that on Monday, December 8, two days after the draft was finished, PUC was disbanded, lock, stock, and barrel, and everyone, POWs, administration, troops, and supplies were put on a convoy of trucks and moved north to the Yalu. The ordeal of Frank Schwable, however, was not over and he had almost nine more very hard months to serve as a war criminal. He was never given the status of POW.

After the war, the inquiry determined "that Colonel Schwable resisted this torture to the limit of his ability to resist." John Pratt, the colonel's civilian attorney, said, "When he submitted, his judgment was impaired and his will to resist was shattered. In short, he was mentally and physically broken." Colonel Paul Sherman, his military counsel, looked at the confession as "a deliberate and calculated lie, conceived not in the mind of this fine American Marine but in the foul recesses of the communist brain." He went further to say that within this document, one can see "a cruel and relentless enemy of mankind with designs against not only men's bodies, but their very souls." Colonel Sherman swelled with anger at the Chinese and dramatically announced to the court of inquiry and the watching, listening, and reading world that it was "only the foulest incarnation of the devil in human form [who] could conceive of, let alone carry out, such a methodical and calculated program of torture of another being."*[50]

---

*See Appendix for the confession.

8

The Transfer

The germ warfare problem, with its appeal to the masses of people, was a prize propaganda issue too valuable to the Communists to give up under any circumstances.
— Col. Frank Schwable, USMC, Court
of Inquiry, Vol. 3, Exhibit 20 (1)

The trucks arrived at 2:30 A.M., December 8, 1952. Two separate small convoys were formed, one carrying the camp's equipment and supplies plus the commander and his staff, while the other few trucks held the POWs and guards from PUC. The trip north to the Yalu River and Camp 5 was going to require two full days of travel and this first day's journey would last 14 hours. Even though it took only two days to reach the main POW camp in North Korea it was still a vast distance from the disbanded collection point/interrogation center. The trucks traveled slowly through rough, snow-covered mountains on extremely narrow roads, many of them better described as wide trails.[1]

Wearing his blue cotton padded Chinese uniform, Colonel Schwable was put into one of the trucks with a number of other American prisoners. The colonel sat on a side bench at the front of the truck bed and, in addition to several Chinese soldiers guarding the men, he had two detached guards with him at all times; "It was his sort of personal escort," remarked one of the prisoners at the hearing. On the same vehicle were many of the enlisted men who spied on him at PUC but no one was permitted to speak, both among themselves and especially not to the colonel.[2]

Shortly after the captors and captives deserted PUC, they stopped the small parade and loaded another prisoner. The convoy had reached Pike's Peak and in the morning darkness, Lt. (j.g.) Andrew Riker climbed aboard the same truck Colonel Schwable was in. When his eyes became accustomed to the darkness, the navy pilot noticed an old man up front, but he wouldn't find out who he was until they stopped and settled down for the night.[3]

At first light, Lieutenant Riker saw the colonel and said his beard looked to be "about the equivalent of a week's growth. Otherwise, he was just as cold [as] the rest of us." Toward the rear of the truck sat Carl Shepard of the army's Third Infantry Division and he suggested that Frank Schwable was not mentally stable. Shepard observed, "I saw him talking to himself. I also saw him take off his coat and he said he was warming up. I was pretty cold that day, too.... I guess it was as cold as it ever gets over there." It seemed that everyone on the truck was watching the senior marine in the corner, including Robert Grover, also of the Third Infantry Division, who noticed that "He didn't seem to have much heart in anything. He wasn't like the rest of them. They were either worrying about the cold, or something of the sort. Nothing seemed to faze him.... He didn't pay any attention. You know, everyone was kind of watching what was going on, and the country around us, and stuff like that. From all I had observed of him, he just sat there and didn't pay too much attention to anything."[4]

A number of soldiers from PUC now in the truck with the colonel had differing opinions as to his mental stability. Sgt. Pearson Porter, USA, said, "He was just staring ahead. He showed no emotion or anything whatsoever," yet Cpl. Melvin Gaynor, USMC, saw a little more. "He just sat there. He would shake his head now and then while we were going along and he would move his lips a lot. Once he mentioned being surrounded by oil. He said, 'I am surrounded by oil. What is all the oil doing here?' There wasn't any oil around. He was just sitting there looking at the floor, talking to himself." One of the guards sternly told the colonel to shut up.[5]

Once in a great while at PUC, Colonel Schwable was given some loose tobacco with paper and he was able to roll a cigarette for himself. After he told the camp commander that he would confess, he was given three packs of "tailor made" cigarettes. He later remarked, "It was so damned cold that was the only thing that kept me going." Sometime during the day, Colonel Schwable removed a pack and gave a few cigarettes to the men. Lieutenant Riker noticed, "He had a couple that he passed out to us that were Chinese cigarettes [which] he passed to the boys. The boys took one puff and passed them around the truck so we could all have them."[6]

It was at 5 on this Monday afternoon when the small convoy stopped for the night at an abandoned Japanese mining camp. Everyone was put into a two-room mud shack, the prisoners being split between the rooms. For a short moment Cpl. Eugene Vavruska, USMC, was only six or seven feet away from the colonel and saw that "all at once he started shadow boxing. I don't know if he was just loosening himself up from the ride, or what the reason was, but he started shadow boxing." This didn't go on for long. While the men were being quartered and fed, Colonel Schwable was removed from the shack and taken to another area to sleep for the night.[7]

The next morning, Frank Schwable was brought back to the two-room shack to have a breakfast of rice. Other men were in one of the small rooms with him, standing, milling about, and eating. No one was permitted to talk but according to Airman Franklin Hall (just recovering from having to dig his own grave more than once), although there were guards, they "didn't stay right in the room the whole time. There was a big door and they stood outside the door. There was several of us in there and they couldn't possibly watch all of us all the time. We were able to make some signs and so forth between each other."[8]

A soldier is not instructed in this (just as they're not taught many other survival techniques for POWs) but, if captured, expose yourself. If you can get your name out and if, by good fortune, your face — a picture — you have just signed up for an excellent life insurance policy. Your name and/or your face has been plastered across the world. It is now much harder to kill you. (Take American POWs in Iraq, for example. The faces shown on television came home. Those captured and not shown never returned.)

Airman Hall was standing close to Colonel Schwable during these early morning hours and saw that he was walking around, like working a room at a cocktail party. While doing so, his hand was slightly raised and he was putting his watchband in front of anyone who would look. On the band was an engraving. Airman Hall observed, "He had a metal watchband with his name and rank on it. He passed that around in the view of the people who were close to him to show that." Soon Colonel Schwable reached Lieutenant Riker, and according to the navy pilot, "He had a wristwatch with his name engraved on it, a metal band. That is when I was sure of how he spelled his name."[9]

Riker knew that the idea of showing the watch was for identification (protection) and now the lieutenant wanted the colonel also to know who he was. They started to whisper. Riker then "passed him a picture of my fiancée." It wasn't actually a picture but "a newspaper clipping of my fiancée, which had a more or less short resume of my background."[10]

It was 8 in the morning when the POWs boarded two trucks, with Colonel Schwable in the lead one. He assumed his same spot in the front corner. This trip lasted seven hours. The temperature was 13 degrees below zero. It was cold, "pretty damn cold."[11]

During midafternoon on Tuesday, the truck carrying Colonel Schwable arrived at Camp 5 and the men were ordered off and lined up on the dirt road. Airman Hall was about three men down the line from Schwable when he heard the man next to the colonel ask him a question that Hall couldn't pick up. The answer, however, was very audible to the airman: "They have been working on me on germ warfare, but I haven't told them anything yet." Almost immediately thereafter, the colonel was snatched out of line and taken away. The remainders were led off into the camp proper except for four men (including Lieutenant Riker) who were driven by jeep to one of the neighbors of Camp 5, either Camp 2 or Camp 3.[12]

* * * *

The town of Pyoktong is a little less than a mile outside the main gate. This is where most prisoners confined to solitary spent their time, and this is where Frank Schwable was taken. To isolate him further, his captors sent him to a remote end of town and put him into a house as far away from the camp as possible. The space he was thrown into was eight feet square, which was room enough to move around; "I could get a little movement," he said. At least, remarked the colonel, "It was a house, not a hut." The walls were of solid mud to protect against the wind and, luxury of luxuries, there was a light bulb. It was 60 watt with wires so old and corroded it was lit about every other day. The system would go out, get fixed, and then come back again for a little while. But when it was on, the colonel said, "I would stand there by hours just holding that little bulb, and that is when I began to get feeling back in my fingers again."[13]

Colonel Schwable was extremely angry. On more than one occasion the Chinese had promised that if he confessed, he would be taken to a main POW camp (which he was) and made a part of the normal POW population (which he wasn't and never would be). The colonel thought that where he was located was even more solitary than before, because during the winter months the door was closed and he was surrounded by darkness. He just sat on a small stool and pondered.[14]

Frank Schwable discovered the broken promise was a result of the system. First they would have to find a man who was willing to live with him and locate one room for both of them. Then they would add another man, then another, until the colonel got accustomed to living with people again. Subsequently, he would be moved back to the camp itself. To this, Colonel Schwable said, "Fine, you just move somebody in with me." The Chinese replied, "All right, we will do that. We will have to look around." Ten days passed and when Schwable asked about his new roommate, the answer was, "Nobody wants to live with you. You are too old." Suffice it to say the colonel spent the next nine months of his captivity alone.[15]

Why? Because once he's integrated into a normal society, he would quickly recover from menticide. Although isolated, the colonel thought that since he was very close to the main camp, "I had the feeling that, well, at least there is another American someplace around here and there are a whole bunch of them — I am getting a little close to it." Close, but no cigar — ever.[16]

The Chinese could not let him see other faces in a general population. Menticide is not permanent; in fact, it is very temporary and one can recover in just days. Dr. J.A.M. Meerloo said that the weakness of menticide "is the danger that the moment they see some friendly faces, they will come back." Therefore, isolation is extremely important. The doctor went on and stated, "When something unexpected happens, a friendly face, or a mistake made by the interrogator, or liberation, then you find [that] the superimposed conditioning disappears, they come back to their old beliefs." Dr. Alan Little takes this recovery concept one step further, directly to its origin, and testified, "Even Pavlov's dogs got over their artificially induced neuroses and returned to normal health when given rest and sleep."[17]

Although the germ warfare statement signed by Colonel Schwable was dated December 6, 1952, that was only a very rough draft and the actual complete document wouldn't be ready for worldwide distribution for seven more weeks — not until Friday, January 30, 1953. There remained some work to be done and for the first two weeks at Camp 5, the colonel "was engaged in extensive expansion and revision of the bacteriological statement," or what Frank Schwable refers to as his "Fleas, flies and mosquitoes confession."[18]

For the most part during the next seven weeks, however, the coin was flipped and the writing belonged to the Chinese. In the lean-to, all of the colonel's scribbling was in bits and pieces, an extract here, an episode there, and it was the captors who took the portions of imagined incidents and pieced them all together to make a coherent whole. The colonel described the seven-week period ending the next to last day in January 1953, as a time when "my confession was rewritten and rewritten many times as the deceitful Chinese kept increasing or broadening the field of bogus B warfare."[19]

From just past the middle of December to the end of the first month of the new year, there was no writing and the Chinese virtually disappeared. The pieces had to be put together and it's not known where but, because of the time lapse involved before the final draft, it certainly wouldn't be straying too far to say that the fragments were sent to Peking for editing. When the final paper was brought to the colonel, he noted that:

> the Chinese had thoroughly edited the type written copy given to me. They had corrected the grammar, changed some phraseology, rearranged my more or less complete 6 December rough draft, omitted some critical parts of that rough draft and inserted extracts from other rough drafts I had submitted. The typewritten statement handed to me had been checked and cleared by "higher authority" over a period from 21 December, 1952 to about 30 January, 1953.[20]

On the last Friday in January, Colonel Schwable, after many weeks of solitary confinement, was handed his confession. He said, "I was presented with the typewritten Chinese document that I was to transcribe [and sign]; they insisted that because I had written one of these papers on the 6th of December, that it was predated. I will be perfectly frank, I didn't argue about it much." Schwable was given legal-size paper and told to rewrite the typed confession in longhand and then sign it. In addition, he was forced to initial each page he read and wrote (from the typed copy) and if he had any corrections to make from the typed versions, those corrections were also to be initialed. Once this marine signed, he had thereby fallen. But worse was to come. "It was only after I had completed this phase," said the colonel, "that I was told I must make a wire recording and later yet, I must be photographed while reading the statement."[21]

Frank Schwable had his midnight meeting with the commandant of PUC during the last few days of November 1952, but didn't actually sign the germ warfare statement until the end of January 1953. During this period, and especially during the six-week term when the bits and pieces were being edited, he was left alone, which raises the question, Why didn't the colonel rethink his actions and when they came back for transcription and signature, tell them he changed his mind and wasn't going to sign? This lack of interrogation, the freedom, almost required that he rescind. It was a very dangerous time for the Chinese and they knew it; they were schooled in menticide. According to the word's "coiner," Dr. Meerloo said that "because there is time that goes in between, there is a time lag, he can recant, he can say it is not true, or he can save all his energy for the time when he is not under torture or, at least, there are witnesses, there are some neutral people [around]." Thus the need for absolutely total isolation; and just as important, according to Meerloo, is repetition. Colonel Schwable, on numerous occasions, was required to write out his confession, either in whole or part, from typewritten sheets prepared by the captors.[22]

* * * *

A confession wasn't all the Chinese wanted. The natural progression of this initial indignity would be the further indignity of personally reading it for the entire world to hear, and that is what Col. Frank Schwable did on Friday, February 20, 1953. He said, "I made recordings for the Chinese," but he noted that he did so "under protest and under duress." At first he resisted the order to record, but his treatment then reverted back to the lean-to days. He said, "Soon realizing that since they had the major propaganda material in their hands — it was useless to persist in my resistance."[23]

Provided with a new Chinese uniform, he was seated in front of a microphone placed on a wooden table and the colonel began to practice. The captors reminded him to be certain he spoke "in a voice that did not display the despair that was in my heart at that time." When he got good enough, the mike was turned on, the tapes began their slow spin, and Colonel Schwable started reading.[24]

The Chinese still weren't finished heaping indignities upon the marine and the next one was motion and still pictures. Within a day or two after making his recording and getting his face cleaned up and hair combed, in his new Chinese uniform he was ready to be photographed. The night before the official photo opportunity, the Chinese brought in and introduced to the colonel Alan Winnington, the correspondent for the *London Daily Worker* who had met General Dean a little less than two years before and left him a bottle of bourbon. They spoke for a few minutes and, although Schwable disliked the man for what and whom he represented, he did say that it felt great "to talk to a white man." The next morning, just before the photo shoot, Winnington and the freshened-up colonel were talking while waiting for a motion picture crew to set up when the correspondent made a humorous remark and Frank Schwable broke out into a hearty laugh. At that exact moment, still picture cameras began clicking and the colonel suddenly realized that "that had been planned so they could represent me to the world as happy-go-lucky while slandering my country. Winnington is a very clever man." Soon everyone began shooting and rolling and, according to the colonel, "Many, many retakes were necessary, as in the wire recordings, before I could ... look like something I didn't feel." During the shoot, Winnington had to go but left behind for Colonel Schwable a bottle of wine.[25]

* * * *

The Foreign Broadcast Information Service is "the organization within the United States government implementing the charge of the National Security Council to monitor all public broadcasts of significance [for] the United States Government," testified Norman Kriebel, a nine-year veteran and field operations manager for FBIS. The principal monitoring station in the Far East was Bolo Point, Okinawa. Many of the broadcasts were in English and Mr. Kriebel, drawing a big picture (but referring to the colonel) said, "The principal target of this broadcast is not the United States." It was specifically directed to "the Far Eastern area, Southeast Asia, and presumably also the English speaking audience in Japan and Korea." The colonel's broadcasts were monitored and recorded on Dictaphone belts and acetate discs.[26]

No matter the route, the tapes arrived in Peking. All broadcasts were made from Peking since it had an extremely powerful transmitter compared to Pyongyang's. The colonel's voice was heard first at 10:30 Sunday evening,

February 22, 1953. The broadcast lasted a half-hour. In this broadcast, Col. Schwable read the first part of his confession but FBIS couldn't understand it because it was very garbled. At the same time the next night, it was picked up. This time, the second half of the confession was intelligible, and it was introduced by an English-speaking Chinese announcer:

> On this transmission yesterday, Radio Peking broadcast a recording of Colonel Schwable's own deposition in which he exposed how the U.S. Joint Chiefs of Staff ordered strategic germ warfare to begin in Korea by means of a secret directive to General Ridgway. Today he will describe how the expansion of germ warfare was ordered and carried out.[27]

During 1952, the Chinese bombarded the airwaves with allegations of germ warfare. Suddenly there was nothing from Radio Peking and for a little over six weeks it was dead quiet. Incidentally, the absolute silence began shortly after Colonel Schwable confessed. In mid-February, the relative peace was shattered with the announcement that Peking had "conclusive evidence" of bacteriological warfare and further evidence that in October and December 1952, the United States "dropped disease-infected spiders and flies and germ-stained handbills." Right after the broadcasts, newspapers began reporting that "Communist China's propaganda machine renewed today its campaign of attack on the United Nations for alleged use of germ warfare in North Korea."[28]

Roy Bley went through exactly the same steps his pilot did, and Bley's confession was broadcast three days after the colonels but it was different. Since he was the wing's ordnance officer, the statement "included elaborate details concerning storage, loading and security measures," he said. Major Bley's broadcast deposition was "confined almost entirely to an account of alleged techniques of storing and delivering germ bombs and enforcing security measures rather than to emotional appeals."[29]

While all this was taking place, Gen. Mark Clark, commander-in-chief of the United Nations Command, was away from his Tokyo headquarters and in Korea on an inspection tour. Propaganda of this magnitude gets around very fast and upon hearing reports of the broadcasts he said that:

> The only possible explanation for this broadcast is that the Communists, in anticipation of new outbursts of disease among their miserable people with the spring thaws, must be seeking desperately to conceal their own criminal responsibility for chaotic public health services by making these fantastic and utterly false charges against the United Nations Command.[30]

* * * *

Every Korean War POW, young or old, black or white, private or general, had a problem to clear. Once the problem was cleared, no matter how trivial or large, treatment got better. After the recordings, the Chinese said to Colonel Schwable that he had "cleared the problem" and that his "case was closed." He was moved into another and somewhat nicer house (still in Pyoktong) because, as they kept pounding into Frank Schwable, "You are finished with this problem. You are cleared for this problem."[31]

At precisely the time Radio Peking was broadcasting to the world the colonel's recordings, his captors began giving him gifts. On February 23, one of the broadcast days, books were brought into the house for Colonel Schwable. Half were propaganda and the other half were fine, including various works by Charles Dickens. The Chinese reaction to all the books was, according to Frank Schwable, that they "had a social implication, always ones that showed the downtrodden man." He liked to sketch and he received blank paper. He had a comb that he had used for the photo shoot and he was told, "Well, here, you can keep this." A thermos bottle was brought for his use so his water wouldn't freeze and he was now permitted to shave once every two weeks, with his constant guard taking the razor from him when he had finished.[32]

It was also at this time that the Chinese began to recognize the colonel's rank. Whenever he received something he was told, "Well, you are a colonel and these other prisoners, they don't have that. We don't have enough to give all prisoners but you are a colonel so we will give you that." They were lying to Schwable. He couldn't possibly know that the POWs in the main compound of Camp 5 were by this time living like kings compared to him. What he also didn't know was that his confession had been broadcast to the world by Radio Peking. He would find this out on April Fools' Day.[33]

* * * *

EZ didn't belong in Korea or for that matter, in the 20th century. One can just imagine him standing at the court of Queen Victoria, splendid in his high-necked scarlet tunic, gold buttons blazing, red-striped black trousers, polished shoes and, of course, the traditional silver sword swaying from his hip, the tip barely dragging the floor. And EZ's speech? It was incredible. He spoke with an elegance reserved for the aristocratic few. For example, one night he was climbing a mountain. Upon reaching the top he saw that it was flat for a short distance, and so he walked on a small trail to the other side so he could go down. But he couldn't go down because it was a straight drop — a cliff without a single hand or foothold — so he had to turn and go back. But EZ will not use the word "cliff." To describe his predicament, he said that he turned around "because of an abrupt change in the structure."[34]

There was a nasty side to EZ, however, which made some people frightened of him, including the Chinese. There was one thing you did not do to

EZ and that was anger him. Don't do it and if you do, get out of town. EZ had a startling reaction to anyone getting him angry and that was to immediately knock him on his backside. Questions would come later.

Major D. Earl Ezelle, USMC,* out of Fort Worth, Texas, was with the First Marine Division and was in a small airplane acting as a forward artillery observer when ground fire shot the plane down. It was March 10, 1953, approximately three weeks after Colonel Schwable's broadcast. The pilot bailed first and EZ followed. When he jumped, the horizontal stabilizer hit his back and as he continued floating earthward, he was being shot at from below. Upon slamming into the ground, he tried to get back to nearby friendly territory but he found himself "surrounded, pinned down, and forced to surrender."[35]

Many captured fliers were initially held by the combat troops who seized them until arrangements could be made to move them to the rear. This was also true for the major. These soldiers took him back to a rear area (either a corps or divisional headquarters), walking 18 miles in 14 hours "through snow and slush and across the hills of northeast Korea," according to EZ. During the march, officers showed him bloodstained maps and questioned him about the lines, but the only reply the major gave was name, rank, and serial number. He said, "They became antagonistic toward me for my attitude." They threatened him with death but that didn't work. He described what he wore:

> That night a heavy rain and snow set in. I was clothed only in dungarees. I had lost my shoes when I bailed out. I had been wearing fleece lined boots and they had given me a pair of old shoes which had been taken off possibly a dead Marine. That was my only clothing except for a flak vest.[36]

For three weeks the major was moved slowly northward and constantly bombarded with questions. Because they knew he was an active front line field grade artillery officer, they were aware that he had current military data, which would be extremely useful to them, but EZ stood by the code of silence. Finally, a Chinese major approached him and asked, "What would you do if we took you out and shot you?" Without hesitation, the marine replied, "'I would ask God to forgive you for committing a sin because that would be wrong and you have no right to shoot American prisoners.' That was the only thing I could think of at the time."[37]

It was on April 1, 1953 (the same day Colonel Schwable was told that his confession had been broadcast worldwide), that EZ was taken to his permanent home somewhere in the mountains of North Korea. It had no name and apparently no other POWs. He was thrown into a four-by-seven-foot mud hut and here he was to remain in total solitary confinement for the next

---

*"The incomparable Major Ezelle," according to John Pratt, counsel to Colonel Schwable.

five months. The hut was in the middle of a Chinese army battalion area of about 200 troops and a squad of these soldiers was specifically detailed to guard the major. The hut itself (the worst in the area) had trails around it that led into and over the surrounding mountains. The newspaper-covered roof was caving in and when the major was forced to stand at attention, he had to bend forward. When it rained, which it seemed to do every day and night, EZ was forced to sit or stand; lying down was out of the question because the floor was nothing but a quagmire of mud and water.[38]

Initially he had a blanket but, he said, "because I was difficult that was taken away from me." There was a nearby stream and EZ was permitted outside for a few minutes each day to wash up and relieve himself. If he had to do the latter any other time, he did it in place:

> Since I had developed a case of dysentery which seemed to stay with me, I was forced to relieve myself in the room in which I was located. The smell, the odor, the flies, the bugs, the Chinese spitting into the door, the constant haranguing, harassing, telling you to admit what you have done and tell the truth [but] the more you tell them the truth, the more they call you a liar.[39]

Major Ezelle had more current strategic and tactical information on him than he would care to admit and this is what the Chinese were after, not germ warfare, not yet. As a career artillery officer, he was a battery commander, battalion S-2 (intelligence) and S-3 (operations), assistant regional S-3 of the Eleventh Marines, and the divisional artillery air observer:

> I knew enough information to assure the defeat of the First Marine Division. I knew the plans for withdrawal. I knew the position of every artillery unit in the First Marine Division area, Army and Marine. I knew where they would reinforce the First Marine Division and the amount of artillery necessary, and that was available to them. I knew the fire defensive plans of the First Marine Division. I worked on them. I had commanded batteries in every sector of the First Marine Division. I designated and worked out the code system for every Marine artillery position [and] every Army position in the First Marine Division sector. I was familiar with the system used by both Corps artillery and Division artillery in our area. It had been an artillery man's war, and I felt that the information which I possessed was of such value that I must not give that information away.[40]

Before he was captured, EZ had read of Frank Schwable and his confession in the armed forces paper *Stars and Stripes*. His initial reaction and continual thought on the article was, "I felt all the time great admiration for Colonel Schwable because I knew, as Chief of Staff, that he must have had the great amount of [military] information which I had possessed and his having admitted to bacteriological warfare seemed to me to be insignificant, if he kept that other information to himself, as I intended to keep the information which I had."[41]

The major's military interrogation was intense. Interrogation, solitary confinement, and filth were beginning to weaken EZ but he was willing to die first rather than jeopardize his fellow combat marines on the ground. During his entire five months alone, never seeing another American, never shaving, and never clean, Major Ezelle felt "degraded and about as low as I could possibly get." Like all other POWs in total isolation, the major fantasized about being with other Americans, leaning on them, getting advice, even having a simple conversation. Later he testified that "When you are alone, with nothing but the enemy, and nothing but death, when you would rather be dead than alive, and they still won't kill you, it is very difficult then to decide what is the proper thing to do."[42]

The principal Chinese officer conducting EZ's military interrogation was vicious. Even this brave marine remarked, "Over a period of months, I got to fear this little man who came to see me." Taking his fear one step further, he said, "I got to the point that I shook and was ever afraid of that man. I could have killed him with my bare hands." The fear, however, was a two-way street and the interrogator was just as scared of EZ as EZ was of him. The Chinese knew never to be alone with the marine since they were aware of his violent nature and knew his thinking, which was, "There is only one man I would like to kill, and that is the Chinese interrogator.... I hated this man with such a hate that I could have done anything to him." Major Ezelle not only refused to give the Chinese the right time of day but he fought back with the only weapons he had — belligerence and physical action. He said, "I am afraid I attempted to get to the interrogator and therefore, the guard always stepped between us and struck me with a burp gun. The interrogator never came close to me because of my attitude." EZ, even as a POW, tried to solve his problems with fists: "I became violent at times and corrective action was taken by them, by either a beating or by knocking me down with a burp gun."[43]

After about the first two weeks of April 1953, Major Ezelle decided that it was time to change tactics because, he said, "I was going to get myself beaten to death or something":

> At the end of two weeks, I thought I had to adopt a completely new system for protecting the information which I possessed, which was so important. I decided that when I felt that I could no longer resist, at that time I would give such information that was common knowledge, I knew, to them and I knew to the general public, things that I had read in Life Magazine and Time Magazine and such as that.[44]

The first piece of military information EZ gave the Chinese was the production in the United States of an atomic cannon. He was an artillery officer, so this was a natural topic to discuss although the major knew nothing about it except, as he said, "I had just read Life Magazine before leaving for my flight and it had a complete article on the new atomic cannon which had been developed by the Army." He would also lecture them and say things like, "Everywhere I look there is artillery, everywhere I look there are tanks, there are thousands of soldiers, an attack by the Chinese would be suicide, you would be cut to pieces with our superior fire power."[45]

As previously noted, the Chinese were rather quick to give up on an interrogation once they saw they had a tough and uncooperative prisoner on their hands, and they gave up on Major Ezelle. Actually, there were only two people the enemy never let up on and they were Colonel Schwable and his co-pilot, Major Bley. For the most part, everyone else who toughed it out got off. But with EZ, although the Chinese quit military questioning, they changed the subject to germ warfare. It was sometime during the middle of April, about five or six weeks after his capture and about two weeks after military questioning, that the interrogator thought EZ had something "in the back of his mind" and wanted to know what it was. The marine had no clue as to what he was talking about until he was given some magazine articles to read that were about the United States conducting germ warfare in Korea. Suddenly the light went on. He said, "I began to realize what they meant by the back of my mind, what was in the back of my mind. I felt that they were actually talking about bacteriological warfare." This made no sense because, he recalled, "I felt they would accuse Colonel Schwable, they might accuse some [other] people bombarding the hills of Korea from airplanes, but an artillery air observer? It did come as a surprise to me." The major, however, still wanted to play hardball and noted, "Up until that time, I had always thought that they were after the knowledge which was so important to me. I decided on this, I would say absolutely nothing; that if they wanted bacteriological warfare, they would have to ask me for it."[46]

The Chinese tried everything in the book to get EZ to mention germ warfare first. They would lead him and say, "We are not supposed to tell you what we are talking about. We are not supposed to tell you what we are interrogating you about. You know what I am talking about." Sure he did, but he would try to make them suffer as much as he could. They had to mention the subject first, and they did. The interrogator, in frustration, finally stated to Major Ezelle, "We know you have participated in bacteriological warfare. We want you to tell your entire story. We want you to tell your part in bacteriological warfare." The Chinese officer then took it one step further and said, "You were Battery Commander of Baker Battery, First Battalion, Eleventh Marines." EZ quickly confirmed the command and essentially relaxed because he felt that this supported the fact that he didn't know anything about germ warfare. Then, like a solid punch in the gut, he was told that since he was a senior artillery officer, "That proves only that you were one of the people that participated in shooting bacteriological shells at our front line troops." They wanted a germ warfare confession from an artillery officer.[47]

After the initial shock wore off, the major began to relax since he could use germ warfare interrogation as a shield to protect military information. If they concentrated on one subject, they'd be required to let go of the other, which they did. EZ felt he could discuss germ warfare with them all day long, every day, since "this was just a bunch of crap, to put it mildly." He would discuss it, but never sign a confession: "[I couldn't] appear before my own people, my own soldiers and marines, and make the statement. I couldn't bring myself to do that. I couldn't bring myself to admit to somebody I hated as much as I hated that interrogator or give him the satisfaction that I had participated in bacteriological warfare."[48]

The Chinese badly wanted his name on a piece of paper and one day they brought in a booklet, that contained photos of POWs who were clean-shaven, relaxed, and playing basketball and touch football.* He could be part of this if only he put his name on a piece of paper admitting that he shot from his guns germ-laden artillery shells. And if he didn't sign?

> Forget your family, forget your country, forget everything, you will never see them again, we know how to deal with our friends, but we also know how to deal with our enemies. Are you prepared to die? You can be hung for this. You are committing crimes against the people. Why don't you admit the truth. Why don't you tell everything you know and be a prisoner of war like these people.[49]

After receiving this threat, Maj. D. Earl Ezelle, USMC, decided it was time to get out of there. He was going to escape.

Supposedly, nothing is impossible, but escape from the interior of North Korea is very close to it. Where are you going? To the north is the vast, somewhat uncharted wilderness of Manchuria, so scratch that. To the east and west are two huge bodies of water, the Sea of Japan and the Yellow Sea. South would probably be the best way but one would have to hike in enemy territory about 200 miles. There's nowhere to go! Not one man ever escaped from a Chinese POW camp in North Korea.

When he was taken out of the solitary shack for his once-a-day head call, EZ constantly reconnoitered the surrounding area. He ignored the much-used main trail, which led into the valley where the camp was located, but studied and memorized the surrounding mountains and minor trails. It was in late April or early May when Major Ezelle got up one night and simply

---

**During 1953, with the war practically over, the photos in the booklet were quite real; this was not propaganda.*

walked out. He was able to do this because, except for one of the permanent camps along the Yalu which in 1953 held about 4,000 surviving American prisoners in total (3,000 had died in captivity during 1950 and 1951) and had towers, barbed wire and guards, any other holding area only had guards. When one fell asleep, left the area, or just wasn't keeping a good watch, it was easy enough to walk out. The major did just that and was gone for eight days with the Chinese army hot on his tail.[50]

EZ decided to head east for the Sea of Japan. When he reached the water, he was going to look for a unit of the U.S. Navy and swim out to it or, if that didn't work (which it probably wouldn't), he would try to steal a boat. During this eight-day adventure, the major walked through a number of North Korean villages at night without being challenged. His training warned him that when evading, you must do so only at night and stay away from occupied areas. He was lucky but had a few close calls.[51]

Shortly after running away, Major Ezelle encountered an armed North Korean militiaman. In the dark, EZ began mumbling to himself and swaying as if he were drunk. The Korean let him pass. While pretending, all the marine had to say was, "Believe me, gentlemen, I prayed." On another night, while walking on a large, flat plain (which aren't easy to find in mountainous North Korea), he felt hundreds of people nearby and saw small red dots surrounding him. EZ was walking right through the Chinese army and the red dots were lit cigarettes. He wasn't challenged so he kept right on hiking through them until he got to the base of a mountain and began to climb. Upon reaching the top, he lay down and waited for first light. He recalled, "I hid in the bushes overlooking this area that I had just come through to discover to my amazement the next day that I had come through a North Korean division reserve area." As light began to appear, the major saw that "there must have been a thousand men running all over the place."[52]

Although it was spring and various wild fruits were growing in the mountains and some food could be stolen from small farms and gardens, the major's strength was beginning to wane. Climbing mountains at night is not simple nor fast and to get to the east coast and the sea quicker, EZ at times traveled during the day, as he says, "from bush to bush, tree to tree, and rock to rock." On his seventh day of his eastward escape, Major Ezelle came upon a small village nestled between two mountains. Not having the strength to climb, EZ decided to wait until dark and, against everything he was taught, walk through the village. His feeling on this was since he got by the militiaman and flowed right through a thousand armed soldiers, it would be a breeze. Of starting down the main village trail, he said, "This was a period when there was no moon, no light, and Korean nights were very dark; it was a total blackout."[53]

But there was something wrong; EZ thought there was a little more activity than usual for that time of night. He became cautious. Slowly walking down the trail, the major came upon several men sitting on the side. He immediately turned 180 degrees and headed back to where he started. However, one of the Koreans got up and began running after him. He then jumped into a nearby creek. The chaser, who knew the area, went around EZ and cut him off. With limited options, he had to try the trail through the village once again.[54]

For his second attempt, Major Ezelle found a large heavy stick and using it as a staff, began to walk "Korean style" down the trail and into the village, bent over about 45 degrees, the top of one hand placed on the small of his back while the other held the pole. Suddenly he happened upon some people smoking and EZ began "hoping that they would just let me pass." When he reached them, one of the smokers said something and in the darkness the major replied, "Wa bu doong, choongwa bing, wa bu doong" which, according to Major Ezelle, meant, "I don't understand; I am a Chinese soldier. I don't understand." After this reply, one of the Koreans began hollering and screaming and the marine reasoned, "My Chinese evidently was not very good." Not in any mood to take the hollering and yelling, EZ calmly walked up to the guy and "hit him across the head with the stick."[55]

Escaping from the village and on the lam again, he climbed up the side of a trail leading to the top of a mountain. At the top was a plateau and the path continued across it until it ended at a cliff on the other side. EZ turned around and in the middle of the flat mountaintop, he sat down. The major was exhausted. He recalled, "The next day I woke up with a Chinese officer holding my hair and shaking my head and the Chinese soldiers were all around me." EZ guessed that he "was within a very few miles of the coast when I was recaptured [and] so my escape attempt had all been in vain."[56]

The soldiers brought the major back down to the village where he was fed some rice and then taken back to the same mud hut from which he escaped. The hated interrogator was waiting. EZ was given some paper and told to write down everything about the escape from the camp and to include his experiences during the eight-day evasion, which he did. The next day the document was brought back to him, told it was unsatisfactory and that he was going in front of a board of officers to be tried as a war criminal. The major was also warned "to be very polite and not to act the way I had acted under interrogation." It took a very short time for the board to convene and, according to EZ, "They found me guilty of whatever the charges were." Major Ezelle was also given the news that he was going to receive either a very long prison term or death.[57]

When he was returned to his isolated mud shack after the board met, EZ was alone for only a few minutes when a small band of soldiers burst in. Amid yelling and cursing, fists and feet began to flail and the major had the living daylights beat out of him. He was hurting bad. When he got a chance to question the interrogator about the reason for the trouncing, he was told, "They hate you. You deserve that. You have done many things against the Chinese people and the Korean people, and these men had to search for you eight days and eight nights. They hate you, and I hate you." The marine was very stubborn, however, and after the beating, he became more determined than ever to fight them. He said, "From then on, I would not speak one word to them. From that time on, which was a period of about three weeks, I refused to answer anything, even to name, rank, serial number, or anything else."[58]

During this period of self-imposed silence, EZ was forced to sit on the mud floor in the middle of the hut with his knees brought up under his chin. Staying like this all day for the injured marine was impossible and shortly after this torture began, he scooted his entire body rearward and leaned his back against the wall. Standing at the door was the guard who immediately ordered him back to the middle. The major just cursed at him. Then, according to EZ, "He threw a round into his chamber, which indicated to me — before I hadn't known that — that they did not load their weapons unless they felt they were going to have to use them." With a loaded burp gun pointed at him, the major struggled to his feet, lifted his dungaree shirt to expose his naked stomach, pointed at it and shouted, "Shoot me across here, you son of a bitch." The guard began hollering for his sergeant. In a characteristic understatement, the marine said, "I was very fortunate that he didn't shoot me." The sergeant came running in, grabbed the weapon from his guard, pointed it at EZ and ordered him to sit in the middle. Still standing, once again the marine pointed to his stomach and yelled at the sergeant, "You shoot me, you son of a bitch, I am tired of living anyway."[59]

It was at this point in Major Ezelle's prison life that the Chinese, either consciously or subconsciously, gave up on him. The sergeant turned to the guard and said, "Sim bing," which the major knew meant "sick." The marine encouraged this and said to both of them, "Sim bing. I am sick." The guards actually thought he was nuts. The weapon was returned and the guard motioned for Major Ezelle to sit down and lean his back against the wall. Previously, this sergeant "had been very difficult to get along with," recalled EZ, but now he was starting to receive small favors. When the sergeant came on duty, he actually stood watch with his guard and "He would see that I had water.... He would bring his own canteen and fill my cup up with that, whereas the others would make me drink from the stream."[60]

One day the sergeant entered the hut and placed the palm of one hand over the back of his other, interlocked the fingers and wiggled them. EZ described it as having "had something to do with bugs, and that I should tell everything so that I could play basketball." The senior guard wanted the marine out of solitary and into a POW camp and, as Major Ezelle described it, "After a period of time, even he felt sorry for me and he made signs that I should write how I was being treated and I was not guilty of this thing I was accused of."[61]

The thinking of EZ was, "If this is what you want, this is what you're going to get." Using supplied pencil and paper, he wrote. He described how roughly the interrogator treated him, the mental and physical torture he went through, not having proper food, the inability to clean himself, the cold and, finally, the lack of medical treatment. He signed it and gave it to the sergeant. But he had forgotten something and wrote on another paper how much he hated the interrogator. He signed this paper, too, and handed it to the sergeant. The next morning, the Chinese officer walked in waving EZ's two signed papers. He pointed out to the major that he was the only English-speaking Chinese in the area and didn't he know that the papers would reach him? He was in a rage. EZ recalled his outrage: "Any mental torture that you are undergoing you are doing it yourself. I am not doing it to you. You are doing it yourself." When the marine tried to say something, the reply was, "Do not argue with me. Do not argue with a Chinese officer." In absolute frustration, the interrogator spit at the major and walked out. It was over. Everything was over except for the sergeant who, EZ said, "disappeared. I never saw him again. I don't know what to assume, whether he was sent to the front lines, whether he was shifted to another organization, or maybe killed."[62]

The Korean War was officially over on July 27, 1953, and the POWs were all going to be slowly released during August and the first week in September. But first all prisoners had to be gathered at a staging area for processing and that area was primarily Camp 5. In early August, the major was permitted to shave, issued a blue Chinese uniform, and then moved to Pyoktong, the small town where Colonel Schwable was imprisoned. He was again thrown into solitary where he remained for three days until a Chinese officer walked in and said to EZ, "Pick up your things and follow me." He was put into the back of a truck with another prisoner for the one-mile trip to the main camp. The other POW was wearing a faded blue uniform and from what EZ observed, "He appeared so frightened that he would not look at me." Ordered not to talk, the forever-obstinate major whistled the Marine Corps hymn so that the other captive would know he was a marine. And, to show he was from Texas, he also whistled "The Eyes of Texas." There was no response.

About halfway to the camp (probably about a 10-minute ride), the truck stopped. The other prisoner was unloaded, taken off the road, and walked into the woods. The truck then continued on with only EZ on board.[63]

When they reached the interior of Camp 5, the major was unloaded, taken into a building, and registered as a POW. Now, for the first time, the marines would know that he was alive and, as EZ noted, "[Registration] was welcome news to me because I didn't know what had happened, why all of a sudden they decided to make me a prisoner of war when all this other time I had been designated a war criminal and I still had not satisfied their desires as to what they wanted." Major Ezelle was given some candy and beer during the signing in process and then an officer came in to accompany him to the officer's compound where American prisoners were held.[64]

At this point, the major had no idea that the war had been over for about 10–12 days. In his own mind he thought it would last for 10 years. About halfway to the compound, the officer stopped and said to EZ, "You sit down and I have something to tell you." He was instructed not to join any underground organizations and then was told to listen carefully because "This is the important information. The war has been over since July sometime and soon you will be going home to your people." The major cried. "When I was told that it was ended and that I would be going home..., I couldn't believe it, it shook me up a great deal. After I recomposed myself, the Chinese officer took me to the little hut where the other men that I would live with were and introduced me to the squad leader."[65]

Reflecting upon his experiences, EZ said, "I think that had the war not ended, I would be a dead man in Korea." Mournfully, Maj. D. Earl Ezelle, USMC, noted, "Even today, I find myself unable to draw on words that I had formally possessed in my vocabulary. I find myself unable to think of those days without it visibly affecting me."[66]

* * * *

On April Fools' Day 1953, Frank Schwable was brought into the camp commander's office and informed that his confession had been publicly released, in both the spoken and written forms. "I almost cried when they told me that...," said the colonel. Expecting the commandant to say, "Why, that is fine. Now I am a fighter for world peace...," and therefore eligible to be placed with the main population, instead he was told that his attitude was horrible and that he would remain in solitary confinement until the war was over.[67]

After he cleared his problem, the colonel was permitted to write his first letter home to Beverly, his wife of 17 years, whom he had married while stationed in Quantico. Colonel Schwable was very concerned about affairs at home and remarked, "A married man finding himself a POW worries very much about the welfare of his family and hopes that at least word can get back home that he is a prisoner." In early March 1953, Frank Schwable wrote home but he wasn't that enthused about it because "It didn't make any difference anyway since they never let a single letter of mine get through to home." Beverly wrote her husband on a regular basis and after February, he did receive one letter from his wife and several from his mother. Unexpectedly, according to the colonel, "they shut off the mail as promptly as they had started the flow. All the time they insisted they were doing everything possible to facilitate exchange of mail!"[68]

Since the publication of the confession, Beverly Schwable and Margaret Bley became absolutely certain that their husbands were alive. When Mrs. Schwable heard that the colonel had signed, her comment on the entire affair was, "That's the same old Communist malarkey. Nobody believes it." On the other hand, Mrs. Bley was so happy to know about the major, she said, "They can accuse him of anything.... They could say he confessed to dropping atomic bombs or anything else as far as I'm concerned."[69]

* * * *

Most of the men from PUC arriving at Camp 5 were further dispersed to either Camps 2 or 3, which were not too distant from the main camp and Pyoktong. The Chinese, at these two camps as at Camp 5, made every effort to inform the prisoners that a marine colonel had signed a germ warfare confession. Even before the colonel's statement was in final written form and on tape, marine corporal Melvin Gaynor was told by a Chinese officer that confessions from various air force officers had been obtained. Gaynor told the captor that he didn't believe him but then was asked, "What would you think if a Marine, a Colonel and a Major all signed confessions that you used germ warfare?" The corporal replied, "Well, I still wouldn't believe it. I have never seen it used and as far as I know, it could have been dope or just cracking up. The colonel is a pretty old man, naturally he might not go through what we could." Suddenly, Corporal Gaynor received a hard slap across the face and was told, "You just do not want to accept the facts that you started using it."[70]

Sgt. James Hale, USMC, was at Camp 3 on the Yalu when in March 1953, he and the approximately 180 enlisted men at the prison were given "thick white pamphlets" that contained photos of Schwable and Bley in addition to their written confessions. The photo of the colonel on page four showed him sitting at a table in front of a microphone. There were also pictures of bomb casings and an assortment of bugs. When Sergeant Hale saw the photo of Frank Schwable, he suddenly recognized who the old man was that he spied on at PUC. The propagranda brochure's impact on the enlisted population of Camp 3 was, according to Hale, "We didn't believe them; that is one thing. We never paid much attention to them. We would read a couple of pages and then drop it.... Our reaction was that we thought maybe the Chinese wrote this article and had the places and dates and so forth, where the bombs were supposed to have been dropped, and had our officers sign them. That was the impression we got."[71]

Most of the less populated camps along the river which were spun off from the main camp (Camp 5 had an average population of 1,500) held both officers and enlisted but in separate compounds as they were not permitted to mingle or interact with each other in any manner. Because of this restriction, during the term of their imprisonment, the enlisted troops had essentially no formal officer corps to lead them; they were on their own. In the officer's compound at Camp 3 (which held about 350 officers), Lt. Col. William Thrash, USMC, upon hearing of the confessions, noted that the officers in the camp "had a certain mature judgment, understanding, and certain technical background. The program, as far as we were concerned, with very few exceptions, the officers considered it a farce." Over at Camp 2 officer's compound, Lt. Col. John McLaughlin, USMC, read the confession in a communist newspaper and didn't believe it. He said, "My reaction was that I thought they must have given Colonel Schwable some very rough treatment in order to obtain such a statement."[72]

Airman First Class Franklin Hall at Camp 2 listened to the announcement over the camp's speaker system: "This is a confession written by Colonel Frank Schwable, United States Marine Corps, telling of his part in germ warfare in Korea." Although the Chinese had numerous confessions in their possession signed by air force officers, Schwable was the star. Practically every one of the approximately 4,000 surviving POWs had the confession drummed into them over loudspeakers and in distributed pamphlets, magazines, and various newspapers. Airman Hall, after hearing the announcement, subsequently read articles about the colonel and discussed them with the other prisoners. The feeling, according to the airman, was

> [They] created in some of the guys' minds that maybe actually there was such a thing going on due to the fact that such a high-ranking officer had written such a confession.... But I think that was just the attitude that was taken immediately, but I think after they read it over for a few times, and had a little time to think about it, we all came to the same conclusion that if he did write it, there was some doubt even as to whether he had written it or not, and if he did write it, we felt confident that he was forced to write it.[73]

* * * *

Camp 2 had an officer's annex that held two platoons consisting of a mixed bag of U.S. army, navy, and air force, two British and two South African officers. Upon arriving at the annex, Maj. Walter Harris found he was the senior United Nations officer present and therefore "[I] appointed myself commanding officer." In the camps, POWs are not noncombatants and the prison is merely an extension of the battlefield. Therefore, it is not a democracy, there is no voting, and Major Harris did exactly what he was supposed to do and that was take charge. Harris said he was "pulled out once or twice by myself and warned to behave myself. I was told that I would be responsible for anything that happened in the compound; that they knew I was senior officer."[74]

Major Harris recalls that the prisoners "received several — I wouldn't call them American newspapers, though they were printed in the United States. We regularly received the New York Daily Worker, the Chicago National Guardian, and the San Francisco People's World. Also, we received the London Daily Worker. In these papers considerable space was given to the confessions, purported confessions, I should say." Having digested everything he could read about the deposition, Harris concluded, "They certainly must have really put the pressure on Colonel Schwable." But at this annex to Camp 2, the propaganda backfired on the Chinese and the total reaction, according to the major, was rage, "from myself down to the lowest ranking man in the compound. There was obvious anger toward the Chinese." Harris said, "My immediate thought was those dirty bastards" and "The language that day about the camp was not very nice; frequently the Chinese communists were pretty well hit with nasty language."[75]

Initially, Frank Schwable wasn't sure whether the Chinese had actually concluded that germ warfare was being committed but as time went on, the colonel became absolutely convinced that the Chinese did believe it. At Camp 2, Capt. Emanuel Amann, USMC, saw with his own eyes this belief in action. B-29s were constantly flying over the area on bombing raids and oftentimes Chinese and North Korean fighters attacked them. To counter these attacks, the bombers would dispense radar-deceiving chaff and, according to the captain, "The Chinese were out in the hills the day after and in the compound itself, picking up a few of the billions of pieces that there must have been, with tweezers and putting them in soda bottles, bringing them to the camp dispensary and disposing of them in a rather dramatic way." When the Chinese were performing this seemingly endless chore, Captain Amann saw that they wore masks, which "seemed to be used, almost SOP, day and night, these cheesecloth breathing masks, face masks. It was ludicrous."[76]

After the confessions were publicized, probably every marine in North Korea took a vicious beating from the army. Two supposedly invincible senior marines, the elite of the armed forces, signed statements defaming their country and corps and marines were savagely hazed. Walter Harris thought that the hazing "was all on a good natured basis" but the major is being more diplomatic than pragmatic. Marine aviator Harris and everyone else tried to refute and/or excuse the confessions because, as the major noted, "I guess the best way to put it is pride in the Marine Corps."[77]

9

The Ship

We were concerned with investigating treason, investigating collaboration in a treasonable manner.
— Lt. Col. Robert C. Matthews, Jr., Counter Intelligence Corps, United States Army, Court of Inquiry, Vol. 1, 422–423

Five weeks before the end of the Korean War, Frank Schwable was moved from the house in Pyoktong to Camp 2, which was about 25 miles to the east. This small camp had four compounds. Two abutting compounds were known as Camp 2 and were within walking distance. The other two were known as Camp 2 Annex. Each compound was commanded by a Chinese company commander who reported to the overall camp commander responsible for the main camp and annex. Colonel Schwable was not integrated into the main population, however; he was once again thrown into an isolated empty house where he would remain in solitary confinement. He was issued swimming trunks and about once a week removed from isolation and taken out to swim and wash his body and clothes. The house itself was a ramshackle affair and every night he listened to rats running back and forth atop the cardboard ceiling just over his head. The colonel was also permitted out of the house to go to the latrine. The toilet, if one can call it that, was somehow situated on top of a hog pen and while squatting, according to him, "the flies go back and forth between you and the hog. To me that is repulsive."[1]

It was sometime during the first week in August 1953, that Colonel Schwable felt a stirring within his environment. Something was going on. A platoon of Chinese soldiers, for example, walked near his house in full marching gear and just past his quarters, the unit stopped. An officer gave a speech; the troops clapped and then marched out of the camp. Soon the colonel observed that there was a noticeable reduction in the camp's guard detachment. Within another day or so, a fairly large group of POWs were marched by the colonel's house, heading for the administration center. A short time later they returned and Frank Schwable figured they didn't go to the center for interrogation and assumed some sort of announcement was made to them. A few days later, on Sunday, August 9, 1953, Colonel Schwable was informed that he was being repatriated. The armistice ending the Korean War had been signed 13 days before.[2]

Even though the conflict was over, the colonel was to continue his isolated imprisonment for close to another month. This was not unusual since almost 4,000 men (out of 7,000 originally captured) had to be processed out and that simply took time. The Chinese held the most senior colonels until the very end; they were the last to leave. Sometime during the daylight hours of Thursday, September 3, 1953, an interrogator walked into the dilapidated house and said to the colonel, "Put on your clothes, you have to go down to the administration building right now." When he got inside, he found a military tribunal. In a solemn ceremony, Frank Schwable was pronounced a war criminal and then immediately returned to the house. The colonel said that he had been "formally convicted by the Korean Peoples Democratic Political Council as a War Criminal, my conviction being formally read to me before five witnesses," which consisted of four Chinese and one North Korean officer.[3]

The colonel was back in the rat-infested house for only a few minutes when someone else entered and said, "Pick up your stuff and come along." Back to the administration building he went, but this time the colonel joined other prisoners who were already there. Frank Schwable had in his possession everything he owned, which wasn't very much, but it did include a batch of drawings he had made with his pencil and any paper he could find at the time. "I'm a little handy with paper and pencil," he said. The colonel was thoroughly searched and the drawings were spotted by an officer who began to confiscate them. Schwable asked if he could keep them, and the searcher agreed, and therefore, he recalled, "I came home with those. I came home with what I wanted."[4]

On the night of September 3, Colonel Schwable was loaded aboard a truck with two air force colonels, Andrew J. Evans, Jr., and Walker Mahurin. From Montgomery, Alabama, Colonel Evans was 34 years old (but after his ordeal looked 54), a West Point graduate (class of '41), and a World War II "ace." After capture, Evans underwent months of interrogation without signing a confession and even attempted suicide by voluntary starvation, so the Chinese began to force-feed him. Finally he was physically and mentally unable to continue and signed a germ warfare confession on September 2, 1953 (predated to August 17), well over a month after the armistice and one day before release. Colonel Mahurin was also 34 and an "ace." From Fort Wayne, Indiana, Mahurin spent eight months in solitary confinement where, day and night, he was continually threatened with death by a team of no less than 15 interrogators. Colonel Mahurin, too, attempted suicide when he somehow obtained a knife and slashed his wrists. He was starting to lose consciousness from loss of blood when a guard came in and stopped the bleeding. The colonel finally collapsed in late May and from then on was kept busy writing and rewriting his germ warfare confession. He also signed after the truce. Both air force colonels were told to either sign or remain prisoners until they died. Walter Mayo, a representative of the United States to the United Nations, on speaking of these confessions, asked, "How seriously do the Communists take the armistice agreement? Their guns cease firing, but still — to the very moment of repatriation — they torture the bodies and minds of prisoners to get ammunition for the spurious propaganda war."[5]

Three months before the armistice, Operation Little Switch took place. Between April 20 and May 3, 1953, sick and wounded Chinese and North Korean prisoners were released by the United Nations command and 149 American POWs were returned to UN custody. The Little Switch people were immediately flown out of Korea to Valley Forge Army Hospital for medical care and recuperation. The Chinese thought Valley Forge to be a psychiatric facility and assumed the former prisoners were taken there because they were mental cases. In passing, a Chinese officer said to Colonel Schwable, "You know what is going to happen to you people? You are going to Valley Forge. That is exactly what happened to the 'Little Switch' people." This did not bother the colonel for he had a much greater concern. Frank Schwable thought that he was going to be met by military police and placed under arrest.[6]

The truck, with Colonels Evans, Mahurin, and Schwable the only passengers, was part of a large convoy of Chinese ambulances, jeeps, and trucks that began to roll southward on this Thursday night, September 3. The ride to freedom lasted 44 hours and during the entire time, the colonels were not permitted to speak with each other nor any other POW who might happen to be milling about during a stop. About halfway through the trip, one of the trucks in the convoy broke down and two of its young occupants were put into Colonel Schwable's truck. Silence continued to prevail.[7]

Operation Big Switch, which returned 3,597 American POWs, began on August 5, 1953, and after 33 days was officially completed on September 6 at 10:30 A.M. For the final leg of their journey, the colonels were taken from the truck and put into a jeep and now they could finally speak; the guards were gone and there was just a driver. To get into Freedom Village at Panmunjom, the large convoy was split into two groups and shortly after 9 A.M., the first convoy rolled in with 50 men aboard for processing. There was very little fanfare; no shouting, no waving of flags, and the former prisoners, mostly

9. The Ship

Colonel Frank Schwable, September 6, 1953, 10:30 A.M.—repatriation. "[This was] the most emotional day I had during my entire experience. Coming home and stepping out of that [jeep] and being met by a good friend.... I put my arms around him and kissed him, much to his embarrassment—but it was to feel that cloud of oppression and depression completely removed in one step. I tell you, it was the most emotional thing I have ever gone through" (official Department of Defense photograph).

officers, "appeared to take their liberation calmly," as a witness said. Finally, at about 10:30 A.M., Operation Big Switch was over and the very last group of trucks (one of which had Roy Bley as a passenger) rolled to freedom with the jeep carrying the three colonels in the lead. A Broadway musical couldn't have been better choreographed.[8]

When observers first saw the jeep with its three senior officers, it was reported that "their hands shook and there were tears in their eyes." Waiting to greet Colonel Schwable as he got out, instead of military police, was Maj. Gen. Vernon E. Megee. Megee was then commanding general of the First Marine Aircraft Wing and had relieved Colonel Schwable's friend General Jerome, eight months earlier. The colonel was overwhelmed at being personally met by "Maggie" Megee and his enormous apprehension about coming home was somewhat alleviated by the "feeling of delight of just putting my arm around General Megee." In describing his arrival, Colonel Schwable said that it was:

> ... the most emotional day I had during my entire experience. Coming home and stepping out of that [jeep] and being met by a good friend, General Megee—I put my arms around him and kissed him, much to his embarrassment—but it was to feel that cloud of oppression and depression completely removed in one step. I tell you, it was the most emotional thing I have ever gone through.[9]

The next two days, Sunday, September 6, and Monday, September 7, were a complete blur as one day blended into another. Shortly after their arrival the former POWs, among them the colonel, were stripped, showered, and issued new clothing, including underwear, shoes, dungarees, and covers.* Colonel Schwable attached to his collar a set of silver eagles of rank that General Megee had brought with him especially for the colonel to put on. Next was a quick physical exam and then everyone was placed on trucks, ambulances, and jeeps and driven south about 30 miles to the large western port city of Inchon.[10]

At the replacement depot in the city, under the guidance and with the authorization of their air force superiors, Colonels Evans and Mahurin were cleared to hold a news conference, which they did. The mass of reporters and photographers hanging around Freedom Village at Panmunjom and at Inchon to the south, however, wanted the senior colonel held by the Chinese and on Monday, September 7, Frank Schwable was called to a press conference. He was confused and didn't know what to do or where to turn. From this point on, Colonel Schwable was constantly requesting direction from the marines, and the marines constantly ignored him. He didn't know who to meet or not meet, what to say or not say, whether to hold a conference or not hold a conference. He had absolutely no help at all. Since he was on his own, the colonel decided to take guidance from the air force. Frank Schwable assumed that if Colonels Evans and Mahurin, both of whom had signed germ warfare confessions, were cleared to go public the day before, this was the guidance he would follow. After all, the First Marine Aircraft Wing was still under the operational orders of Fifth Air Force.[11]

In a room filled with reporters from all the major papers and wire services, Colonel Schwable told the assembled group that if he hadn't signed, he would have faced imminent death. The colonel also pointed out that it was "utterly fantastic" that people would believe any of the confessions: "They've got enough fleas, flies and mosquitoes in North Korea without our adding to it." After the articles on the conference had been written, published, and read, the colonel was to remark, "I have been grossly misquoted in numerous instances."[12]

At Inchon, psychiatrists, psychologists, social workers, lawyers, medical doctors, and the Counter Intelligence Corps — especially the Counter Intelligence Corps of the United States Army — were all over the place. All of them were like bears on honey. The first doctor to meet with Colonel Schwable, almost immediately upon his release, was Lt. Col. Vincent J. Cassone (M.D.), USA, who had been a practicing psychiatrist for 19 years. The colonel's interview was split into two days at Inchon and practically every former POW went through these same examinations.[13]

Colonel Cassone's observations of Frank Schwable took place at the 509 Replacement Depot at Inchon during the evening of September 6 and the

---

*At that time, the work/combat uniform was commonly known as "utilities," not dungarees.

morning of September 7, 1953. The total time for the examination was about an hour. Colonel Schwable spoke freely of his experiences and Colonel Cassone, as he was taught to do, simply listened and evaluated. The doctor was looking at the manner of Colonel Schwable's "responses to questions that I asked, his manner of speaking. His behavior manner was evaluated. His touch of reality was estimated. Memory, intellectual resources were investigated, and whether or not there existed any pertinent mental or nervous symptoms."[14]

Frank Schwable was extremely nervous. He was filled, almost overwhelmed, with remorse. Colonel Schwable was a walking guilt trip if there ever was one. When Dr. Cassone questioned him about the obvious anxiousness, the reply was, "You don't brush this cloud of oppression off you immediately ... you don't get rid of it, you don't get it out of your mind, you don't get it out of your nightmares for a long time." To the doctor, these fears were normal and he stated that Colonel Schwable had "an excellent memory," was coherent, his speech relevant and, according to the colonel, "he showed none of the phantasy, or disconnection, with reality that one would expect in a mental disorder." Dr. Cassone did particularly note, however, that "Colonel Schwable was anxious over what might occur upon his return to the States. He showed a certain amount of uneasiness as to what lay ahead."[15]

Colonel Schwable was very concerned that he would be viewed as a traitor and he knew, without question, that he had done something that was absolutely contrary to regulations. According to Dr. Cassone, Frank Schwable had regret but it "was not overtly expressed, but merely a statement that he had a feeling that he had done what he should not have done."[16]

* * * *

Having been pronounced a war criminal and sentenced to death, Capt. John Patrick Flynn, USMC, was taken out of the interrogation center somewhere in Korea and shipped north to Camp 2 on the Yalu. For the next 12 months, although occasionally interrogated, he was basically a normal prisoner living with other POWs. Although he had a death penalty hanging over his head, nothing ever happened. When Colonel Schwable's confession was distributed throughout Camp 2 and the annex, after reading it Captain Flynn said, "I was affected — I didn't know.... The other prisoners didn't believe it and we joked about it a good deal, to the effect that it was a farce." Maj. Walter Harris was also in the camp and he and Flynn spoke about the confession several times. Major Harris recalls that Captain Flynn had critiqued it and indicated to him that "there were many, many discrepancies that pointed to the fact that it was a false statement."[17]

On July 16, 1953, without notice or expectation, John Flynn was pulled out of his compound and taken to Camp 3. Thrown into a ten-foot-by-six-foot room in a Korean house, he remained in solitary confinement for exactly one month. He was pulled from Camp 2 11 days before the war was over.[18]

After one year of being left alone, why suddenly this drastic move? The confession of Colonel Schwable, a former night fighter pilot, stated unequivocally that night fighters were the first aircraft to initiate germ warfare operations in North Korea. But not just any night fighters — specifically, all of the fighters in Marine Night Fighter Squadron 513. VMF(N)-513 once had a pilot in the squadron named John Patrick Flynn. What better cake could one make; the chief of staff, the ordnance officer, and a pilot from the squadron who actually flew the missions and dropped the bombs. This certainly would shatter the defenses of many skeptics.[19]

For a little over three weeks at Camp 3, Captain Flynn was interrogated for one to four hours each day on his participation in germ warfare. At one point, the interrogators actually brought into his solitary room duplicates of the signed confessions of Schwable and Bley. Within the restricted limits of paraphrasing, they essentially said to the young night fighter pilot, "If these two field grade officers can sign, why can't you?" They handed the confessions to him to keep but the marine refused.[20]

On the last four days during the middle of August 1953, according to Flynn, "They went all day and the last three nights, they went all night and all day." On Saturday, August 15 (the war had been over for 19 days), Captain Flynn was removed from his house and taken to the headquarters of a Chinese general who, with an interpreter, was waiting for him. When Flynn arrived, the general motioned to walk and they went to a pagoda perched on the side of a hill. Moving to the front porch, they looked down upon numerous trucks on the road, all moving south. The general stared at Captain Flynn and reminded him that he, too, could be on one of the vehicles loaded with Americans. All he needed to do was sign. Incidentally, the senior officer, almost as an afterthought, notified the captain that the military tribunal, which had judged him a war criminal almost a year ago, suspended his death sentence and instead sentenced him to 20 years in a Chinese prison. John Flynn said:

> I had mixed emotions. I believed him. Now I would say, "This can't be true; they wouldn't do this to me." My general emotion was that of belief since he was not very friendly at the time. And believing he was a general, I was quite impressed with that.

The interpreter, in order to reinforce the general and support Flynn, said, "that the General thought I should go ahead and confess and not worry about it. [He] said, 'It is not serious, just sign it and everything will be fine.'"[21]

General or no general, Captain Flynn was not signing a thing. The general was as angry as one can get and the marine recalled, "I was almost thrown out of the place." Two days later, on August 17, 1953, John Patrick Flynn, Jr., was on a truck headed south to Freedom Village; the captors wanted nothing further to do with this captain of marines.[22]

* * * *

Lt. Col. Robert C. Matthews, Jr., USA, first got into the intelligence field during World War II in 1944 when he was assigned to the Office of Strategic Services (OSS). His OSS basic training lasted about four months and then he was sent for special exercises on Catalina Island, off the southern California coast. In 1945, he returned to Washington and almost immediately was ordered to Nationalist China where he remained for two years. The colonel said, "I stayed in China doing work of that sort until June of 1947. I say work of that sort; I was in intelligence work proper. I was in the secret intelligence portion of the OSS effort."*[23]

After his return from China, the colonel was ordered to engineer school. Upon completion, he was sent to another school in Monterey, California, to learn the Chinese language. In late 1948, he was transferred to the Counter Intelligence Corps (CIC)† of the United States Army and sent for special training at Camp Holabird, Maryland, which was CIC headquarters. With training completed, he was assigned to Sixth Army at the Presidio of San Francisco where he became operations officer for the 115 CIC detachment and also operations officer with the counterintelligence division of Sixth Army G-2. After about 18 months at the Presidio, on October 2, 1951, he was ordered to Far East Headquarters in Tokyo, but he didn't remain long, for in December, he was sent to Korea. In six months, however, he was returned to Japan for treatment of an eye infection. That taken care of, Colonel Matthews was then assigned to his permanent unit, the 441 CIC detachment where he became, and remained, liaison officer, as he describes it, "between the 441 Counterintelligence Corps detachment and the section of G-2 (intelligence) of the United States Armed Forces, Far East, which is concerned with the staff work, counterintelligence; the security group, it is called." Colonel Matthews's job was to chase spies and saboteurs; he was a spy going after spies. Why, then, was an officer of Matthews's caliber, training, and experience about to

---

*The OSS was established in 1942 for the purpose of gathering intelligence on the enemy and to sabotage their war effort and morale. It was disbanded in 1945 and its functions taken over by the newly formed Central Intelligence Agency (CIA) in 1947. The OSS was the first U.S. intelligence agency. Prior thereto, each service and certain branches of government had their own intelligence gathering networks and information was generally not shared.

†Counterintelligence: "The activity of an intelligence service employed in thwarting the efforts of an enemy's intelligence agents to gather information or commit sabotage." (Webster's Encyclopedic Unabridged Dictionary)

embark a ship anchored in Inchon Harbor and sail in that vessel, loaded with former American prisoners of war, to San Francisco?

Lieutenant Colonel Matthews boarded the USNS *General R.L. Howze* during the early morning hours of Tuesday, September 8, 1953.[24]

* * * *

The USNS *General R.L. Howze* (T-AP-134)* was a 10,000-ton troop transport. She had a single screw which moved her bulk at an average speed of 16 knots, was 522 feet long, 71 feet wide, and usually carried a crew, depending on the mission, of between 200 and 400 men. *Howze* had a troop capacity of over 3,300. She was armed with four 5" 38s, four twin 40s, and sixteen 20mm guns. When *Howze* was originally commissioned in 1944, the ship was a USS but after the war and several transfers to various commands, she became a USNS, retaining her name. This ship received six battle stars for Korean service. The *Howze* arrived at Inchon on September 2, dropped anchor in the harbor, and waited for her human cargo, who were gradually brought aboard by barge and launch. The ship remained at anchor until the last of the POWs and other passengers were settled in, including Colonel Schwable, and at 3:43 on Tuesday afternoon, September 8, the entry was logged in: "Anchor aweigh. Shift colors." It took 17 days to cross the vast Pacific, a trip of exactly 5,790 miles.† Many years later (30 to be precise), when the Naval Historical Center was developing its oral history for the colonel, he was questioned about the ships bringing men home (rather than planes) and he said, "It was a decompression thing." The prisoners settled down, got into the habit of eating proper foods again, and just got civilized. Frank Schwable noted, "We sort of felt like a human being when we got to San Francisco."[25]

There were a total of nine ships (eight transports and one hospital ship) that embarked the prisoners and set sail; *Howze* was the last ship to leave. Dubbed "Freedom Ships" by the press, they had the mission of moving soldiers from Korea to California and this movement was called "Operation Homecoming." But make no mistake, these were not "Freedom" ships for those passengers who were former prisoners of war. They were prison ships. What better place to retain prisoners than in the hold, albeit a comfortable one, of a ship in the middle of the ocean? Obviously, everyone could have been put on planes (there weren't that many POWs) and could have been with their

---

**See notation following endnote 24.*

†*Counting the days on a 1953 calendar, it would be 16 days, but on Wednesday, September 16, the ship crossed the International Date Line so there are recorded in the ship's log two September 16's. "0200.—All clocks advanced 1 hour to time zone -12, 180th meridian, bridge and engine room clocks synchronized."*

USNS *R.L. Howze*, T-AP-134. One of nine ships transporting soldiers, marines, and former POWs from Inchon to the West Coast of the United States in Operation Homecoming. The press dubbed the transports "Freedom Ships" but for the ex-prisoners, they were no such thing; they were prison ships (official U.S. Navy photograph).

families in just days, but that was not to be. About 450 repatriated prisoners who were sick were flown to Tokyo but the remainder were still prisoners — and suspect. Suspected of what? Suspected of returning to the United States with the intent to subvert and eventually overthrow the government. Many of the prisoners, whom the Chinese labeled "students," had learned their lessons well — too well.[26]

Lt. Col. Robert Matthews was "Chairman of the Joint Intelligence Processing Board No. 9" aboard *Howze*; number 9 because it was the ninth and last ship to leave Korea. The seven previous transports (all USNS "Generals"; *General Walker, General Pope, General Brewster*, and so on) all had a "chairman" on board, all lieutenant colonels and all CIC. Each chair was responsible for directing and supervising all the investigations and interrogations aboard that particular vessel. This was temporary duty for all and Colonel Matthews, for example, was still permanently attached to the 441 CIC Detachment, U.S. Armed Forces, Far East.[27]

The "Processing Board" on *Howze* had seven members, including Matthews as chair, and he supervised the progress of the other six members and their staff of officers who roamed the ship day and night. Unless otherwise noted, everyone was army and this was strictly an army show. The army was in complete charge of everything. On the board were mostly senior officers and they included a psychiatrist, a CIC officer from the army and the air force, a Marine Corps representative (a Captain Stevens), a psychological warfare expert, and a lawyer attached to the Judge Advocate General's office. Colonel Matthews reviewed their function: "Now, under the board operated an administrative team and counterintelligence interrogation teams and military intelligence or Phase 3 teams, as we called them." Teams were swarming the ship like hornets. Each team had a "chief" who, according to the colonel, was "normally in control of the immediate assignment of investigation, [the] decision as to when the investigation would begin, and the like." Colonel Matthews never spoke with or interviewed any of the former POWs; he let his board and their respective staffs do that and none of these teams, except for medical, ever bothered Frank Schwable. They were after much bigger fish, primarily young, impressionable, and naive army enlisted personnel. Colonel Matthews and his staff knew what Frank Schwable had done but not the other, mostly enlisted, former POWs. Before the ship reached the United States, however, they would "have the goods" on everyone.[28]

Howze sailed carrying "192 crew members, 258 cabin class [and] 1,727 troop class passengers." Most of the men were soldiers returning from war but segregated from them were nearly 300 former POWs. Matthews said that his teams "completely processed" ("intelligence processing," according to the colonel) 288 men, comprising 209 army, 51 air force and 28 navy and marine. Of this total, many of the investigators were assigned to concentrate on 34 air force officers (not counting Schwable and Bley) who had been intensely interrogated by the Chinese "with a view toward making them 'confess' to bacteriological warfare," according to Matthews. Before the ship reached San Francisco, to their total disbelief, the CIC interrogators discovered that of the total officers on board, 22 of them had signed confessions — and this was only on *Howze* although, Matthews said, "I had the majority." The colonel claims that his teams didn't suspect that this many officers had signed because, he said, "I don't believe the Chinese had published many of those confessions. I believe there were many of them which had not been publicized at the time the Truce was effected."[29]

Certainly it would have been propaganda overkill to make public every signed germ warfare confession since the Chinese already had three colonels, two majors and, according to Matthews, "There were some captains and I would say the majority perhaps were lieutenants." Although the colonel made no criticism of those officers who signed, there were men who were not officers (generally bomber crews) who were also viciously grilled but wouldn't concede anything. Colonel Matthews complimented these men when he said, "There were also some enlisted personnel among those who were questioned [by the

Chinese], who successfully resisted the efforts to break them and make them confess." This is true for a small minority of air force enlisted but the CIC investigation aboard *Howze* found that the vast majority of returning prisoners of war had signed one thing or another. These signatures were not an admission of doing something but were an appeal for something to happen, and that would be "peace." Matthews illustrates how bad the situation was of former POWs giving aid and comfort to the enemy when he said, "An entire camp signed a peace appeal at the request of the Chinese. There were other examples of that sort in which large numbers of people became involved. Those signatures could have been considered of some benefit to the enemy."[30]

* * * *

On Thursday, September 10, *Howze* was doing an average speed of 15.88 knots and the visibility stayed at 15 miles all day. The waves were a little high, averaging five feet during the day and reaching 12 at night, but other than that, the remaining 5,083 miles appeared to be a smooth sail. It was on this day that one of the psychiatrists approached his board member and requested a psychological evaluation be conducted on Frank Schwable. The medical board member approved it and assigned the task to 1st Lt. Martin E. Gluck (Ph.D.), USA.[31]

Lieutenant Gluck was 26 years old and had joined the army in July 1951. Having completed his degree work at the University of Pittsburgh, while in the service he interned at Fitzsimons Army Hospital. Upon finishing, the army sent him back to Pittsburgh to earn his doctorate, which he did in June 1953. Dr. Gluck's specialty was clinical psychology, or the evaluation and understanding of human behavior. Actually, Dr. Gluck did not receive his physical diploma until August 26, 1953, and on August 27, two weeks before meeting Colonel Schwable, the lieutenant found himself on a plane headed for Korea as a medical staff member of "Processing Board No. 9."[32]

Meeting in a private compartment with Colonel Schwable, Lieutenant Gluck administered four different psychological tests and although the colonel was "quite friendly, very cooperative," the doctor added that he was very fidgety while sitting. The first test was the Bender-Gestalt in which Dr. Gluck held nine cards of various designs, displayed each one in front of the colonel for five seconds and, after each display, asked the colonel to draw what he saw. "Primarily, it is a test of the individual's apperception of [his] environment," said the doctor, "how accurate, how well he is aware of his environment." The average person can do the Bender-Gestalt in 10 minutes; Colonel Schwable took an hour. This was a simple test of drawing what one saw but Dr. Gluck said, "He frequently asked for very specific instructions which, of course, I didn't give."[33]

In the Draw-a-Picture Test, a single picture of any person is drawn. The colonel chose to sketch a man in a tuxedo with a cocktail glass in his hand. This, also, took some time. The colonel was an excellent artist, so his drawings throughout had various dark and light shadings. The colonel was given the Thematic Apperception Test, in which the patient is asked to make up a short story for a series of pictures ranging from very clear images to the obscure. Also administered was the Rorschach, the classic 10-card "ink blot" examination. In this last test, according to Dr. Gluck, the colonel saw "bullets smashing through things, shattered glass but these again are a reflection of stirred-up feelings, tension within the individual."[34]

The lieutenant's function was not to diagnose but according to the doctor, "simply to present to the psychiatrist a personality picture of various strengths or weaknesses in the person, various techniques that the individual has at his command for adjusting, getting along." Colonel Paul Sherman, counsel to Colonel Schwable, although he didn't use the word "kid," was angered that the lieutenant was allowed to get even close to Colonel Schwable and thought that to be in the same room with him was absolutely unacceptable. He said:

> Surely, with so much at stake, our country could have afforded the services of an experienced psychologist. That this task should have been assigned to the officer it was is a deplorable commentary on the lackadaisical way the repatriation of all these fine American citizens was accomplished.... Under no circumstances should anyone with the meager experience of the young man, who was allowed to give his opinions, have been assigned to this important task.

Colonel Sherman (and all others during the inquiry) rarely protested anything but in this instance, the colonel may have protested too much.[35]

* * * *

Two days after sailing, Colonel Matthews gathered all the former POWs together, including Frank Schwable, for a "security briefing" but all it really amounted to was ordering them not to speak with anyone outside of their cloistered community. At that time, Matthews didn't recognize Colonel Schwable but a few days later did so, he said, "primarily because he was the only full Marine Colonel aboard."[36]

On Saturday, September 19, the ship had been at sea for 13 days. *Howze* was heading due east and, the record shows, "Steaming in accordance with NCSO Classified order #5–10." She had a mere 1,335 miles to go. It was another beautiful Pacific day with "clear sky, visibility good, vessel riding easily." Becoming more and more anxious the closer the California coast came, Colonel Schwable, as the senior officer among all the prisoners, decided to approach Matthews and have a talk with him.[37]

Frank Schwable needed help. According to the colonel, some form of guidance was necessary prior to docking "so that all of us fleas, flies and mosquito people could have a conference in a room and have this guidance ... told to all of us, so that all of us would be on exactly the same firm footing before we hit the shore and dispersed to the four winds." He continued:

> What I asked for on that ship, as the senior officer, was policy guidance, not on whether we should talk to the press, or whether we shouldn't, but if and when we eventually did, and it was inevitable that sooner or later we would be faced with the press, what the policy was, what the government's policy was; should we just categorically deny the use of germs and acknowledge that our statements were false, and stop there, or should we go into our treatment [on] how did they get these things from us.[38]

Walking down a passageway on this Saturday, Colonel Schwable saw Colonel Matthews approaching and decided to stop and speak with him for the first time during the voyage. Schwable asked the senior CIC officer to send a message to the Department of Defense (DOD) requesting guidance for all the officers who had signed germ warfare confessions; they just didn't know what to do when the ship docked, which would be in only four more days. Time was getting short and tensions were building the closer they got to California.[39]

Colonel Matthews agreed that guidance for everyone, including his own people, was essential and said, "It was an excellent idea at that time [because] the matters concerned were obviously of such nature that they needed to be brought to the attention of the services concerned." Frank Schwable asked that the transmission be directed to the Defense Department since there were no army personnel involved with signing germ warfare statements, only air force officers and two marines.* Colonel Matthews, however, refused to direct any messages to DOD; he insisted that everything go through the army. As a matter of fact, he wouldn't even send copies of his message to the air force or navy. The colonel justified his tunnel vision by saying, "I was under the Department of the Army, who was the exclusive agent during the program. I had no instructions regarding information copies to the Department of the Navy and to the Department of the Air Force." Colonel Matthews did make a request in the text, however, "that this message be passed to the interested services as soon as possible. In other words, I did not send it directly to them as information, but I sent it to them in effect by requesting that the Department of the Army immediately call it to their attention, which they did, I believe."[40]

---

*Most army POWs, both officers and enlisted on Howze and all the other ships, were intensely interrogated for something else, and that was collaboration with the enemy.

The radio room of the ship was archaic. The coding and decoding of messages was very slow and therefore, all messages had to be kept short. Colonel Matthews, knowing this and also knowing that the ship would be docking in four days, did not request a reply since it would arrive too late anyway. The colonel said, "A great deal has been made of the failure of the Defense Department to supply guidance. I did not make any specific request [to] the Defense Department, or from any other department under the Defense Department, for a specific reply by message." With time slipping by, another transmission fracture took place with the message (in addition to slowness) and that was when the radio room received the draft but diminished its importance. This slowed things even further, "particularly at the Pentagon end," noted Matthews. He said:

> I submitted the message as an "operational immediate" message. I intended and desired that it should have that type of attention and handling. I believe that if the ship had sent the message in that form in accordance with my request, the effect of the message would certainly have provided for action as fast and as expeditiously as desired. The ship, without consulting me, as a matter of fact, downgraded that — perhaps that is the wrong word — changed the precedence on the message from "operational immediate" to priority and informed me about it later.[41]

Colonel Matthews did not send the message solely at Frank Schwable's request. Said the colonel, "It was a message which summarized the condition[s] aboard the ship with respect to the number of persons who had been involved in the Chinese propaganda concerning bacteriological warfare." The message was also an urgent request for help; the colonel and his board were almost in over their heads. The communication did ask for press guidance for the flyers but in addition, Matthews said that it further "requested that in view of the time that was available at that time, it requested that fully briefed and qualified intelligence personnel from the various services come aboard the ship prior to its docking and to give me such guidance as they could offer at that time." The message from Matthews also contained a warning to DOD: "It also indicated that psychiatry reports indicated, and that the board unanimously concurred, that certain press contacts were not desirable. It indicated that frequent access by the press to personnel involved was not considered advisable."[42]

* * * *

It was 6 P.M. on Tuesday, September 22, 1953, when Colonel Schwable spotted Matthews and asked if he could speak with him privately. Colonel Matthews invited Colonel Schwable to come to his cabin in two hours. At 8 on the evening before docking, the two officers met. Matthews recalled, "Colonel Schwable indicated to me that he was in doubt as to whether or not he should submit a statement of some sort." The air force officers aboard ship had all prepared and submitted statements of their experiences and why they signed confessions, and without Marine Corps guidance, Frank Schwable figured it would be safe to follow suit. He had been working on it while at sea and noted, "Well, here, I have this stuff on paper, I might as well at least give a copy of it to Matthews so he could complete his records on me." Matthews assured Schwable that he could make any statement he wanted, sworn or not, but warned him "that if he did make a statement he must realize that anything which he said or wrote could be used against him in a court-martial."[43]

Colonel Schwable had left the statement in his cabin. Matthews recalled, "that he had typed up painfully and without a great deal of accuracy, a summary of his experiences. He said that it was chopped up, or words to that effect, that it had many corrections on it; that he had scratched out portions and made corrections, and that it was not in the condition in which he would like to have it for submission." The CIC officer mentioned to Schwable that he had typists who would help in putting the summary in proper format. Colonel Schwable asked if the administrative people had the necessary security clearance and, secondly, if he could receive a copy. Matthews replied in the affirmative to both questions. Schwable then went to his cabin, returned with the messy statement and handed it to the colonel. Matthews said, "I took it to my compartment where the board formally met and where the administrative section was located, and had the statement typed — rather poorly, I might say." Matthews and another officer proofed it, typos were noted in the margin and when they were finished, at 1 A.M., Colonel Matthews delivered it to Colonel Schwable. There was no light showing under the cabin door, however, so Matthews decided to hold it until Colonel Schwable awoke.[44]

The *Howze* was very busy on the morning of arrival:

0524 — Farallone Is. Lt. abeam 2.9 mi off, various courses and speeds as per Masters orders to Pilot station.
0642 — Pilot boat alongside.
0643 — Pilot, Capt. Gatergig aboard; various courses and speeds to.
0727 — Mile Rock at 0.6 miles off.
0735 — SBE.
0736 — Arrival — Passing under Golden Gate Bridge.
0737 — Stop.
0745 — U.S. Army tug, Lt. Col. W. R. Kendrick alongside with boarding party.
0755 — Tug away.

It was 7 A.M., precisely the moment of sunrise, when Matthews caught up with the senior marine and showed him the newly typed statement. Again he warned Colonel Schwable of his rights concerning self-incrimination. He reminded Schwable that he didn't have to do this and anything he wrote or said could be held against him at a trial. He pointed out the penciled corrections he had made and, in ink, Colonel Schwable approved those corrections within the text and initialed each one. Frank Schwable signed it and Colonel Matthews recalled, "I then entered my name as the witness and that was the way the statement was taken." It was on legal-size paper, 10 pages long, single-spaced with a small font. Colonel Schwable's last request to Matthews was that the long statement be gotten "to the Marine Corps as quickly as possible."[45]

With the California beach in view, Colonel Schwable was extremely uneasy. He was well aware that what he did was wrong and said, "as a military man, [I] know that that is not according to our Marine Corps or Navy regulations. I was bound to have apprehension." His anxiousness was partly due to Colonel Matthews using the word "treason" on more than one occasion.[46]

While meeting with Frank Schwable in his cabin, Colonel Matthews admits, "I am quite certain that I implied he was being investigated for collaboration in a treasonable manner." At another time, he mentioned to Schwable "that the nature of the offense [I was] investigating is as follows: collaboration with the enemy in a treasonable manner." In a third instance, Matthews told the marine that he could not advise him as to whether he should submit a statement because "he must realize that we were there in the capacity of investigating collaboration in a treasonable manner." Colonel Matthews also told his board to pass down to their respective staffs that right from the beginning, each soldier or airman was to be warned, prior to interrogation, that he "was suspected of an offense that did involve collaboration in a manner which could be considered treasonable in that it rendered aid and comfort to the enemy."[47]

Colonel Matthews, together with every other officer in the armed forces, especially attorneys, made a serious mistake in vernacular because he, and all the others, simply didn't know any better. Nothing like what was taking place with returned POWs had ever happened before in the history of the military: all 4,000 repatriates were suspected of treacherous acts. Certainly not all committed them but according to the definition, the majority did.

Using the army as an example but applicable to all services, officers should be warned to eliminate the word "treason" from their vocabulary. Why? Treason is a federal crime and therefore, can only be tried in a federal court. This being the case, the army must then turn over its prisoner to the federal authorities and this, of course, was not acceptable to them because control over that man would be forever lost.

In order to maintain jurisdiction over its people, the army came up with a relatively new charge and that was collaboration. Collaboration with the enemy carried with it the death penalty. For all intents and purposes, treason versus collaboration, after the Korean War, was a distinction without a difference except that control continued to rest with the military.

For two years after the war, army general courts-martial were taking place across the United States against American soldiers on charges of collaboration with the enemy and many of those tried received very long prison terms. One of the best defenses to these charges was when the prosecutor mentioned the word "treason," which happened often. At that point, the defense immediately objected and requested that the venue be changed from a military to a civilian court. None of the objections carried much weight, so the trial continued, but they did create a stir. During the court-martial of Maj. Ronald Alley, for example, the defense said:

> Major Alley is no less a citizen of the United States because he has on a uniform of the United States Army. We come to you with the argument that, if he is a citizen of the United States, first you should dismiss this entire proceeding, because he is charged here only with treason — exclusively with treason. This can't be anything else in the light of the English language — the construction of the English language from the earliest times of Chaucer and Bacon down to Funk and Wagnall's Dictionary.... [The charges] spell out treason, if anything; and I don't mean to be humorous, but an egg, if it is scrambled, or hard boiled or soft boiled or poached, it is still an egg. Now, there is nothing on this sheet of paper that is not treason.[48]

In a similar vein, defense counsel for Cpl. Thomas Bayes said that he "was charged with treason, found guilty of treason, and punished for treason, all without the necessity of proving an intent on his part to betray the United States, and the overt acts by two witnesses."[49]

The army was the only service to court-martial its men. The marines held a court of inquiry and the air force convened a board of review, which is an inquiry. Of the 220 repatriated air force personnel, almost half that number were suspected of signing germ warfare confessions. In the end, four officers left the service and the remainder were retained.[50]

As *Howze* tied up to the San Francisco pier, is it any wonder that Col. Frank Schwable felt "apprehension"?

10

The Arrival

> *This miserable experience was — and still is — so fantastic in its concept, so vile in its execution, and yet so very serious in its results, that at times I cannot believe now that such things can take place among civilized humans — and yet how bitterly I realize that it did happen and that I, albeit unwillingly, personally was a central figure in this dreadful fraud.*
> — Col. Frank H. Schwable, USMC, Court of Inquiry, Vol. 3, Exhibit 10 (11)

0823 — Let go stbd anchor 4 shots in water.
0841 — Tug a/s with docking pilot Capt. Rode.
0905 — Start heaving stbd anchor.
0914 — Anchor aweigh.
0945 — First line on dock. All secure portside to Pier #2 Fort Mason, Calif.
1011 — Start debark troops.
1200 — Vessel still debarking troops.[1]

Boarding *Howze* while she was still anchored was a marine lieutenant colonel from the Public Information Office (PIO) at Marine Corps Headquarters, Department of the Pacific, located on Harrison Street in San Francisco. He immediately asked to see Frank Schwable and upon meeting, the colonel handed him his written orders dated the day before. The orders, signed by Gen. Ray Robinson, read as follows:

> 1. By direction of the Commandant of the Marine Corps, you are hereby directed not to make any statement whatsoever to representatives of the press, radio, television, or other public information media or to any other civilians until authorized to do so by the Commandant of the Marine Corps.
>
> 2. This does not prohibit private communications, within security restrictions, with members of your immediate family.[2]

The PIO officer told Colonel Schwable these were the only instructions he was to receive but at least this gag order furnished the firm guidance Frank

Schwable was seeking.* The colonel was also informed by the courier that Col. A.T. Mason, chief of staff of the Department of the Pacific, was waiting for him at dockside with a car and that Schwable's mother and sister were with him. Maude Schwable made the long trip north from San Diego to be with her son while his wife, Beverly, together with the children, David and Susan, anxiously waited at home in Arlington, Virginia, for the return of Colonel Schwable to the east coast.[3]

The colonel was one of the first to leave the ship, and he was warmly greeted by his mother and sister. Colonel Schwable and the two women were quickly hustled through a mass of reporters by Colonel Mason to the waiting car. Driven to Marine Memorial Hotel, Frank Schwable was given a room and told to change into the winter green uniform prepared for him and in one hour report to headquarters.[4]

Shortly after 11 A.M., the smartly dressed marine left the hotel and was driven to Harrison Street. He was ushered into the office of Ray Robinson, commanding general of the Department of the Pacific, an old "China Salt," and a 36-year veteran of the corps. Ray Robinson spent quite a bit of time alone with Schwable and they reviewed together current events, the general bringing the colonel up to date on changes that took place during his absence from the wing and corps. Sometime during this meeting, Colonel Schwable was handed a message from the U.S.

General Ray A. Robinson, Commanding General, Marine Corps Headquarters, Department of the Pacific. The general was one of the first officers Colonel Schwable met after docking in San Francisco. His direct order from General Robinson was, "You are hereby directed not to make any statement whatsoever to representatives of the press, radio, television, or other public media or to any other civilians until authorized to do so by the Commandant of the Marine Corps" (official U.S. Marine Corps photograph).

*Roy Bley received the same order but one day after debarking they went their separate ways.

Ambassador to the United Nations, Henry Cabot Lodge, directing him to answer four specific questions, the answers to which Ambassador Lodge could use in the biological warfare battle fiercely raging in New York. None of the questions asked why he signed but all four made reference to his treatment. Because of this and other factors, while most of the former POWs were "dispersed to the four winds," Frank Schwable remained on the West Coast for the next three days.[5]

Just after 1 P.M. on Wednesday, the chief of staff walked into the general's office and shocked them both when he announced that the commandant, General Shepherd, had cancelled the gag order and stated that Colonel Schwable was to hold a press conference in one hour. In amazement, the colonel asked General Robinson what he should or shouldn't say to the press but Ray Robinson himself had no idea and could only reply, "Probably the less you say, the better." Colonel Schwable was livid. He later remarked, "I had no guidance whatsoever. I had been told by letter to keep quiet and then that was revoked and there I was ... being thrown to the wolves." Frank Schwable asked Colonel Mason to come with him, which he did, but in reality there was nothing the chief of staff could do. Once again, Frank Schwable was alone.[6]

The media meeting was uneventful and although the colonel revealed some of the tortures he underwent, both in body and mind, it wouldn't be until much later that Frank Schwable realized that he had undergone menticide. After the conference he returned to his room at the Marine Memorial Hotel where he would spend what was left of the day. That night he restlessly slept.

On Thursday and Friday, the colonel shuffled back and forth from his hotel to the headquarters building where he was given a small office that contained a desk, chair, and typewriter and there Frank Schwable sat, wrote, and typed. He was, as the colonel remarked, "totally unassisted" and, in a sense, back in solitary confinement. The marines did not furnish him a secretary or navy yeoman who could take down what was dictated or do his typing. This was a terrible way to treat a full marine colonel but, unfortunately, this was also only the beginning of that treatment. The colonel felt that he could have used a ghostwriter, someone to dictate to so that he himself could simply "sit down and put in good words — to bring out the proper emphasis — our counterpropaganda program" that Ambassador Lodge could use at the United Nations. In the final analysis, Frank Schwable said, he didn't "think much of the statement I wrote."[7]

Meanwhile, in the same city, and not too distant from where the marine colonel was writing, so was an army lieutenant colonel. Robert Matthews was occupied in penning a memo to the commanding general of Sixth Army at the Presidio of San Francisco. He described the massive collaboration that took place, uncovered on the long trip home aboard *Howze,* and the numerous germ warfare confessions signed by airmen (and that was only aboard his ship). So that the general didn't think that everyone collaborated with the enemy in one way or another, he singled out 14 airmen (including Major Ezelle and Captain Flynn) who didn't. Although these officers were in the minority, he related to the general in his lengthy memorandum that they wouldn't give in, even though:

> ... placed in solitary confinement in a small space; being sent to the "hole"; jail, or isolation, suffering beatings with fists, rifle butts, and/or hatchets; being tied hand and foot and hanging from a pole; being forced to face a firing squad; being stood at rigid attention for up to thirty hours; court-martial with death sentence; having cocked pistols placed against their heads; being handcuffed and chained for extended periods; and having threats made against their families.[8]

On Friday, Frank Schwable completed his reply to Ambassador Lodge and later in the day was forced to hold another press conference at Headquarters, Department of the Pacific. During this conference, he repudiated his germ warfare confession and was filmed. The motion picture was later shown at the United Nations as "counter-propaganda" and the colonel remarked, "It was the most half-baked way of taking a picture that I have ever seen."[9]

By Friday afternoon he had finished in San Francisco and the next evening, Saturday, September 26, Colonel Schwable boarded a plane for the long flight to the East Coast. He arrived at Washington National Airport at 10 A.M. Sunday. Beverly and the children were waiting for him together with a few friends and neighbors. The marines did not send anyone to meet the colonel. His ostracism by the corps was beginning.[10]

The colonel spent Sunday afternoon and evening at his home in Arlington, alone with his family. He had to be a little nervous, however, because he had orders to report to the Pentagon the next day at 9 A.M. There the assistant commandant of the Marine Corps and director of Marine Aviation, Lt. Gen. William Brice, would be waiting for him.[11]

* * * *

The North Koreans initially launched the germ warfare charge against the United States in May 1951. At that time, virtually everyone ignored it, including Radio Peking and Radio Moscow. Nine months later, toward the middle of February 1952, both Moscow and Peking blasted the airwaves with a massive and furious attack on the United States. Charges of germ warfare were viciously spread, reaching even the lowest communist front organizations worldwide. In the last days of February, the Soviet Union finally levied these charges at the United Nations in New York.

Almost immediately, Dean Acheson, secretary of state, "categorically denied these charges" while at the same time, so did Trygve Lie, secretary-general of the United Nations, who called them "utterly false." Secretary of Defense Robert Lovett labeled them "abominable, malicious falsehoods" while Gen. Matthew Ridgway "denied that any element under his command had employed germ warfare at any time or in any form."[12]

As if to excuse itself for fabrication, in the middle of this controversy, on March 18, 1952, to be precise, Radio Moscow broadcast a statement saying that "the basis of Communist morality, Lenin thought, is the struggle for strengthening and achieving Communism. For the Soviet people, everything is moral that serves the victory of the Communist Order."[13]

In March 1952, Dean Acheson went to the International Red Cross and asked it to examine the matter and it accepted. The Red Cross agreed "to establish an investigating body composed of persons who would offer every guarantee of moral and scientific integrity." The communists refused. Then in June, the United States went to the Security Council of the United Nations and requested intervention and asked the Red Cross again to investigate. All members of the council voted yes with the exception of the Soviet Union, which used its veto power to kill the idea.[14]

Though the idea died, it shouldn't be forgotten that only a few months later Colonel Schwable and Major Bley were captured and while Frank Schwable and Roy Bley were undergoing menticide and torture respectively, newspapers all over the world were continually reporting on the battle taking place in New York. This war of words was going to continue for many months (and years) to come and one can see how vitally important it would be for the Soviet delegation to have the germ warfare confessions of both officers. Schwable and Bley were really the big fish in the propaganda pond.

The two confessions would not be ready for publication and distribution until the end of February 1953, but five months before, on October 1, 1952, while Colonel Schwable was resisting in his lean-to half a world away, the Soviet Union introduced to the delegates a document entitled "Report of the International Scientific Commission for the Investigation of Facts Concerning Bacterial Warfare in Korea and China."* Appended to the report were the handwritten germ warfare confessions of four air force lieutenants.[15]

The big day came five months later when on March 12, 1953, Andrey Vyshinsky, the permanent representative of the Soviet Union, presented to the First Committee of the United Nations the complete and signed germ warfare confessions of Frank Schwable and Roy Bley. Vyshinsky then requested that the confessions be entered into the proceedings of the General Assembly "and distributed to the delegations of all States Members of the United

---

The Soviet Union acted on its own behalf but also on behalf of North Korea and China since neither of these two countries were members of the United Nations at that time.

Nations." This was all done only six weeks after Colonel Schwable put his final signature on the document at Camp 5.[16]

The timing seemed to be right on the money, or so the United States thought. The General Assembly reconvened on February 24, 1953, and the delegates received the circulated confessions on March 12, only 16 days later. "In other words," said Charles Mayo, the U.S. representative, "the tortures of Colonel Schwable and Major Bley evidentially were an integral part of Soviet preparations for the General Assembly."[17]

Two weeks later, the United States introduced to the General Assembly nine signed statements denying germ warfare from eight marines and one soldier. The soldier was the Chairman of the Joint Chiefs of Staff, Gen. Omar N. Bradley, and the marines included two major generals, one brigadier general, four colonels, and one master sergeant. The statements were not all that creative, however, since they were boilerplate, one a copy of the other. It was the same as submitting one statement with all nine signing. The two marine major generals, nevertheless, had something to say privately. Gen. Christian F. Schilt, former commanding officer of the First Marine Aircraft Wing prior to Gen. Clayton Jerome (with Colonel Schwable as chief of staff), said about the confession, "None of the statements on the subject attributed to me are true." More dramatically, General Jerome held, "It's all a damn lie and I would like to go up to the U.N. and tell them so under oath." In spite of this, it would appear that it was too little too late.[18]

Six weeks after the Soviets submitted the confessions of the two marines, a vote was taken at the United Nations to perform an investigation into germ warfare. It passed by an overwhelming majority. The investigating committee consisted of Brazil, Egypt, Pakistan, Sweden, and Uruguay. The Soviets said no and stated that the five-country committee was handpicked by the United States and that the International Scientific Commission report introduced by them on October 1, 1952, was sufficient. On that note, all the United States could say was that "an unbiased investigation is one under which the investigators will do exactly what the Soviet Union requires them to do."[19]

This battle at the United Nations over germ warfare went on for months (and eventually years) after the war was over. Three months after the truce, Charles Mayo described the attitude of the United States:

> The question before us — the charge that the United States forces engaged in bacteriological warfare in Korea — plainly involves the honor and integrity not only of my country and her soldiers but also of the United Nations itself, under whose banner sixteen member nations fought in Korea. It is therefore a subject which my country in particular, but in a larger sense all of us here, must treat in the most serious way. We cannot allow this whole distorted story to slide away like water off a duck's back.
>
> [Nothing] could fully express the indignation which every citizen of my country

feels at the vicious slander which Communist Imperialism has cast upon our national honor, upon the dignity of our soldiers, and upon the concept of truth.[20]

* * * *

The confession itself was a work of art and very believable. It was thorough, exact, and extremely well edited. Although the colonel was literally freezing when writing, his mind was hard at work, as he said, "to insert ideas into the statement that could be used to show that it was false, ridiculous, and subject to refutation." It was a good try, but every time he got back an edited portion to rewrite, most of those ideas had been deleted — except one. He was trying desperately to get messages out within the text in the hope that they "would be taken up promptly and used to demonstrate to all people that this whole thing was a hoax, thus warning other pilots of what might be expected should they be shot down." It was very hard to make a false statement, however, because the Chinese knew quite a bit about the First Marine Aircraft Wing. Frank Schwable said, "In formulating the plans and operations I assumed in my statement, I had to make them realistic enough for the Chinese to accept them since they knew our basic organizations, locations, names, etc., but I also tried to make general operational features relatively normal because I knew other POWs would be forced to guess at my operations and to 'confirm' them."[21]

The one idea (actually word) that the colonel did insert into the text four times and the Chinese left alone was "suprop." When the Chinese questioned it, Schwable alleged that it was the code the United States used when referring to germ warfare in Korea. Actually, he was trying to send the message that his confession was "super propaganda." Later, several air force officers told him that they caught on right away but the ones who counted — that is, the United Nations, the marines, and the press — didn't. The colonel noted, "This code name naturally does not appear in a single official record, paper, report, code book or elsewhere in the entire U.S. military establishment except in connection with my own false 'confession.'" In his own personal definition of "suprop," Frank Schwable said, "that that is what this was, that it is super propaganda, it is super duper."[22]

Anyone reading the confession should immediately notice that if the Chinese didn't write it, it was thoroughly edited by them. How? Apparently, the editors did not know the difference between American English and British English. Here are some examples:

Defense spelled defence — once
Center spelled centre — once
Connection spelled connexion — once
Program spelled programme — 12 times

The confession was distributed to all the POW camps in North Korea. Maj. Walter Harris, during the spring of 1953, was interned at Camp 2 Annex on the Yalu. Once he read it, he recalled, "It signified to me that somebody with a British background had composed it and knowing that many Chinese had been educated under the British, I felt that there was a good possibility, and many of the other men in the camp felt there was a good possibility, it had been written by the Chinese." At the court of inquiry, Major Harris became a little annoyed when he was asked if he knew whether Colonel Schwable had a British education. His reply was, "No, sir, we could only go on a system of odds. Odds were against Colonel Schwable being British."[23]

There were other irregularities in the statement that a seasoned observer could pick up. Schwable explains that there was no way a massive germ warfare operation, as claimed by the Chinese, could have taken place without something put on paper, but there wasn't a word. "It would be utterly impossible," remarked the colonel, "to conduct operations on such a large scale from so many bases with such involved logistics" without something in writing. Furthermore, where were the casualties? The enemy never produced a single person, civilian or military, who had been infected by any disease caused by germs from American bombs. During his time in prison, Frank Schwable said, "I often wondered in my solitude whether the U.S. would insist upon an international on-the-spot investigation in Korea to tabulate the tremendous number of casualties that must have resulted from the thousands of bombs 'I dropped' all over Korea since it would be next to impossible to inoculate all the Chinese and Koreans against the ridiculous variety of diseases all of our statements together claimed to being in the [germ warfare] program."[24]

The Chinese claimed three diseases had been used in the Korean War: cholera, yellow fever, and typhus. However, flies and mosquitoes spread cholera and yellow fever yet neither could survive the North Korean winter and, as a matter of fact, flies and mosquitoes disappeared from all the prison camps in early October and didn't reappear until June. And, in one other inconsistency, the confession mentions that an aircraft named Banshee was used at times to drop bombs but it is designated as the F2H-2P. This is the version of the Banshee used for photo recon and therefore it didn't have the ability to carry bombs, fly at altitude, or make horizontal bomb runs. Nor did it have bombsights. In fact, the Marine Corps did not inventory sights for the F2H-2P.[25]

The confession revealed quite a bit of classified information. For our purposes, classified could mean anything from secret down to a violation of security. During the investigation into the conduct of the colonel prior to the inquiry, Lt. Col. Chester A. Henry, G-2 (Intelligence), Headquarters, Marine Corps, was given the task of informing the court what classified data was contained in Schwable's statement. It turns out that it reeked with it. Not a little on every page either, but seemingly every paragraph. Colonel Henry compiled an amazingly long list. Here is just some of the classified material disclosed:

1. Identifies the commanding generals of the wing.
2. Identifies the wing's G-1, G-2, G-3, and G-4.
3. Identifies the group commanders.
4. Enumerates the station lists of the wing (part of the order of battle).
5. Identifies bases and the geographic locations of MAG-12 and MAG-33.
6. States that VMF-513 was a unit of MAG-33, which is order of battle information.
7. Notes that VMF-513 was operating out of K-8 and identifies Kusan.
8. Identifies VMF-513 as a night fighter squadron operating on night fighter missions.
9. Describes the form issued by Fifth Air Force to be used for filling out mission reports.
10. Explains the navy's area of operations as being on the east coast of Korea and extending several miles inland.

"The use of personal names in my 'confession,'" added the colonel, "was the bitterest pill I had to swallow."[26]

* * * *

At 9 sharp on Monday morning, September 28, 1953, Frank Schwable walked into the Pentagon and went directly to the offices of Lt. Gen. William O. Brice, assistant commandant of the Marine Corps and director of Marine Aviation. Brice was quite cordial and for about an hour he and the colonel spoke. At the conclusion of their conversation, the director handed to Colonel Schwable a memorandum from Gen. Lemuel Shepherd, the commandant. Contained in the memo were charges against the colonel (signing and broadcasting), and there were various enclosures including newspaper clippings and transcripts of all broadcasts made by him and transmitted by Radios Peking and Pyongyang. General Shepherd gave Schwable three days in which to reply.[27]

The message also contained a caution. It stated, "You are privileged to submit such statement as you may desire relative to the allegations" but warned him that he should familiarize himself with Article 31 of the Uniform Code of Military Justice. Article 31 is entitled "Compulsory Self-Incrimination Prohibited." The colonel, in essence, was being read what would now be called his Miranda rights. Then General Brice told Colonel Schwable that there was no office space available at the Pentagon and suggested that he return to his residence and draft the reply. The colonel recalled, "I went right home and for three days and the good part of three nights, I wrote as fast as I could."²⁸

After his release and up to his hour-long conversation with General Brice, Colonel Schwable had no clue as to what trouble he was in. It wasn't until the general handed him his orders from the commandant that it hit him over the head like a hammer. Beverly Schwable knew from reading newspaper articles about her husband, and through her contacts in the corps, that he was in difficulty but didn't say anything to him on his first day home. "Bless my wife's heart," commented Frank Schwable, "the first night I was home she had not told me what she had read in the newspapers about the so-called 'harsh attitude.'" It wasn't until he was writing the day following the meeting with General Brice that Beverly showed her husband some articles. Only then did Frank Schwable realize the "attitude" held toward him. Suffice it to say that there were many senior marine officers who wished he were dead.²⁹

Lieutenant General William O. Brice, Assistant Commandant of the Marine Corps and Director of Marine Aviation. After arriving at the general's office in the Pentagon, Colonel Schwable was handed a memorandum containing all the charges against him (official U.S. Marine Corps photograph).

The colonel's reply to the commandant contained an overall view of what happened to him in North Korea that made him do what he did, but it didn't go into minute detail. He felt that could be taken as making excuses: "I wouldn't make an excuse to the Commandant and I won't make excuses now to anyone." Schwable felt that his letter was "complete in its essentials." Colonel Schwable did complain, however, about the limited time afforded him to answer and thought, "I was trying to cover fourteen months experience on a pretty difficult situation in the first three days I had been home with my family [in] two years." In his rejoinder, Frank Schwable did have the daring to compare writing his reply to writing his confession by remarking to General Shepherd, "Those papers too, were written under pressure and with a very short time limit." On October 1, 1953, exactly on time, the colonel's 24-page, single-spaced, typewritten reply was submitted to his commandant.[30]

The Marine Corps, according to the *New York Times*, "was stunned by the Schwable case. In the top command, there were demands for swift, summary punishment. The Defense Department, however, restrained the Marine generals." The colonel, therefore, did not receive immediate punishment, not even confinement to quarters, but his fate was almost worse than that — he was completely ignored until the corps could figure out what to do with him. He had no office, no job; he didn't even have to report in since there was no one to report to. He was told to simply stay around the house and wait until the commandant contacted him. Shepherd's advisors wanted to hang Frank Schwable from the proverbial yardarm but since the corps is not a democracy, the future of this marine aviator, a hero of World War II, lay in the hands of Lemuel Cornick Shepherd, Jr.[31]

A frustrated Frank Schwable said, "I was getting fidgety — let's do something — let's say yes or no; ... what's going to happen? What are we going to do? When do I go back to work again? Where do I go?" The colonel's time in limbo lasted four months and all the while he wondered whether there would be a court-martial, an inquiry, or would he simply be "asked" to retire. Colonel Schwable actually believed that it was going to be relatively easy for him upon his return to the United States to repudiate what he had done; call it a lie, call it a misstatement, call it something, but it didn't work. "I was dreadfully disappointed," said Schwable, "with the fact that the one thing I thought I could do when I came home was to try to effectively counter my own statements." He quickly learned that the official position toward him and other former POWs who signed germ warfare confessions or any other anti–American statements was, as he put it, "in general terms, to condemn, crucify and disgrace them." By doing this and having this attitude, according to the colonel, the government was telling future soldiers, sailors, marines, and airmen "that if they are captured in the execution of their loyal duty to their country, they must then sacrifice their lives, if sufficiently pressed, in futile resistance to propaganda measures or they will return home as disgraced men."[32]

After repatriation and back home in Virginia, Schwable still stood before the entire communist world as a formally convicted war criminal. But within his own corps, he said, "I have been repatriated to my own country under a cloud of doubt, suspicion and lack of understanding." In service clubs, cocktail hours, and even in the press, he was seen as the one officer who confessed without any physical punishment or torture. What is known now wasn't known then.[33]

At first, the commandant wanted to leave well enough alone. He knew Beverly through her father (Capt. John Pollard, USN), and mother because Dr. Pollard and General Shepherd were stationed together in Haiti. He liked

Beverly's parents and their daughter. He felt, however, that he had to do something since the army was haphazardly court-martialing former POWs all over the United States for collaboration with the enemy and the air force was holding a Board of Review for the scores of their officers who signed germ warfare confessions. Swaying opinion in the other direction, however, was that General Shepherd knew "there were others, among those who will never return, who no doubt resisted as long as the breath of life remained." There are many who falsely believe that a POW is a noncombatant, which is nonsense. The commandant firmly held that the POW camp was, indeed, an extension of the battlefield, which it is. He thought, "Men who become prisoners of war must learn to accept the implications of their fate with the same fortitude with which they have learned in the past to steel themselves to accept the stark reality of death in battle."[34]

In addition to the army and air force conducting trials and tribunals respectively, the commandant was receiving enormous pressure from senior officers within his staff to court-martial Frank Schwable. One officer was Maj. Gen. Merrill "Bill" Twining, deputy chief of staff, Headquarters, Marine Corps, and another was Colonel (later lieutenant general) Victor "Brute" Krulak, secretary of the general staff, whose son would in 1995 become commandant. These two men wanted so badly for Colonel Schwable to pay the price for collaboration that they could taste it. They didn't want an investigation (except as mandated by the UCMJ), they didn't want a court of inquiry, they wanted and pressured the commandant for an immediate court-martial. The result of this type of trial could be life imprisonment or even death. Colonel Schwable knew who his enemies were. The colonel said of General Twining, "I think he disliked or hated my guts. If [Shepherd] had been a Bill Twining, I would have had a general court-martial right off the bat." On Col. "Brute" Krulak, Schwable remarked that he "was never a friend of mine." But the man in charge, the decision maker, was the commandant and, according to Frank Schwable, "there is Lem Shepherd here that leans my way and the two top advisors lean definitely the other way."[35]

While all this was going on, the *New York Times* asked whether the corps had "the right to expect that marines will stand firm where other men have failed?" Hanson W. Baldwin, the military correspondent, answered the question for the paper when he said, "The personal welfare of any individual in a military organization must be subordinated to the good of the whole.... More important than any individual's safe return, the Corps believes, is loyalty to the country and the Corps." Mr. Baldwin may have just put it in reverse order. Death before dishonor.[36]

* * * *

On Thursday, January 21, 1954, General Shepherd ordered that a court of inquiry be convened in the case of Col. Frank H. Schwable. The waiting was over.

Dr. William Overholser, a renowned psychiatrist, was asked to examine the colonel. The doctor did his undergraduate work at Harvard and received his doctor of medicine degree from Boston University. He was an advisor to many departments of government and was a professor of psychiatry at George Washington University. Six days before the inquiry, Overholser and Schwable met. The meeting lasted for about an hour and the doctor noticed that the colonel was sweating and "troubled and anxious." The colonel explained his anxiety by saying, "You can't have that sort of thing stay in your mind day after day. I have never been able to get rid of it. Every time I wake up at night now, I still wake up thinking about this thing."[37]

After spending time with Frank Schwable, Dr. Overholser concluded that at the closing stages of his menticide in the lean-to, Colonel Schwable's "judgment was badly impaired, his ability to act as a willing and reasonable individual was seriously impaired." The doctor took it one step further and added that at the time, the colonel was so "mentally incompetent" that he could not "exercise any substantial degree of judgment as to what he was about; that he was unable to judge the demands of the situation fully; that he was really in essence without a will."[38]

Being without a free will, however, does not necessarily mean that one cannot say yes or no, because one can. Yes means life and no means death. As J.A.M. Meerloo and Alan Little both described, being without a will means that there's no gray area; there's absolutely nothing to think about. It's either yes or no—period. Free will does not enter the equation except for yes or no—life or death. Colonel Schwable chose life:

> The type of treatment used to extract a false and damning so-called "confession" from me was a new way of handling POWs—it is the communist way—it is a diabolical, methodical, unrelenting system of breaking down a human being to the point where he can no longer resist.
> At the cost of my Marine Corps career, and perhaps at the cost of my reputation among certain groups of people, but not at the cost of my own personal integrity and self-respect, I believe that sacrificing my life in a North Korean prison camp for a futile cause would have been of far less benefit to the United States than living to bring back my experiences and knowledge with which to combat this new and vile means of conducting modern warfare.

"I am positive in my own mind," said Colonel Schwable, "that had I not capitulated to them, I would today still be a prisoner of war or else in my grave."[39]

"A strange chapter in the proud history of the Marine Corps will open tomorrow morning as three generals and an admiral sit in judgment on Col.

Frank Hawse Schwable," reported the *New York Times*. Prior to the proceeding, Charles Mayo at the United Nations, speaking on the subject of Korean prisoners of war, stated to the assembled delegates:

> The total picture presented is one of human beings reduced to a status lower than that of animals; filthy, full of lice, festered wounds full of maggots; their sickness regulated to a point just short of death; unshaven, without haircuts or baths for as much as a year; men in rags, exposed to the elements; fed with carefully measured minimum quantities and lowest quality of food and unsanitary water, served often in rusty cans; isolated, faced with squads of trained interrogators, deprived of sleep and browbeaten into mental anguish. Imagine a human being in this condition.[40]

Unfortunately, it is easy for us to understand why Hanson W. Baldwin said, "The 'men who broke' are among the most tragic figures of the Korean War."[41]

Epilogue

It seems to me that every principal of fairness and justice requires that [Colonel Schwable] not be subjected to further suspicion, calumny, and slander.
— John H. Pratt, Esq., Court of Inquiry, Vol. 3, 1142

It took only three days for the members of the court to deliberate and, according to orders, develop and draft the facts, form their opinions, and provide recommendations. "Marine officers were unable to recall any comparable court of inquiry that completed its deliberations so quickly," reported the *New York Times*.[1]

There were 61 facts, 12 opinions, and just 3 recommendations, all classified "Secret, Security Information." The facts are as stated throughout this work, including fact number 7 which states, "That, Article 1223, U.S. Navy Regulations, and Section 0919 of the U.S. Navy Security Manual, 1951, were effective at that time and, taken together, prohibited prisoners of war from disclosing to the enemy any information other than name, rank, serial number, home address, and place and date of birth." Somewhat offsetting this strictness, however, the last two facts (60 and 61) pointed out "That, there is no evidence that Colonel Schwable, during his period of captivity, revealed any substantial military information to the enemy" and "That there is no evidence Colonel Schwable betrayed his fellow prisoners."

Some of the 12 opinions that the three major generals and rear admiral formed were harsh while others were friendly:

1. Colonel Schwable absolutely knew while he was writing about his involvement in planning the germ warfare campaign, in company with the Joint Chiefs of Staff, that it "would be used by the enemy for propaganda purposes."
2. "That this propaganda weapon was of aid and comfort to the enemy."

3. His actions caused "embarrassment to and brought discredit upon the United States in its international relations and required official denials."
4. That the Chinese had perfected the science of menticide to the point where it was "aimed at the destruction of the individual's will to resist."
5. Using menticide, it was inevitable that "a. The victim's will to resist is broken, and he responds as the enemy desires. b. The victim becomes insane. c. The victim dies."
6. Time is of no concern — a week, a month, a year, 10 years — it doesn't matter; capitulation will happen.
7. Because he was a colonel and chief of staff of a marine aircraft wing, there was an "intensified application of the torture" of degradation, deprivation and mental harassment.
8. "That Colonel Schwable resisted this torture to the limit of his ability to resist."
9. The confession and recordings were the "result of mental torture of such severity and compelling nature as constituted reasonable justification for entering into such acts."
10. The press release brought about his downfall and "gave important information to the enemy concerning Colonel Schwable's status."
11. "That there exists, and existed at the time of Colonel Schwable's capture, contradictory and confusing doctrines within the various services of the Armed Forces of the United States as to what information or misinformation a prisoner of war may, or may not, give to his captors."
12. "That Colonel Schwable's record of military service, covering 23 years prior to 8 July 1952, showed him to be an officer of demonstrated courage and for the last fifteen years of the period, of outstanding efficiency."

Here are the recommendations:

1. "That no disciplinary action be taken in the case of Colonel Schwable by reason of acts which he committed while a prisoner of war between the dates of 8 July 1952 and 6 September 1953."
2. "That action be taken on a Department of Defense level to formulate and promulgate to the Armed Forces of the United States instructions relative to the conduct of United States military personnel who may become prisoners of war."
3. "That such instructions be binding on all services of the Armed Forces of the United States, and not left to separate interpretation or action by an individual department or service."

Signed:

    Henry D. Linscott　　　　Christian F. Schilt
    Major General　　　　　　Major General
    U.S. Marine Corps　　　　U.S. Marine Corps
    President　　　　　　　　Member

    Robert O. Bare　　　　　　Thomas F. Cooper
    Major General　　　　　　Rear Admiral
    U.S. Marine Corps　　　　U.S. Navy
    Member　　　　　　　　　Member

"The days of POWs being required to furnish only their names, ranks and serial numbers in accordance with the Geneva Convention, so often quoted by the Chinese," according to Frank Schwable, "[are] gone forever, I am sure." In the 21st century, in agreement with the Code of Conduct developed primarily because of the Korean War and the prisoner of war humiliation, the rule—with very minor variations—still stands: name, rank, and serial number only. Gen. William Dean said, "Under the tenets of the Geneva Convention, that ... was all that a prisoner of war was required to give. That is what I had been instructed in all my years of service, and that is what I always instructed my men, that that is all they were to give if captured." People may be ready to say "practice what you preach," but General Dean admits that during his captivity, "I failed to do so."[2]

On April 14, 1954, General Shepherd accepted, in full, the findings of the court and these findings were passed on to the secretary of the navy who, one week later, also agreed to them. In a long reply to the findings, the commandant concurred that the confession was forced but stated:

> The fact remains however, that it was used as a principal circumstantial buttress in support of one of the most enormous fabrications of modern times, a monstrous falsehood which was used as a major propaganda instrument by the communists to the great detriment of the influence and prestige of the United States among those less developed peoples of the world who are now pondering the decision between communism and the way of freedom. In this connection, Colonel Schwable's confession, despite its falsity, constituted a severe blow to national interest by one whose sole motivation should have been to foster and preserve it.[3]

Opinions of the court notwithstanding, Lemuel Shepherd wanted to punish Colonel Schwable. Through the secretary of the navy, the commandant contacted Secretary of Defense Charles Wilson as to the type of reprimand that should be imposed upon his colonel and Wilson told him, "I am leaving this matter to your discretion to handle in a manner that will serve the best interests of the Naval Service." Therefore, even though the general knew and agreed that Frank Schwable acted under mental and physical duress:

... nevertheless, he has been an instrument, however unwilling, of causing damage to his country. Cognizance of this fact must, in my judgment, be taken into account in regard to his future assignment potential with the application of such restrictions of his service to those military activities involving duties of a type making minimum demands for their successful performance."[4]

Colonel Frank Schwable was prohibited from ever commanding troops again.

The colonel remained at home while deliberations were taking place and when he finally heard of the court's opinions and recommendations, he was "greatly relieved," but at the same time disappointed that the responsibility of command never again be his. At a press conference, President Eisenhower commented on the disciplinary action by remarking, "You couldn't take back such people [as Colonel Schwable] and ask young Americans to follow them enthusiastically." The colonel suggests that it was General Twining that sponsored this action to the commandant and "That one cut my throat completely. That finished my career.... That is the thing that killed me right off the bat. I mean that finished me up completely."[5]

From his return to the East Coast until after the inquiry, Colonel Schwable was without a job. Officially, his assignment was at the Pentagon, which housed the headquarters for marine aviation under Lt. Gen. William Brice, but Frank Schwable had nothing to do so he rarely went there. Essentially, his base of operations was his home in Arlington. Shortly after the court's findings and the commandant's censure were internally released, General Brice called Colonel Schwable into his office and said, "If you want to retire, we will expedite your retirement." "No," replied the colonel, "I've been a Marine all my life and I'm going to stay in." All the general said was, "Okay." Now the problem was what to do with this experienced aviator who could not command and whose retirement did not come up for another five years. What they did was set up a new unit named the Aviation Safety Office at the Pentagon under the deputy chief of naval operations (air). Colonel Schwable and a navy captain who was about to retire were assigned to this entity and that's all it was composed of: just the two of them. Their function was to review all accident reports that came in and make recommendations.[6]

Colonel Schwable stayed at the Pentagon for several months and then was transferred to Fleet Marine Force (FMF), Atlantic, headquartered in Norfolk, Virginia, where he became the aviation safety officer. At this new post, Colonel Schwable was to "help with the study of accident reports and flight procedures as part of the continuing effort to make service flying safer." Prior to assuming his new position at FMF, Atlantic, he reported to Marine Air Station, Cherry Point, North Carolina, to take a flight refresher course. While in training, on June 22, 1954, with no public announcement, he was decorated with the coveted Legion of Merit for his outstanding service as chief of staff of the First Marine Aircraft Wing. Actually, according to Schwable's biography, "He was awarded a Gold Star in lieu of his third Legion of Merit." Maj. Gen. Clayton Jerome recommended this honor, as the general had been his commanding officer in Korea. General Brice flew into Cherry Point from Washington to make the presentation and General Jerome, then commanding general of FMF, Atlantic, attended. Colonel Schwable remained aviation safety officer until the day of his retirement.[7]

In closing, Hanson W. Baldwin said:

> The record of the court of inquiry in the Schwable case, or at least an abstract, together with the court's recommendations, and the reasoning behind those recommendations, should be circulated widely to all officers of the services and to the general public. The United States in general and the armed forces in particular, must understand the terrible issues posed by this case if service morale is not to suffer.[8]

* * * *

A little over a half-century has passed since these events took place. All of the senior field and flag grade officers are now deceased. Of the junior officers, many of them are gone, too. They lived a life in the service of their corps and country that was exciting, adventurous, and noble. Many were promoted to senior field grade and flag rank positions, and deservedly so. Gen. William Dean, for his actions on July 20 and July 21, 1950, as commanding general of the 24th Infantry Division, was awarded the Medal of Honor, which was presented by President Truman and accepted by the general's wife on January 9, 1951, while he was a prisoner. General Dean died in 1981. The reporters Burchett and Winnington are dead. Maj. Roy Bley left the marines in 1958 and died in 2004. Lieutenant General Thrash was awarded the Legion of Merit, as was Major Walter Harris, which is quite unusual because this decoration is normally reserved for a senior officer of staff or flag rank. For his bravery while a POW, Capt. John Patrick Flynn received the Navy and Marine Corps Medal. He stayed in the marines and became a lieutenant colonel. John Pratt later served on the U.S. District Court for the District of Columbia and died of cancer at 84 years of age. General Shepherd died in 1990. General Jerome died in 1978 in Arlington, Virginia. General Linscott died in 1973 and General Bare in 1980. General Schlit died in 1987 and is buried in Arlington National Cemetery. Brigadier General Paul Sherman died in 1987. Gen. Ray Robinson and Gen. William Brice are gone. General Twining is dead and so are many of the others. They did their duty as they saw fit to do their duty.

Col. Frank Schwable, after 30 years of service, retired on June 30, 1959. Also on that date, the colonel was meritoriously promoted to brigadier general "by reason of having been specially commended for heroism in combat during World War II." General Schwable's son, David, died from injuries suffered in a car accident while in Florida in 1971. He was 33. Susan has four children and presently resides in Virginia. General Schwable died from natural causes on October 28, 1988, and Beverly, in June 2000. The general, together with David and Beverly, are buried in Ebenezer Cemetery in Loudoun County, Virginia, 25 miles outside Washington, D.C.

"Your first transition was indeed death, the second an ideal sleep, and now the third metamorphosis is the true rest, the relaxation of the ages."[9]

Appendix: Deposition by the Captured United States Colonel Frank H. Schwable

I am Colonel Frank H. Schwable, 04429, and was Chief of Staff of the First Marine Aircraft Wing until shot down and captured on July 8, 1952.

My service with the Marine Corps began in 1929 and I was designated an aviator in 1931, seeing duty in many parts of the world. Just before I came to Korea, I completed a tour of duty in the Division of Aviation at Marine Corps headquarters.

Directive of the Joint Chiefs of Staff

I arrived in Korea on April 10, 1952, to take over my duties as Chief of Staff of the First Marine Aircraft Wing. All my instructions and decisions were subject to confirmation by the Assistant Commanding General, Lamson-Scribner. Just as I assumed full responsibility for the duties of Chief of Staff, General Lamson-Scribner called me into his office to talk over various problems of the wing. During this conversation he said: "Has Binney given you all the background on the special mission run by V.M.F.-513?" I asked if he meant "Suprop" (our code name for bacteriological bombs) and he confirmed this. I told him I had been given all of the background by Colonel Binney.

Colonel Arthur A. Binney, the officer I relieved as Chief of Staff, had given me, as his duties required that he should, an outline of the general plan of bacteriological warfare in Korea and the details of the part played, up to that time, by the First Marine Aircraft Wing.

The general plan for bacteriological warfare in Korea was directed by the United States Joint Chiefs of Staff in October, 1951. In that month the Joint Chiefs of Staff sent a directive, by hand, to the Commanding General, Far East Command (at that time General Ridgway), directing the initiation of bacteriological warfare in Korea on an initially small experimental stage, but in expanding proportions.

This directive was passed to the Commanding General, Far East Air Force, General Weyland, in Tokyo. General Weyland then called into personal conference General Everest, Commanding General of the Fifth Air Force in Korea, and also the Commander of the 19th Bomb Wing in Okinawa, which unit operates directly under F.E.A.F.

The plan that I shall now outline was gone over, the broad aspects of the problem were agreed upon and the following information was brought back to Korea by General Everest, personally and verbally, since for security purposes, it was decided not to have anything in writing on this matter in Korea.

Objectives

The basic objective was at that time to test, under field conditions, the various elements of bacteriological warfare, and gradually to expand the field tests, at a later date, into an element of the regular combat operations, depending on the results obtained and the situation in Korea.

The effectiveness of the different diseases available was to be tested, especially for their spreading of epidemic qualities under various circumstances, and to test whether each disease caused a serious disruption to enemy operations and civilian routine or just minor inconveniences, or was contained completely, causing no difficulties.

Various types of armament or containers were to be tried out under field conditions and various types of aircraft were to be used to test their suitability as bacteriological bomb vehicles.

Terrain types to be tested included high areas, sea coast areas, open spaces, areas enclosed by mountains, isolated areas, areas relatively adjacent to one another, large and small towns and cities, congested cities and those relatively spread out. Every possible type or combination of areas was to be tested.

These experiments were to continue for an indefinite period which would make it possible to carry them out in the most diversified meteorological conditions found in Korea.

All possible methods of delivery were to be tested as well as tactics developed to include initially, night attacks and then expanding into day attacks by specialized squadrons. Various types of bombing were to be tried out and various combinations of bombing, from single planes up to and including formations of planes, were to be tried out with bacteriological bombs used in conjunction with conventional bombs. Enemy reactions were particularly to be tested or observed by any means available to ascertain what his countermeasures would be, what propaganda steps he would take, and to what extent his military operations would be affected by this type of warfare.

Security measures were to be thoroughly tested — both friendly and enemy. On the friendly side, all possible steps were to be taken to confine knowledge of the use of this weapon and to control information on the subject. On the enemy side, every possible means were to be used to deceive the enemy and prevent his actual proof that the weapon was being used.

Finally, if the situation warranted, while continuing the experimental phase of bacteriological warfare according to the Joint Chiefs of Staff directive, it might be expanded to become part of the military or tactical effort in Korea.

Initial Stage

The B.29s from Okinawa began using bacteriological bombs in November, 1951, covering targets all over North Korea in what might be called random bombing. One night the target might be in Northeast Korea and the next night, Northwest Korea. Their bacteriological bomb operations were conducted in combination with normal night armed reconnaissance as a measure of economy and security.

Early in January, 1952, General Schilt, then Commanding General of the First Marine Aircraft Wing, was called to the Fifth Air Force H.Q. in Seoul, where General Everest told him of the directive issued by the joint C.G.S. and ordered him to have V.M.F. 513 — Marine Night Fighter Squadron 513 of the Marine Aircraft Group 33 of the First Marine Aircraft Wing — participate in the germ warfare programme [sic]. V.M.F. 513 was based at K8, the air force base at Kunsan of the Third Bomb Wing, whose B.26s had already begun bacteriological operations. V.M.F. 513 was to be serviced by the Third Bomb Wing.

At that time, all the aircraft of the Marine Corps (combat type) based on the Korean coast were under the direct command of the Fifth Air Force and the First Marine Aircraft Wing was constantly informed of all their operations; whenever new flights were undertaken or old ones continued in connection with the programme [sic] for bacterial warfare, the Fifth Air Force Command usually informed the Aircraft Wing beforehand.

By the end of January 1952, night fighters of the 513th Squadron making isolated night reconnaissance flights and conducting operations in connexion [*sic*] with bacterial bombs shared their targets and objectives with the B.26 bombers, which operated in the southern part of North Korea and concentrated mainly on its western regions. The 513th Squadron co-ordinated its operations in all these flights with the Third Bomb Wing, using "F7F" (Tiger Cat) aircraft for these operations, because of their twin-engine safety.

K.8 (Kunsan) offered the advantage of a take-off directly over the water, in the event of engine failure, and both the safety and security of over-water flights to enemy territory.

For security reasons, no information on the types of bacteria being used was given to the First Marine Aircraft Wing.

In March, 1952, General Schilt was again called to the Fifth Air Force headquarters and verbally directed by General Everest to prepare Marine Photographic Squadron One (V.M.J.1 Squadron) of Marine Aircraft Group 33 to enter the programme [*sic*]. V.M.J.1 based at K.3, Marine Aircraft Group 33's base at Pohang, Korea, was to use F2H-2P Photographic Reconnaissance Aircraft (Banshees).

The missions would be intermittent and combined with normal photographic missions and would be scheduled by the Fifth Air Force in separate, top secret orders.

The Banshees were brought into the programme [*sic*] because of their specialized operations, equipment facilities and isolated area of operations at K.3. They could penetrate further into North Korea as far as the enemy counter-action was concerned and worked in two plane sections involving a minimum of crews and disturbance of normal missions. They could also try out bombing from high altitudes in horizontal flight in conjunction with photographic runs.

During March 1952, the Banshees of the Marine Photographic Squadron One, commenced bacteriological operations, continuing and expanding the bacteriological bombing of North Korean towns, always combining these operations with normal photographic missions. Only a minimum of bomb supplies were kept on hand to reduce storage problems and the Fifth Air Force sent a team of two officers and several men to K.3 (Pohang) to instruct the marine specialists in handing [*sic*] the bombs.

The Navy's part in the programme [*sic*] was with the F.9F (Panthers) AD (Skyraiders) and standard-type F2H (Banshees) aircraft, which, unlike the aircraft of the type used for photographic reconnaissance, were based on aircraft carriers operating along the east coast of Korea.

The Air Force also extended its operations, using squadrons of various types of aircraft, using various operational methods and tactics of bacterial warfare.

Such was the situation on the eve of my arrival in Korea. The important events described below then took place:

Operational Stage

In the second half of May, the new Commanding General of the First Marine Aircraft Wing, General Jerome, was called to the Fifth Air Force Headquarters and given a directive for expanding bacteriological operations. The directive was given personally and verbally by the new Commanding General of the Fifth Air Force, General Barcus.

On May 25, General Jerome outlined the new stage of bacteriological operations to the wing staff at a meeting in his office at which I was present in my capacity as Chief of Staff. The other staff members of the First Marine Aircraft Wing present were: General Lamson-Scribner, Assistant Commanding General; Colonel Stage, intelligence officer (G.2); Colonel Windt [*sic*], operations officer (G.3) and Colonel Clark, logistics officer (G.4).

The directive from General Barcus, transmitted to and discussed by us that morning was as follows: A contamination belt was to be established across Korea in an effort to make the interdiction programme [*sic*] effective in stopping enemy supplies from reaching the front lines. The Marines would take the left flank of this belt, to include the two cities of Sinanju and Kunuri and the area between and around them. The remainder of the belt would be handled by the Air Force in the centre and the navy in the east or right flank.

Marine Squadron 513 would be diverted from its random targets to the concentrated target, operating from K.8 (Kunsan), still serviced by the Third Bomb Wing using F.7F's (Tiger Cats). The squadron was short of these aircraft but more were promised.

The responsibility for contaminating the left flank and maintaining the contamination was assigned to the commander of squadron 513 and the schedule of operations left to the squadron's discretion, subject to the limitations that the initial contamination of the area was to be completed as soon as possible and the areas must then be replenished, at periods not to exceed ten days.

The crews of the aircraft carrying out these operations were to be given orders for the regular night reconnaissance carried out over Haeju peninsula. On the way to the target, however, the aircraft were to fly over Sonanchu [*sic*] or Kunuri, drop their bacterial bombs there and then carry out their regular tasks. That was done for greater security and also to interfere as little as possible with the regular operations.

Reports on this programme [*sic*] of maintaining the contamination belt would go direct to the Fifth Air Force, reporting normal mission number so and so had been completed "via Sinanju" on [sic] "Via Kanuri" [sic] and stating how many "superpropaganda" bombs had been dropped.

Squadron 513 was directed to make a more accurate "truck count" at night than had been customary in order to determine or detect any significant change in the flow of traffic through its operating area.

General Barcus also directed that Marine Aircraft Group 12 of the First Marine Aircraft Wing was to prepare to enter the bacteriological programme [sic]. First the A.Ds (Skyraiders) and then the F.4Us (Corsairs) were to take part in the expanded programme [sic], initially, however, only as substitutes for the F.7Fs.

General Jerome further reported that the air force required Marine Photographic Squadron One to continue their current bacteriological operations, operating from K.3 (Pohang). At the same time, Marine Aircraft Group 33 at K.3 was placed on a standby, last resort, basis. Owing to the distance of K.3 from the target area, large scale participation in the programme [sic] by Marine Aircraft Group 33 was not desired. Because the F.9Fs (Panthers) would only be used in an emergency, no special bomb supply would be established over and above that needed to supply the photographic reconnaissance aircraft. Bombs could be brought up from Ulsan in a few hours if necessary.

These plans and the ramifications thereof were discussed at General Jerome's conference and arrangements made to transmit the directive to the officers concerned with carrying out the new programme [sic].

It was decided that Colonel Wendt would initially transmit this information to the commanders concerned and that the details could be discussed by the cognizant staff officers as soon as they were worked out.

First M.A.W.s Operations
Marine Night Fighter Squadron 513

The next day then, May 26, Colonel Wendt held a conference with the Commanding Officer of Squadron 513 and I believe, the K.8 Air Base Commander and the Commanding Officer of the Third Bomb Wing and discussed the details.

The personnel of the Fifth Air Force were already cognizant of the plan, having been directly informed by Fifth Air Force Headquarters.

Since the plan constituted, for Squadron 513, merely a change of target and additional responsibility to maintain their own schedule of contamination of their area, these were no real problems to be solved.

During the week of June, Squadron 513 started operations on the concentrated contamination belt, using cholera bombs. (The plan given to General Jerome indicated that at a later, unspecified date — depending on the results, or lack of results — yellow fever and then typhus in that order would probably be tried out in the contamination belt.)

Squadron 513 operated in this manner throughout June and during the first week in July that I was with the Wing, without any incidents of an unusual nature.

An average of five aircraft a night normally covered the main supply routes along the western coast of Korea up to the Chong Chon River but with emphasis on the area from Pyongyang southwards. They diverted as necessary to Sinanju or Kunuri and the area between in order to maintain the ten-day bacteriological replenishment cycle.

We estimated that if each airplane carried two bacteriological bombs, two good nights were ample to cover both Sinanju and Kunuri and a third night would cover the area around and between these cities.

About the middle of June, as best I remember, the squadron received a modification to the plan from the Fifth Air Force via the Third Bomb Wing. This new directive included an area of about ten miles surrounding the two principal cities in the squadron's schedule, with particular emphasis on towns or hamlets on the lines of supply and any bypass roads.

Marine Aircraft Group 12

Colonel Wendt later held a conference at K.6 (Pyongtaek) at which were present the commanding officer, Colonel Gaylor [sic], the executive officer and the operations officer of Marine Aircraft Group 12. Colonel Wendt informed them that they were to make preparations to take part in the bacteriological operations and to work out security problems which would become serious if they got into daylight operations and had to bomb up at their own base, K.6. They were to inform the squadron commanders concerned, but only the absolute barest number of additional personnel, and were to have a list of a limited number of handpicked pilots ready to be used on short notice. Colonel Wendt informed them that an air force team would soon be provided to assist with logistic problems, this team actually arriving the last week in June.

Before my capture on July 8, both the A.Ds (Skyraiders) and the F.4U's (Corsairs) of Marine Aircraft Group 12 had participated in very small numbers, once or twice, in daylight bacteriological operations as part of regular scheduled, normal, day missions, bombing up at K.8 (Kunsan) and rendezvousing with the rest of the formation on the way to the target. These missions were directed at small towns in Western Korea along the main road leading south from Kunuri and were a part of the normal interdiction programme [*sic*].

Marine Aircraft Group 33

Colonel Wendt passed the plan for the Wing's participation in bacteriological operations to Colonel Condon, commanding officer of Marine Aircraft Group 33 on approximately May 27–28.

Since the Panthers (F.9Fs) at the group's base at Pohang would only be used as last resort aircraft, it was left to Colonel Condon's discretion as to just what personnel he would pass the information on to, but it was to be an absolute minimum.

During the time I was with the Wing, none of these aircraft had been scheduled for bacteriological missions through [*sic*] the photographic reconnaissance planes of the group's V.M.J. One Squadron continued their missions from that base.

Scheduling and Security

Security was far the most pressing problem affecting the First Marine Aircraft Wing, since the operational phase of bacteriological warfare, as well as other type combat operations, is controlled by the Fifth Air Force.

Absolutely nothing could appear in writing on the subject. The word "bacteria" was not to be mentioned in any circumstances in Korea, except initially to identify "superpropaganda" or "Suprop."

Apart from the routine replenishment operations of Squadron 513, which required no scheduling, bacteriological missions were scheduled by separate, top secret mission orders (or frag orders). These stated only to include "Super Propaganda" or "Suprop" on mission number so and so of the routine, secret "frag" order for the day's operations. Mission reports went back the same way, by separate, top secret dispatch, stating the number of "Suprop" bombs dropped on a specified, specially numbered mission.

Other than this, Squadron 513 reported their bacteriological mission by adding "via Kunuri" or "via Sinanju" to their normal mission reports.

Every means was taken to deceive the enemy and to deny knowledge of these operations even to friendly personnel, the latter being most important since 300 to 400 men of the wing are rotated back to the United States each month.

Orders were issued that bacteriological bombs were only to be dropped in conjunction with ordinary bombs or napalm, to give the attack the appearance of a normal attack against enemy supply lines. For added security over enemy territory, a napalm bomb was to remain on aircraft until after the release of the bacteriological bombs so that if the aircraft crashed it would almost certainly burn and destroy the evidence.

All officers were prohibited from discussing the subject except officially and behind closed doors. Every briefing was to emphasize that this was not only a military secret, but a matter of national policy.

Personally I have never once heard the subject mentioned or even referred to outside of the office, and I ate all of my meals in the commanding general's small private mess where many classified matters were discussed.

Assessment of Results

In the wing, our consensus of opinion was that the results of these bacteriological operations could not be accurately assessed. Routine methods of assessment are by presumably spies, by questioning prisoners of war, by watching the nightly truck count very carefully to observe variations from the normal traffic, and by observing public announcements of Korean and Chinese authorities, upon which very heavy dependence was placed, since it was felt that no large epidemic could occur without news leaking to the outside and that the authorities would announce it.

Information from the above sources is correlated at the base commander-in-chief's Far East level in Tokyo but the overall assessment of results is not passed down to the wing level. Hence the complete lack of knowledge of the results.

When I took over from Colonel Binney, I asked him for results. And he specifically said, "Not worth a damn."

No one that I knew of has indicated that the results are anywhere near commensurate with the effort, danger and dishonesty involved, although the Korean and Chinese authorities have made quite a public report of early bacteriological bomb efforts. The sum total of results known to me are that they are disappointing and no good.

Personal Impressions

I do not say the following in defence [*sic*] of anyone, myself included, I merely say it as an absolute direct observation that every officer when first informed that the U.S. is using bacteriological warfare in Korea is both shocked and ashamed.

I believe, without exception, that we come to Korea as officers who had always been told about bacteriological warfare—that it is being developed only for use in retaliation in the third world war.

Those officers who arrived in Korea and there learned that the Government was deceiving them so crudely by announcing to the whole world that it was not using bacterial weapons, are now forced to doubt the truth of everything else that the Government states about war in general and about the Korean war in particular.

None of us considered that bacterial weapons could be given any given place in war, since the main purpose of bacterial bombs was the mass annihilation of the civilian population, which is absolutely contrary to the human conscience. The spread of diseases cannot be foreseen and there are probably no limits to the development of an epidemic. Furthermore, a feeling of cowardice and dishonestly [sic] is engendered in any one who realized that he is dealing with a weapon which is being used surreptitiously against an unarmed and unwarned people.

I remember specifically asking Colonel Wendt what were Colonel Gaylor's [sic] reactions, when he was first informed and he reported to me that: Colonel Gaylor [sic] was both horrified and stupefied. Everyone felt like that when they first heard of it, and their reactions are what might well be expected from a fair-minded, self-respecting nation of people.

Tactically, this type of weapon is totally unwarranted—it is not even a Marine Corps weapon—morally it is damnation itself: administratively and logistically as planned for use, it is hopeless: and from the point of view of self-respect and loyalty, it is shameful.

F. H. Schwable, 04429, Colonel, U.S.M.C.
December 6, 1952, North Korea

A TRUE COPY, ATTEST:

N. M. BENNETT
Captain, U.S. Marine Corps
Ass't Counsel, Court of Inquiry

EXHIBIT 10

Chapter Notes

The primary research document is the court of inquiry transcript, which has three volumes, numbered consecutively, ending on page 1,170. For example, in a note that reads C3:1169. C is the Court of Inquiry transcript, the digit after the letter is the volume, and the page number(s) appear after the colon.

The inquiry transcript also has hundreds of pages of documents attached, such as exhibits, addendums, and judicial notices. These documents have been made part of the bibliography in the traditional manner and are specifically mentioned in the endnotes, not made part of the transcript pages, per se.

There's one other abbreviation used in the endnotes and that's OH, which will be followed by a page number. This is the 232-page oral history transcript of Frank Schwable (included in the bibliography).

Preface

1. Schwable biography.
2. *Ibid.*; OH: 39–40.
3. Schwable biography.
4. C1: 284–285.
5. C3: 1169.
6. C3: Exhibit 21 (1–2).

Chapter 1

1. C3: 885.
2. C1: Appendix "A"; C3: 1140, 1143.
3. C1: Appendix "A".
4. C3: 1118, 1143.
5. C2: 470.
6. C1: 440; C3: 1144.
7. C1: Appendix "A".
8. C1: 1.
9. Linscott biography.
10. C1: 396; C3: Exhibit 17 (2); Schilt biography.
11. Bare biography.
12. Cooper biography.
13. *Ibid.*
14. Sherman biography.
15. OH: 198–199; Abel, "Schwable Case Shows," 5.
16. C3: 1156–1157.
17. OH: 200–201.
18. "John H. Pratt Dies," *Washington Post*, August 12, 1995, B6.
19. OH: 200–201.
20. C1: 110–113.
21. C1: Appendix "B" (1–2).
22. "Schwable Case," *New York Times*, 2; Baldwin, "Inquiries and Morale," *New York Times*, 18.
23. Abel, "Schwable Case Shows," 5.
24. C3: 955.
25. C3: 1119; Abel, "Schwable Case Shows," 5; "Court Opens Case," 4.
26. OH: 209; "Court Opens Case," *New York Times*, 4.
27. OH: 203; Abel, "Schwable Case Shows" *New York Times*, 6.
28. C1: 2.
29. OH: 208.
30. C3: 798–799, 802, 838, 844–847.
31. C3: 803–805.
32. C3: 811–812, 814.
33. C3: 817, 841.
34. C3: 847.
35. *Ibid.*
36. C3: 826, 841, 856.
37. C3: 806, 842.
38. C3: Exhibit 22 (2).
39. C3: 861.
40. C3: 826.
41. C3: 801.
42. C3: 822.
43. C3: 855.
44. C3: 827, 861.
45. C3: 830.
46. C3: 863.
47. C3: 827.
48. C3: 828.
49. C3: 831–834, 840.

50. C3: 848.
51. C3: 847; Exhibit 22 (4).
52. C3: 835–836.
53. C3: Exhibit 10 (16).
54. "Dean Bulwarks," *New York Times*, 10.
55. C3: 959, 1129; Abel, "Schwable Tells of P.O.W. Ordeal," 1.
56. C3: 1167.
57. C3: 1170.

Chapter 2

1. C3: Exhibits 6 (3), 7 (6–7).
2. C3: Exhibits 10 (4), 17 (3); Jerome biography. Certain documents have a one-day difference in dates; e.g., some say General Jerome arrived on April 10 and assumed command on the 11th. This can be attributed to where the document originated. If its origin was in Washington, it would be in one time zone and if in Korea, another, which could extend to one day before or after the date of the documents source.
3. C3: 896; OH: 157.
4. C1: 9, 42–43.
5. C1: 43; Jerome biography.
6. C1: 52–54; Schwable biography.
7. OH: 114, 118.
8. OH: 102, 104.
9. C1: 52.
10. Schwable biography.
11. *Ibid.*; C1: 52; C3: 1011–1012; OH: 143.
12. C3: Exhibit 7 (9–10).
13. *Ibid.*
14. C3: 1087–1088.
15. C3: Exhibits 6 (3), 7 (6–7, 9), 8, 10 (15), 16 (4).
16. C1: 314, 318; Abel, "Schwable Case Shows," 5.
17. C1: 323, 337.
18. C1: 323, 325–326.
19. C1: 325–327.
20. C1: 334–335.
21. C1: 326–329.
22. C1: 328–329.
23. *Ibid.*

24. C1: 329–330.
25. *Ibid.*
26. *Ibid.*; C1: 333–334.
27. C1: 337.
28. C1: 43.
29. *Ibid.*; C2: 742–744, 756.
30. C2: 745, 752.
31. C2: 517–518, 530, 534–535, 548.
32. C2: 551.
33. C2: 518–520, 549.
34. C2: 547.
35. C2: 530–531, 548.
36. C2: 521–522, 543, 545–546.
37. C2: 532.
38. C2: 541.
39. C2: 522, 524.
40. C2: 523.
41. C2: 546–548.
42. C2: 538–539.
43. C2: 523–524.
44. C2: 525–526.
45. C2: 524–526.
46. C2: 537–538.
47. C2: 524.
48. C2: 759, 782.
49. C2: 744–745.
50. C2: 761–762.

Chapter 3

1. C1: 47–48.
2. C3: Exhibit 7 (12).
3. C1: 44.
4. C1: 45.
5. C1: 102–103; C3: Exhibit 10 (4).
6. C1: 88–89; C3: Exhibit 17 (6).
7. C1: 85–87.
8. C1: 5–6, 86–87.
9. C3: Exhibit 10 (4); OH: 158.
10. C3: Exhibit 10 (4, 16).
11. C3: Exhibit 10 (4).
12. OH: 158.
13. C1: 30–32, 88.
14. C1: 38–39.
15. C1: 53–54; C2: 631, 639; "Finding of Facts," no. 7.
16. C1: 90–91; C2: 612.
17. C2: 734–736.
18. *Ibid.*, 737, 740.
19. "Finding of Opinions," no. 11.
20. C2: 604–605.

21. C2: 598–601.
22. C1: 92–93.
23. C2: 732–733, 749–750.
24. C2: 769–770, 772, 778–780.
25. C3: 969; Exhibit 10 (16).
26. C1: 331–332.
27. C1: 345–346.
28. Shepherd, "Report on and Reply to Findings, Opinion and Recommendations of Court of Inquiry," 2.
29. C1: 87; C3: 1110, Exhibit 8.
30. C1: 93–94, 102, 106–107.
31. C1: 93–94, 106–107.
32. C3: Exhibit 20 (1); OH: 159.
33. C3: Exhibit 41 (2).

Chapter 4

1. C1: 94; C3: Exhibit 10 (4).
2. *Ibid.*; OH: 162.
3. C1: 94, 103–104.
4. C1: 94–95; C3: Exhibit 10 (4); OH: 162.
5. OH: 162.
6. C1: 95, 104; C3: 1002, Exhibit 10 (4).
7. C1: 44–45.
8. C1: 105; OH: 177.
9. 1: 45–46.
10. *Ibid.*
11. *Ibid.*, 95.
12. C3: 1002–1003. .
13. C1: 95–96.
14. C1: 96; C3: 1002–1003.
15. *Ibid.*; C3: Exhibit 10 (5).
16. *Ibid.*; C3: 1012.
17. C3: 971; OH: 163.
18. C3: 1004, 1007.
19. C3: 1012.
20. C3: 1003, 1076, Exhibit 10 (5).
21. C1: 96, 119; C3: 1005, Exhibit 10 (5).
22. C1: 127.
23. Lech, 92, 106.
24. C3: 1064–1065.
25. C3: 1148.
26. C3: 1006, Exhibit 10 (5).

27. C3: 971–972.
28. C3: Exhibit 10 (5).
29. C1: 97; C3: 1006–1008.
30. C1: 97; C3: Exhibit 10 (5).
31. C3: 1006–1007, Exhibit 10 (5).
32. C3: 1007–1008.
33. C1: 97–98, 107–108.
34. C1: 97–98.
35. *Ibid.*; C1: 107–108; C3: Exhibit 10 (5).
36. C3: 1008–1009, Exhibit 10 (5).
37. C3: 998–999.
38. C3: 1008–1009.
39. *Ibid.*; C1: 98; C3: Exhibit 10 (6).
40. C1: 98.

Chapter 5

1. C1: 157, 252, 314; C2: 517; C3: Exhibit 21 (8).
2. C1: 192, 201, 235, 245; C3: 1041, 1124, Exhibit 10 (6).
3. C3: Exhibit 18 (3).
4. C3: 975–977.
5. C3: 1008.
6. C3: 1010–1011.
7. C3: 1154–1155, Exhibit 36.
8. C3: 1010–1011.
9. C3: 1127; Shepherd, "Report on and Reply to Findings," 4.
10. C3: Exhibit 10 (6).
11. C3: 964–965, 973.
12. C3: 965, 1049, Exhibit 10 (6).
13. C3: 963–964.
14. C3: 1071.
15. C3: 965.
16. C3: 993–994, Exhibit 18 (3).
17. C3: 1014, Exhibit 10 (9).
18. C3: 1050, 1052.
19. C3: 1015, Exhibit 22 (4–5).
20. C3: 1041–1042, 1077.
21. C3: 1015, 1043, 1080, Exhibit 10 (6).
22. C3: 1015.
23. C3: 1017.
24. C3: Exhibit 18 (4).
25. *Ibid.*

26. C3: Exhibit 10 (8).
27. C3: Exhibit 10 (6); "Finding of Facts," no. 34.
28. C3: 1050, Exhibit 10 (6), Exhibit 18 (4).
29. C3: 1017, Exhibit 18 (4).
30. C3: 1051.
31. C3: 1016–1017.
32. C3: 978, 1015, Exhibit 18 (3–4).
33. C2: 640–643.
34. C2: 642, 673.
35. C2: 688.
36. C2: 646–647, 653.
37. C2: 655–656; C3: 978.
38. C2: 653; C3: Exhibit 33 (3).
39. C2: 645; C3: 907.
40. C3: 898–900.
41. C3: 900–902.
42. C3: 902–904.
43. *Ibid.*
44. C3: 898–900, 904–906.
45. C3: 960–961, Exhibit 18 (2).
46. C2: 692–693, 704; C3: 915.
47. C2: 665; C3: 912.
48. C3: 914.
49. C3: 913, 916, 925.
50. C3: Exhibit 21 (8).
51. C3: 1150, 1164.

Chapter 6

1. C1: 246; C3: 977–978; 987, 1022, 1112, Exhibit 10 (7).
2. C3: 1052, Exhibit 18 (6); OH: 167.
3. C3: 1013–1014.
4. C3: 1073–1074; OH: 179.
5. C3: 1075; OH: 171.
6. C3: 1053–1054.
7. C3: 979, Exhibit 18 (10).
8. C3: Exhibit 20 (5).
9. C3: 1068, 1077.
10. C3: 967.
11. C3: 1015–1016, 1052–1053.
12. C3: 981.
13. Lech, 102.
14. C3: 915–916.
15. C3: 992.

16. C3: 996.
17. C3: 917, 920.
18. C3: Exhibit 18 (5).
19. Bley biography.
20. C1: 99; C3: 975.
21. C1: 119–121.
22. *Ibid.*
23. C1: 100, 120.
24. C1: 122.
25. C1: 125.
26. C1: 121–122.
27. C1: 122–123.
28. C1: 126.
29. C1: 123–124.
30. *Ibid.*
31. C1: 123–125.
32. *Ibid.*
33. *Ibid.*
34. "Red China Steps Up Germ Warfare Charges," *New York Times*, 3.
35. C3: 1033, Exhibit 21 (5).
36. C1: 145, 202; C3: Exhibit 18 (5).
37. C1: 130–131, 134; C3: 974.
38. C1: 132–133; C3: 1066.
39. C1: 132; C3: 1083–1084, Exhibit 20 (3).
40. C1: 150–151, 155.
41. C1: 141, 143, 147.
42. C1: 148.
43. C1: 146, 155.
44. C1: 142.
45. C1: 145.
46. C1: 157–163, 229.
47. C1: 162–164.
48. C3: 988.
49. C3: 989–990.
50. C3: 990–991.
51. C3: 991–992.
52. OH: 170–171.
53. C1: 191, 195, 201.
54. C1: 192, 276–277.
55. *Ibid.*, 193; C3: 1055.
56. C1: 268–269; OH: 173.
57. C3: 1000, 1079.
58. C1: 194.
59. C1: 225–226; C3: 983, 1042.
60. C3: 963.
61. C1: 235–237, 245–246.
62. C3: 1054–1055.
63. C1: 248–249; C3: Exhibit 21 (9).

Chapter 7

1. C3: Exhibit 10 (10).
2. C3: 1164–1166.
3. C3: 984–985, 1045, Exhibit 18 (7).
4. C3: 1079–1080, Exhibit 18 (7).
5. C3: 985, 1045–1046.
6. C3: 983–985.
7. C3: 997; OH: 170.
8. C3: Exhibit 10 (9).
9. C3: 969–970, 1038–1039.
10. C3: 1038–1039, 1057.
11. C3: 1000–1001.
12. C3: 1013, 1018–1019.
13. C1: 206–207, 213–214, 221–222.
14. C1: 217–218, 221.
15. C1: 219–220.
16. C1: 216.
17. C1: 215–217.
18. C1: 215, 218.
19. C1: 215–216, 218.
20. C1: 283–284, 294, 301.
21. C1: 285–286, 305.
22. C1: 294, 369.
23. C1: 293.
24. C1: 285–286, 290.
25. C1: 305–306.
26. C1: 227; C3: 1043, Exhibit 10 (11).
27. C3: 996.
28. C3: 1019–1020.
29. *Ibid.*, C3: Exhibit 10 (10), Exhibit 20 (4).
30. C3: 970.
31. C3: 1020, 1032, Exhibit 10 (7, 17).
32. C3: 1057–1058.
33. C3: Exhibit 10 (16).
34. C3: Exhibit 10 (10).
35. C3: Exhibit 10 (17).
36. C3: Exhibit 10 (10).
37. C3: Exhibit 20 (2).
38. C3: Exhibit 18 (5).
39. C3: Exhibit 10 (10).
40. C3: Exhibit 10 (8).
41. C3: 1020.
42. C3: Exhibit 10 (9, 13).
43. C3: 1074–1075, 1080–1081.
44. C3: Exhibit 10 (11).
45. *Ibid.*
46. C3: Exhibit 10 (7), Exhibit 18 (7), Exhibit 20 (4).
47. C3: 1113, Exhibit 10 (7, 11); "Finding of Facts," no. 40.
48. C3: 1024–1025.
49. C3: 1025, 1067, Exhibit 10 (3).
50. C3: 1139, 1145, 1149, 1166; "Finding of Opinions," no. 8.

Chapter 8

1. C1: 165–166; C3: Exhibit 10 (12).
2. C1: 165–166, 197–199, 210, 260, 271; C3: Exhibit 10 (7).
3. C1: 207.
4. C1: 207–208, 265, 271.
5. C1: 165–166, 169, 175–176, 197–199, 208, 214.
6. C1: 208; C3: 1057.
7. C1: 166, 176–177, 209.
8. C1: 209–210, 247–248.
9. C1: 211, 238.
10. C1: 208–211, 213.
11. C1: 166, 209–210.
12. C1: 201, 210–212, 232, 240, 272.
13. C3: 985, 1023, 1056, 1081–1082.
14. C3: 1023, 1057, 1114.
15. C3: 1081–1082.
16. C3: 1056.
17. C3: 936, 940–941, Exhibit 33 (4).
18. C3: Exhibit 18 (2); "Finding of Facts," no. 45.
19. C3: 1056, 1131, Exhibit 18 (8).
20. C3: 1131, Exhibit 10 (7, 13); "Finding of Facts," no. 46, no. 47.
21. C3: 1067, 1131, Exhibit 10 (3, 7), Exhibit 18 (10); "Finding of Facts," no. 46, no. 47.
22. C3: 924.
23. C3: 1034, Exhibit 10 (3, 12).
24. C3: Exhibit 10 (12); "Finding of Facts," no. 48, no. 49.
25. C3: 1034–1035, 1061, Exhibit 10 (12).
26. C1: 376–378, 382–383. For a review of Bolo Point, see Lech, 123.
27. C3: Exhibit 10 (3), Exhibit 15, Exhibit 16; "Finding of Facts," no. 51; "Clark Denounces Germ Warfare Charges," *New York Times*, 2.
28. C3: Exhibit 9.
29. "Red China Steps Up," 3.
30. "Clark Denounces," 2.
31. C3: 1060, Exhibit 10 (7); "Finding of Facts," no. 50.
32. C3: 1060–1061, 1083.
33. C3: 1065–1066.
34. C2: 571.
35. C2: 554, 567; C3: 1140; "Marine Ex-POW Backs Schwable," *New York Times*, 5.
36. C2: 554–556.
37. C2: 555.
38. C2: 555–556, 558, 563–564, 569–570.
39. C2: 563–564.
40. C2: 559.
41. C2: 586–587.
42. C2: 565, 568, 596.
43. C2: 558–559, 571, 588, 592.
44. C2: 560.
45. C2: 560–561.
46. C2: 561–562, 591.
47. C2: 562, 564.
48. C2: 562–563, 587.
49. C2: 564–565.
50. C2: 565, 569.
51. C2: 565, 572.
52. *Ibid.*
53. C2: 572–573.
54. C2: 573.
55. C2: 573–574.
56. C2: 572, 574.
57. C2: 574–575.
58. C2: 575–578.
59. C2: 579–580.
60. C2: 560–561.
61. C2: 581.
62. C2: 581–583.
63. C2: 568, 583–584.
64. C2: 584.
65. C2: 585.
66. C2: 577, 588.
67. C3: 1081–1082, Exhibit 10 (13), Exhibit 18 (11).
68. C3: Exhibit 18 (6), Exhibit 20 (2); OH: 72.
69. "Red Germ Charges Cite 2 U.S. Marines," *New York Times*, 3.

Notes—Chapters 9–10

70. C1: 168.
71. C1: 141, 145, 149–150, 153.
72. C1: 289, 350, 353.
73. C1: 241–243.
74. C1: 315, 332, 340.
75. C1: 315–316, 319, 323.
76. C1: 389–390; C3: 1021–1022.
77. C1: 317, 320.

Chapter 9

1. C1: 367, 384; C3: 972, 991, 1062, 1080, 1083.
2. C3: 981–982.
3. C3: 1063–1064, 1116–1117, Exhibit 18 (11), Exhibit 20 (5).
4. C3: 1063–1064; OH: 90.
5. C3: 987, Exhibit 10, Exhibit 11, Exhibit 12, Exhibit 13, Exhibit 21 (6–8).
6. C3: 1068.
7. C3: Exhibit 18 (11); OH: 180–181.
8. "Finding of Facts," no. 56; OH: 180–181; "Last P.O.W.'S Freed," 1; "Two Tried Suicide," 2.
9. C2: 505; C3: 1044, 1070; "Two Tried Suicide," 2.
10. OH: 180–182.
11. C3: Exhibit 10 (3).
12. C3: Exhibit 10 (3, 27).
13. C2: 491–493, 510; C3: 1044.
14. C2: 493–494.
15. C2: 494–496; C3: 1070.
16. C2: 496–497, 499.
17. C1: 317; C2: 551.
18. C2: 527–528, 544–545.
19. C1: 317.
20. C2: 527–528, 542, 552.
21. C2: 528–529, 542, 552.
22. C2: 551–552.
23. C1: 408, 427.
24. C1: 408, 427–429. There are major differences between a USS (United States Ship) and a USNS (United States Naval Ship) and one of the differences can be looked at as ownership—who owns what. An accountant would hypothetically list on the asset side of the balance sheet of the United States of America a United States Ship (USS) while the balance sheet of the United States Navy would carry a United States Naval Ship (USNS) as an asset. Beside ownership, another major difference is function. A USNS is always a noncombatant, and various support and logistical vessels such as tankers, ammunition ships, general cargo ships, troop transports, and an assortment of other noncombatants would be, and are, owned by the navy. If it is a combatant ship—that is, one that can undertake offensive operations—it belongs to the United States.
25. C3: Exhibit 10 (28); OH: 182–183; Ship's Log.
26. "POW Ship," AP Wire.
27. C1: 408, 424, 429.
28. C1: 424–425, 429–430.
29. C1: 430–433, 438, 446; Ship's Log.
30. C1: 430–432, 438.
31. C2: 460–2; Ship's Log.
32. C2: 460–462, 466–470.
33. C2: 462–465.
34. C2: 462–464, 476–477; C3: 1151.
35. C2: 462–464; C3: 1151–1152.
36. C1: 408.
37. Ship's Log.
38. C3: 1027–1029.
39. C1: 415–416.
40. C1: 417–418; C2: 451–452; C3: 1028.
41. C2: 448–449, 453.
42. C1: 417–418; C2: 448–449.
43. C1: 409–410, 419; C3: 1069.
44. C1: 411–413.
45. C1: 413, 420; C3: Exhibit 18 (11); Ship's Log.
46. C3: 1070.
47. C1: 411, 421–423; C3: Exhibit 18 (1).
48. Lech, 255.
49. Ibid., 275.
50. Ibid., 222–223.

Chapter 10

1. Ship's Log.
2. C2: 449–450, 459; C3: Exhibit 39.
3. C3: 1029–1032, Exhibit 20 (5); OH: 51; Schwable biography.
4. C3: 1030.
5. C3: 1026, 1030–1031, 1078–1079; OH: 186.
6. C3: 1030–1031, 1078–1079.
7. C3: 1026; OH: 186.
8. C3: Exhibit 19 (1–2).
9. C3: 1027; "Finding of Facts," no. 58.
10. C3: 956–957; OH: 188.
11. Ibid.
12. C3: Exhibit 21 (3).
13. C3: Exhibit 21 (11).
14. C3: Exhibit 21 (3).
15. C3: Exhibit 21 (4).
16. Ibid.; C3: Exhibit 10 (19); "Finding of Facts," no. 52.
17. C3: Exhibit 21 (5).
18. C3: Exhibit 17 (2–10).
19. C3: Exhibit 22 (2).
20. C3: Exhibit 21 (2, 11).
21. C3: Exhibit 10 (13).
22. C3: 1073, Exhibit 10 (14).
23. C1: 321–322.
24. C3: Exhibit 10 (14), Exhibit 18 (10).
25. C3: Exhibit 10 (14–15).
26. C3: 1086, 1091, Exhibit 10 (11).
27. C3: 957–958.
28. C3: 957–958, Exhibit 10 (2).
29. C3: 958–959.
30. Ibid., C3: 1117, Exhibit 10 (13, 18).
31. OH: 187; Abel, "Schwable Case," 6.
32. C3: 1026, Exhibit 10 (17); OH: 187.

33. C3: 1149, Exhibit 10 (7).
34. OH:188–191; Report of April 14, 1954, 5–6; Lech, *Broken Soldiers*.
35. OH: 188–191, 197.
36. Abel, "Schwable Case," 6, Baldwin, "The Prisoner Issue—III," *New York Times*, 4.
37. C2: 692–693, 702; C3: 950.
38. C2: 703, 715.
39. C3: Exhibit 10 (16–18, Exhibit 20 (4).
40. C3: Exhibit 21 (9).
41. Baldwin, "Prisoner Issue," 4.

Epilogue

1. "Schwable Case Findings," *New York Times*, 6.
2. C3: 820, 844; Exhibit 18 (4).
3. Shepherd, "Report on and Reply to Findings," 1; Memorandum from Secretary of the Navy to Secretary of Defense, April 21, 1954.
4. Shepherd, "Report on and Reply to Findings," 1; Memorandum from Secretary of Defense to Secretary of the Navy, April 27, 1954.
5. OH: 193, 209; Abel, "Eisenhower Gives View on Schwable," *New York Times*, 15; "Schwable Case," *New York Times*, 2; "Schwable Freed but Is Criticized," *New York Times*, 1.
6. OH: 212; Schwable biography.
7. Schwable biography; "Schwable Assigned to Air Safety Post," *New York Times*, 3; "Marines Award Schwable Medal," *New York Times*, 8.
8. Baldwin, "Inquiries and Morale," 18.
9. Various biographies; *The Urantia Book*, 297.

Bibliography

Abel, Ellie. "Eisenhower Gives View on Schwable." *New York Times*, March 11, 1954, 15.
_____. "Schwable Case: 'The Caine Mutiny' in Real Life." *New York Times*, Section IV, February 21, 1954, 6.
_____. "Schwable Case Shows How Communist Torture Works." *New York Times*, Section IV, March 14, 1954, 5.
_____. "Schwable Tells of P.O.W. Ordeal." *New York Times*, March 12, 1954, 1.
Aircraft Clearance and Flight Plan for Col. Frank Schwable. July 8, 1952. Inquiry Exhibit 8.
Ambrose, Steven E. *Citizen Soldiers*. New York: Simon & Schuster, 1997.
Baldwin, Hanson W. "Inquiries and Morale." *New York Times*, March 18, 1954, 18.
_____. "The Prisoner Issue — III." *New York Times*, January 28, 1954, 4.
Biographies of Brig. Gen. Frank H. Schwable, Brig. Gen. Robert E. Galer, Lt. Gen. Henry D. Linscott, Gen. Christian F. Schilt, Lt. Gen. Robert O. Bare, Lt. Gen. Clayton C. Jerome, Gen. Lemuel C. Shepherd, Jr., Maj. Roy H. Bley, and Brig. Gen. Paul D. Sherman. Headquarters, U.S. Marine Corps, Marine Corps Historical Center, Washington, D.C.
Biography of Vice Adm. Thomas F. Cooper, U.S. Navy. Department of the Navy, Naval Historical Center, Washington, D.C.
"Clark Denounces Germ Warfare Charges." *New York Times*, February 24, 1953, 2.
"Col. Schwable, Marine Flyer, Is Shot Down." Unknown Newspaper Article Presented to Inquiry. Undated. Inquiry Exhibit 41(2).
"Court Opens Case of P.O.W. Colonel." *New York Times*, February 17, 1954, 4.
"Dean Bulwarks Schwable Case." *New York Times*, March 9, 1954, 10.
"Ex–P.O.W. Insisted He'd Give in Again." *New York Times*, February 18, 1954, 7.
Excerpts from *The Times Herald*. September 8, 1952. Inquiry Exhibit 10 (27–28).
Finding of [61] Facts, [12] Opinions, and [3] Recommendations of Court of Inquiry. Undated. Classified "Secret, Security Information." Follows Last Page (1170) of Transcripts.
"Former P.O.W. Faces Inquiry." *New York Times*, January 24, 1954, 4.
Gawande, Atul. "Hellhole: The U.S. Holds Tens of Thousands of Inmates in Long-Term Solitary Confinement. Is This Torture?" *The New Yorker*, March 30, 2009.
Geneva Convention Relative to the Treatment of Prisoners of War. (47 Stat. 2021; Treaty Series No. 846; Malloy Treaties, Vol. IV, p. 5224.) July 27, 1929. Inquiry Judicial Notice "C" (1–15).
Hodenfield, G.K. POW Ship. Associated Press wire forwarded to the author by the AP. San Francisco, September 23, 1954.
"John H. Pratt Dies at 84; U.S. District Judge in D.C." *Washington Post*, August 12, 1995, B6.
"Last P.O.W.'S Freed in Korea Exchange by Allies and Reds." *New York Times*, September 6, 1953, 1.
Lech, Raymond B. *Broken Soldiers*. Urbana and Chicago: University of Illinois Press, 2000.
Little, A. "Pavlov and the American GI." Undated manuscript. Inquiry Exhibit 3 (1–4).

"Marine Air Wing Leader Missing in Korean Action." *New York Times*, July 13, 1952, 2.

"Marine Colonel Will Face Inquiry Today on 'Confession' to Reds on Germ Warfare." *New York Times*, February 16, 1954, 2.

"Marine Ex–P.O.W. Backs Schwable." *New York Times*, March 3, 1954, 5.

"Marines Award Schwable Medal." *New York Times*, July 8, 1954, 8.

Memorandum from Col. Frank Schwable to Commandant of the Marine Corps. Statement Regarding Subject Allegation. October 1, 1953. Inquiry Exhibit 10 (3–18).

Memorandum from Commandant of the Marine Corps to Col. Frank Schwable. Allegation of Participation in Germ Warfare. September 28, 1953. Inquiry Exhibit 10 (2).

Memorandum from Commandant of the Marine Corps to Major General Henry D. Linscott, USMC. Appointing Order for Court of Inquiry. January 21, 1954. Inquiry Appendix "A."

Memorandum from Commandant of the Marine Corps to Major General Henry D. Linscott, USMC. Court of Inquiry in Case of Colonel Frank H. Schwable. February 18, 1954. Inquiry Appendix "B" (2).

Memorandum from Commanding General, Department of the Pacific, USMC, to Col. Frank H. Schwable. Orders. September 22, 1953. Inquiry Exhibit 39.

Memorandum from Headquarters, U.S. Army Forces, Far East, Joint Intelligence Processing Board #9 (Lt. Col. Robert Matthews, Chairman) to Commanding General, Sixth Army. Personnel Who Withstood Interrogation on Bacteriological Warfare. September 24, 1953. Inquiry Exhibit 19 (1–2).

Memorandum from President, Court of Inquiry, to Commandant of the Marine Corps. Court of Inquiry in Case of Colonel Frank H. Schwable. February 18, 1954. Inquiry Appendix "B."

Memorandum from President, Court of Inquiry, to Secretary of the Navy. Personnel of the U.S. Air Force: Witnesses Before Court of Inquiry. February 23, 1954. Inquiry Appendix "C" (1–3).

Memorandum from Secretary of the Air Force to Secretary of the Navy. Personnel of the U.S. Air Force: Witnesses Before a Court of Inquiry. March 8, 1954. Inquiry Appendix "C" (5).

Memorandum from Secretary of Defense to Secretary of the Navy. Reply to Findings, Opinions and Recommendations of Court of Inquiry. Office of the Secretary of Defense. April 27, 1954.

Memorandum from Secretary of the Navy to Secretary of Defense. Reply to Findings, Opinions and Recommendations of Court of Inquiry. Office of Secretary of Defense. April 21, 1954.

Operation Order Number 1-52. Naval Forces Far East, HQ, TF 91 MarForFE, Po'Hang, Korea. Classified "Secret, Security Information." Signed by Col. Frank Schwable, Chief of Staff, for Brig. Gen. Clayton C. Jerome. May 19, 1952. Inquiry Exhibit 7 (1–12).

Oral history transcript of Brigadier General Frank H. Schwable, U.S. Marine Corps (Retired). Interviewer: Benis M. Frank. Marine Corps Combat Development Command, Marine Corps University, Research Archives, Gray Research Center, Quantico, Virginia, 1983.

Press Release No. 1786. Issued by the U.S. Delegation to the General Assembly of the United Nations. Verbatim Transcript of Statement of Charles W. Mayo, U.S. Alternate Representative at the 648th Meeting of the Political Committee of the Eighth General Assembly. The Question of Impartial Investigation of Charges of Bacteriological Warfare. October 26, 1953. Inquiry Exhibit 21 (1–12).

Press Release 1796. Issued by the U.S. Delegation to the General Assembly of the United Nations 653rd Meeting of Committee I of the Eighth General Assembly. Additional Statement by the Honorable Charles W. Mayo. October 31, 1953. Inquiry Exhibit 22 (1–7).

Principles of Evasion for Marine Aviation. G-2 Branch, Division of Aviation, Headquarters, U.S. Marine Corps. April 8, 1953. Inquiry Exhibit 35 (1–2).

Record of Proceedings of a Court of Inquiry. Convened at Building Four, Henderson Hall, Arlington, Virginia, by Order of Commandant of the Marine Corps on January 21, 1954. Three Vols.

"Red China Steps Up Germ Warfare Charges." *New York Times*, February 25, 1953, 3.
"Red Germ Charges Cite 2 U.S. Marines." *New York Times*, February 23, 1953, 3.
Schwable, F.H., Deposition by the Captured U.S. Colonel Frank H. Schwable. December 6, 1952, North Korea. Inquiry Exhibit 10.
"Schwable Assigned to Air Safety Post." *New York Times*, May 12, 1954, 3.
"The Schwable Case." *New York Times*, Section IV, March 14, 1954, 2.
"Schwable Case Findings." *New York Times*, March 20, 1954, 6.
"Schwable Freed but Is Criticized." *New York Times*, April 28, 1954, 1.
Shepherd, Lemuel C., General, U.S. Marine Corps, Commandant of the Marine Corps. Report on and Reply to Findings, Opinion and Recommendations of Court of Inquiry. Department of the Navy, Headquarters, U.S. Marine Corps. April 14, 1954.
Ship's Log, USNS *General R.L. Howze* (T-AP 134). September 1–September 30, 1953. Military Sealift Command, Washington Navy Yard, D.C.
Statement by Frank H. Schwable to Robert Matthews Aboard USNS *General R.L. Howze*. Outline of Experiences of Col. F. H. Schwable. September 23, 1953. Inquiry Exhibit 18 (1–11).
Statement of Colonel Frank H. Schwable, 04429, U.S. Marine Corps. Prepared at Headquarters, Department of the Pacific, U.S. Marine Corps, San Francisco, California. September 25, 1953. Inquiry Exhibit 20 (1–5).
Transcription of Broadcast from Radio Peking by Frank Schwable. February 23, 1953. Inquiry Exhibits 15–16.
"Two Tried Suicide Under Red Torture." *New York Times*, September 7, 1953, 2.
United Nations General Assembly, First Committee, Seventh Session, Agenda Item 73, Introduced by A. Vyshinsky. Question of Impartial Investigation. March 12, 1953. Inquiry Exhibit 10 (19).
United Nations Seventh General Assembly, Document A/C.1/L.37 A/2231, Agenda Item 73. Statements by Certain Members of the U.S. Armed Forces. March 27, 1953. Inquiry Exhibit 17 (1–10).
The Urantia Book. Chicago: Urantia Foundation, 1955.
"U.S. Film Shown to U.N. Delegates Refutes Germ-Warfare Confession." *New York Times*, October 7, 1953, 1.

Index

Numbers in **_bold italics_** indicate pages with photographs.

Acheson, Secretary of State Dean 153–154
Amann, Capt. Emanuel, USMC 130

Bare, Maj. Gen. Robert E., USMC 8–**_9_**
Beechcraft SNB **_41_**, 57
Bennett, Capt. Nalton M., USMC 9
Bley, Maj. Roy, USMC 12–13, 40, 82–87, 135; agrees to sign germ warfare confession 86; captured 51–53; docking in San Francisco 151n; education of interrogators 53; main POW camp 84, 99; in Pick-up Camp (PUC) 82–87; and press release 62–63; in punishment cave 83–84; radio broadcast 87, 116; shot down 49–50; takes off 47; tape recordings 116; travels 56–57
bomb line 37–38
brainwashing 79–80
Brice, Lt. Gen. William, USMC 153, 158–**_159_**
Burchett, Wilfred **_20_**–21

Cassone, Lt. Col. Vincent J. (M.D.), USA 136–137
composing fake confession 105–108
Cooper, Rear Adm. Thomas F. (M.D.), USN 8, **_10_**
court of inquiry 5–7, 8, 67, 108, 164–165

Dean, Maj. Gen. William F., USA **_15–16_**; General Walker and 16–17; interrogation 17–19; and name, rank, serial number 166; South Korean hostility toward 17; as war criminal 18–19
death 168–169

education of Chinese captors 53–54
Evans, Col. Andrew J., Jr., USAF 133–136
EZ 118; silent treatment 125; solitary confinement 118–119; see also Ezelle, D. Earl

Ezelle, Maj. D. Earl, USMC 17; classified information and 119, 121–122; escape and recapture 122–125; fear of Chinese interrogator 120; release 126–127; see also EZ

fake confession analysis 156–158
final flight preparations 40, **_41_**, 42
First Marine Aircraft Wing 24–26, 29–30
Flynn, Capt. John Patrick, Jr., USMC 33; and germ warfare 34; interrogation 34–37, 138; meets with Chinese general 138–139
Foreign Broadcast Information Service (FBIS) 115–116
Frey, Maj. Leroy, USMC 43

Galer, Col. Robert, USMC 40–42, 47
Gaynor, Cpl. Melvin, USMC 90–91, 128
USNS _General R.L. Howze_ (T-AP-134) 140–141; radio room 146
Geneva Conventions 80
germ warfare 72, 130, 142–143
Gluck, 1st Lt. Martin E., USA 143–144

Hale, Sgt. James L., USMC 89–90, 128
Hall, Airman 1st Class Franklin, USAF 94–95, 111, 129
Harris, Maj. Walter, USMC 30–31, 130–131, 137, 157
Henderson Hall 13
House 60, 63–65
Hwachon Reservoir 47

Inchon Replacement Depot 136, 140

Jerome, Maj. Gen. Clayton C., USMC 24–**_25_**, 50

Lean-to 60, 76
Linscott, Maj. Gen. Henry D., USMC 8, 12–13; cursing **_14_**; open-door policy **_14_**

191

Little, Alan M.G. (Ph.D.) 113; definition of menticide 69–71
Lodge, US Ambassador to the UN Henry Cabot 152–153

Mahurin, Col. Walker, USAF 133, 135–136
Marines 160
Mason, Col. A.T., USMC 151
Matthews, Lt. Col. Robert C., USA 139–142, 145–149, 152–153
Mayo, Charles W. (M.D.) 74–75, 155
McLaughlin, Lt. Col. John, USMC 80–81, 129
Meerloo, Joost Abraham Maurits (J.A.M.) M.D., Ph.D. 71–73, 80–82, 113–114
Menticide 74–75, 79, 80, 104–105; recovery from 112–113
Murphy, Lt. Col. Kenneth E., USMCR 9

name, rank, serial number 2; adherence to 43; disobedience by 5th Air Force of 44–46; interpretations 44–46, 63, 74, 79

Oehl, Sidney, USMC 94
Operations Big and Little Switch 134–135
Overholser, William (M.D.) 162

Pak's Palace 64
Pike's Peak 34
Porter, Sgt. Pearson, USA 92
POW locations 33–34
Pratt, John H., Esq. 5, 11–12, 108
press release announcement 61–62
prisoners of war 21–22, 116–117, 127
psychological evaluation 143–144
PUC (Pick-up Camp) 59–60, 87, 108, 109
PV-1 Vega Ventura 26–27
Pyoktong 112, 128

race war 53–54
Riker, Lt. (j.g.) Andrew L., USN 100–101, 109–112
Robinson, Gen. Ray, USMC 151–153

Schilt, Maj. Gen. Christian F., USMC 8–9
Schwable, Beverly 13–14, 48, 50, 62, 127–128, 151; death 169; discusses charges against her husband 159; greets husband 153
Schwable, Col. Frank H., USMC 1–2, 23–25, 28 32–33; arrival at Camp 5 111; and back pain 57, 64; capture 51–53; chief of staff position 57, 61; Chinese editing of confession 113–114; death 168–169; despair 78; diarrhea 91–92; duties after repatriation 167–168; final collapse 103–105; freezing 97–98; hatred by senior marines 161; mental stability 110; military interrogation 54–57; military secrets 33, 39–40; orders upon docking 150; promoted to brigadeer general 168; reasons for flight 42; repatriation 132–135; shoot down of 49–50; solitary confinement 55, 58, 65, 77, 81; suicide thoughts 79; take off 47; tape recordings 115–116; torture 73, 75, 98; transfer to main camp 132; treason and 79; war criminal conviction 80, 133
Shepherd, Gen. Lemuel C., Jr. (Commandant of the Marine Corps) 5, 6, 7, 50, 152, 158, 160; punishment of Col. Schwable 166–167
Sherman, Col. Paul D., USMC 10–11, 108, 144
Shockley, William, USMC 87–88
sleep deprivation 81

the tent 60, 65–68
Thrash, Lt. Col. William G., USMC 101–103, 129

United Nations 4, 153–155
United States Air Force 28–29

Winnington, Alan 20–21, 115
wood gathering details 92–94

Yalu River camps 137–138

www.ingramcontent.com/pod-product-compliance
Ingram Content Group UK Ltd.
Pitfield, Milton Keynes, MK11 3LW, UK
UKHW042009140426
5217IPUK00015B/1073